ATLAS OF THE ROMAN EMPIRE

BATTLES CONQUESTS
LEGIONS AND RULERS

DAVID POTTER

ATLAS OF THE ROMAN EMPIRE

BATTLES CONQUESTS LEGIONS AND RULERS

DAVID POTTER

RIVERSIDE PRESS

CONTENTS

INTRODUCTION
6

MAPPING THE ROMAN WORLD
12

CHAPTER 1
CAESAR'S HEIR
20

CHAPTER 2
MUTINIES, MURDERS AND COUPS
68

CHAPTER 3
EXPANSIONISTS AND CONSOLIDATORS
112

CHAPTER 4
IMPERIAL CHURN, IMPERIAL FAILURE
150

CHAPTER 5
EMPIRE RESHAPED AND REFORMED
190

CHAPTER 6
ENEMIES AT THE GATE
234

CHAPTER 7
FINAL CONVULSIONS
270

EPILOGUE
300

FURTHER READING
306

INDEX
308

ACKNOWLEDGEMENTS
318

PICTURE CREDITS
318

ABOUT THE AUTHOR
319

INTRODUCTION

From *caesars* to gladiators, from martyrs to ceremonies of martial triumph, and from architectural feats to sculptural masterpieces, the Roman Empire remains vivid in our modern imagination. What made it so successful that it continues to provide such resonant images of ambition and courage, power and success, as well as darker tales of excess and immorality, cruelty and calamity?

This story of the Roman Empire begins in the last decades of the first century BCE, with the road to power followed by the first emperor, Augustus. As the grandnephew and adoptive son of Julius Caesar, he inherited not only a formidable military apparatus loyal to Caesar's memory, but also the bureaucracy to support it. Those factors enabled him to triumph in the wars that followed, and they provided the foundation upon which the government of the Roman Empire was built.

Augustus was able to reassemble the pieces of a traumatized society to create a political system that would survive for centuries, adapting to circumstance and binding together the people of what would become a vast state stretching from Britain through France to central Europe, North Africa and the Near East. The strength of Augustus's system was such that it could even survive the antics of colourful and notorious successors, such as Caligula and Nero, and continue to grow. Moreover, the Augustan system created space for people born in the provinces to move into positions of power within the government, and brought a military organization that could (usually) ensure the security of the empire's subjects.

The great secret of empire, revealed in the aftermath of Nero's failure in the role, was that an emperor could be made away from Rome. So said Tacitus, Rome's greatest historian. The rocky year 69 CE, which saw no fewer than four emperors, gave rise to the period of Rome's greatest prosperity, leading Edward Gibbon to write in the eighteenth century that if a person was 'called to fix the period in the history of the world, during which the condition of the human race was most happy and prosperous', that person 'would, without hesitation, name that which elapsed from the death of Domitian to the accession of Commodus'.

The Roman Empire would indeed achieve its greatest power, relative to its neighbours, in the second century CE. The emperors of this period represent the success of the Augustan programme to promote imperial unity through the support of shared cultural values. Emperors Trajan, Hadrian and Marcus Aurelius were from families that could trace their origins to Spain, while Antoninus Pius was descended from a family with roots in southern France. A substantial proportion of their colleagues in the governing class were now from western Turkey, Syria and North Africa. Many of the most eloquent proponents of the imperial system from this point onwards wrote in Greek rather than Latin.

The great crisis of empire, beginning in the later second century CE, stemmed not from politics – for the imperial system had long since proven its resilience in the face of an inadequate chief executive – but from pandemics. A great plague swept across the empire, eliminating about 10 per cent of the total population and bringing on an economic crisis when the tax base could no longer support the government's infrastructure (especially the army, which represented around 75 per cent of expenditure). These internal difficulties were compounded by the emergence of an aggressive new regime in Persia (present-day Iran), whose threat lured Rome into weakening its defences of other frontiers, with catastrophic effects. Roughly 20 per cent of the army was destroyed in a series of defeats in 251–52 CE, ushering in a period of increased political insecurity that was solved only with the accession of Diocletian in 284 CE.

There were other problems besides. Loss of confidence in the central government undermined the empire's cultural unity, as people looked to new intellectual and religious movements. The second half of the third century CE saw the rise of Neoplatonism, Manichaeism (whose dualistic ideas originated in Persia) and a great expansion of Christianity, the last of which was recognized as a legal entity in 262 CE. Diocletian could tolerate Neoplatonists but not Manichaeans or Christians, against whom he launched major persecutions on the grounds that they were 'un-Roman' activities. His hostility to Christianity played some role in the choice made by his ultimate successor, Constantine, to convert and offer a new look to the imperial government. Perhaps the most famous piece of imperial legislation still with us is the creed he imposed on the Christian Church at the Council of Nicaea in 325 CE.

By aligning the imperial court with the Christian Church, Constantine shifted the intellectual life of the Roman Empire in a new direction. And in accepting Diocletian's view that the empire could no longer be governed from a single centre, Constantine set in motion the permanent division of the empire, between eastern and western zones, that would henceforth characterize it. Like Diocletian, Constantine believed that the division of the empire could be controlled if the junior rulers were obedient to a single senior ruler. But that proved impossible, and division was essentially institutionalized in the later part of the fourth century CE. The biggest problem to emerge from the division of the empire was that an emperor of one portion could not summon overwhelming force against Rome's neighbours. The peril inherent to this development was underscored when Emperor Valens allowed large numbers of Goths, pressured by the Huns to their east, to enter the empire; Valens would die in battle against them in 378 CE.

That disaster, which took place in Adrianople (now Edirne, Turkey), set in motion the gradual disintegration of the Roman Empire as it lost control of its frontiers, and as new Germanic groups took over Roman provinces as their own kingdoms. It was a process of collapse that, with the Vandals' occupation of Carthage in 439 CE, brought the effective end of the empire.

*

The Roman Empire lasted around 500 years. It did not emerge from nothing, of course, for it was the ultimate failure of a previous half-millennium of history – the Roman Republic – that paved the imperial way.

Republican government had emerged from an era of Roman kings. However, by the first century BCE it was clear that it lacked the institutions needed to run the burgeoning expanse of Roman provinces across Europe,

Figures I and II

Lucius Cornelius Sulla (left) was the brutal dictator who set the tone for the politics of Caesar's generation. Gnaeus Pompey (right), an immensely successful general from an early age, took to calling himself Pompey the Great after Alexander the Great, whose hairstyle he adopts in this image.

the Near East and North Africa. Taxes were collected, armies supplied and public works managed by private corporations, which contracted with the state. Traditionally, these corporations stayed out of direct involvement in politics; it was not worth the risk of alienating members of the senate (the governing council of state) who controlled the handing out of new contracts. But the resources were there – if an ambitious politician could convince corporate leaders to support him – to supply whole armies against the state. The first man to exploit resources to this end was Lucius Cornelius Sulla.

Sulla had been given command of a war in Rome's eastern provinces in the early 80s BCE. However, as he was concluding hostilities, his political enemies declared him a public enemy, at which point he made a treaty with the ruler he was fighting, Mithridates. By the terms of their agreement, Mithridates would supply him with a significant portion of the resources necessary to invade Italy. Sulla then imposed a massive fine on Rome's subjects, gathered by the private corporations that collected taxes in the province, to enhance his resources for the war. Better financed, and with a better army, Sulla triumphed in the civil war, battling his way into Rome. He absorbed powers as 'dictator for life', massacred his enemies, and 'reformed' the constitution to make it impossible for anyone else to do what he had done – or so he thought – until he stepped down from power in 79 BCE, dying the next year.

INTRODUCTION

While civil conflict had sundered Roman life in the 80s CE, external challenges pressed in during the next decade. Mithridates, still on the loose, attacked Rome again in the mid-70s BCE. At the same time, large numbers of pirates roamed the Mediterranean. When the campaign against Mithridates faltered in the early 60s BCE, and the pirates became especially aggressive, the senate was forced to create special commands – first against the pirates, then against Mithridates – which were awarded to the able and ambitious Gnaeus Pompey.

Pompey was given unlimited power to crush his enemies, a project in which he succeeded; he returned to Italy as the most powerful man of his time, and easily the wealthiest. But his political skill was limited, so he required the assistance of a person who could manage the final settlement of the terms he had imposed in the east (from which he derived further profit). The man who fulfilled that role was Julius Caesar.

Caesar turned out to be every bit as ambitious as Pompey. In return for helping Pompey, he required Pompey's assistance in establishing a special term in office for himself: the governorship of three Roman provinces for five years, gained in 59 BCE, when Pompey was carrying out his term as one of Rome's consuls. Caesar then saw to it that his governorship was extended to ten years, during which time he conquered Gaul (the area of what is now France) and acquired a fortune as vast as Pompey's, while building an army that was fiercely loyal to himself.

Jealously observing what Caesar had achieved, and the potential challenge he represented, Pompey obtained a special command for himself and began to build up his own army. While Caesar wrote that the Roman state was best served by an alliance between Pompey and himself, in their extra-constitutional positions, Pompey disagreed; he could not bear the idea of an equal. The strain proved too great for the peace of Rome to bear.

The civil war that broke out in January 49 BCE pitted Caesar's private army against the combined forces of the army Pompey had built up in Spain and the Republic's army. Caesar had more legions, more money and a much better organization. As a result, Pompey's army was destroyed in less than two years, and a victorious Caesar emerged as a new dictator in Rome. Now, the bureaucracy that Caesar had built to support his war effort continued to exist alongside, and often atop, the traditional government of the Republic. Caesar appeared untouchable.

Ironically, it was fear that Caesar would make himself untouchable that curtailed his rule, that threw the Republic into its death throes, and that would, in time, give birth to the age of empire. The pivotal year was 44 BCE.

Figure III

This portrait of Julius Caesar, which was made for a fan in the years after his death, catches the penetrating intelligence noted by his contemporaries – and the receding hairline he tried to conceal.

MAPPING THE ROMAN WORLD

The Romans were very keen on maps, as both administrative tools and artistic products. As Roman rule stretched around Italy, from the fourth to the second centuries BCE, officials routinely created detailed local maps. They laid out the territory that Rome claimed from communities around the peninsula, as well as the land that had been left to those communities – a habit that continued as Roman power expanded beyond Italy. Copies of these maps would be erected in stone in these communities, as statements of Roman power.

The first larger-scale map of a bigger region that we know of depicted Sardinia. In the later second century BCE a Roman consul who had campaigned in the island's conquest installed the map in the Temple of Mater Matuta, on the north side of the Forum Boarium in Rome. Victorious generals displayed maps in their triumphs, too. And in the first century BCE Gnaeus Pompey ('the Great') included a map of the peoples he had conquered in the portico of the theatre he built to celebrate himself at Rome. A map of Rome was also on display in the city's Temple of Tellus (Earth). These were joined at the end of the first century BCE by a large-scale map engraved in Rome's Porticus Vipsania (Portico of Agrippa), once located near the site of the Temple of Hadrian today. It depicted the world as then known, placing Rome roughly in the middle, shown as a circle, and providing measurements for the areas under Roman rule. In the early third century CE Emperor Septimius Severus commissioned the plan of Rome that was placed in a portico near what is now the Church of Santi Cosimo e Damiano (Saints Cosmas and Damian), along the Via dei Fori Imperiali; its remains still provide important information about portions of the ancient city (Fig. III).

Figure I (right)

This section of the *Peutinger Table* shows Rome with the major roads leading from it. The city goddess is in the centre; also shown is Rome's major port at the mouth of the Tiber, and the lighthouse built by Emperor Claudius in 42 CE.

Figure II (overleaf)

The elongated shape of the world in the *Peutinger Table* is a result of the mapmaker's stress on the communication system, showing distances as measurable despite the lack of projection techniques that have since been developed. This detail has Constantinople alongside the great 'burnt column' that survives today in the heart of what was once Constantine's forum, supporting an image of the emperor in heroic nudity resembling the god Apollo.

The interest the Romans took in depictions of the world is perhaps most strongly illustrated by the Staffordshire Trulla – also known as the Staffordshire Moorlands Pan (Fig. IV) – a bronze drinking cup commissioned in the second century CE by a man named Draco and listing the last four forts at the western end of Hadrian's Wall. The most dramatic statement of what a map could mean to the Romans appears in a speech delivered in honour of Constantius I, the father of Constantine, when he was still *caesar* in 197 CE. The speaker thanks Constantius for restoring the school in Autun, whose portico is decorated with a map enabling young men to see, daily, 'every land and all the seas and whatever cities, peoples and nations the invincible rulers either restore by piety or conquer by courage or bind by fear'. Here are shown 'the sites of all locations with their names, their extent and the distances between them, the places where rivers arise and terminate, the curves of all the shores and the Ocean, both where its circuit surrounds the earth, and where its pressure breaks into it' (*Panegyric*, 9.20).

The map described by the speaker sounds very much as if it was designed along the lines of the most important surviving map from antiquity, the

Figure III

Septimius Severus commissioned a massive map of the city of Rome, the *Forma Urbis Romae*, based on contemporary property records. The map was detailed enough to show the floor plans of nearly every public and private building in the city. The section illustrated here appears to show a temple surrounded by private houses.

Figure IV

The Staffordshire Trulla is ornamented in the Celtic style with eight roundels and pairs of intervening triangles, all inlaid with turquoise and yellow enamel. The inscription around the top names four forts on Hadrian's Wall: Camboglanna (Castlesteads), Coggabata (Drumburgh), Mais (Bowness-on-Solway) and Uxelodunum (Stanwix).

so-called *Tabula Peutingeriana* or *Peutinger Table*, named after the sixteenth-century German humanist Konrad Peutinger, into whose hands it passed (Figs I and II; see also pages 26–27). It depicted the world from Britain to India and Sri Lanka on 14 plates, 11 of which survive. The map was probably copied from another that was displayed originally during the era of the Tetrarchy at Rome, in the late third and early fourth centuries CE. It was then updated when Constantinople became an imperial capital after 330 CE. The *Tabula Peutingeriana* shows the land routes that stretch from Rome around the empire and beyond. Like the map evoked at Autun, it allows us to visualize the way a person could pass around the known world, and, since it is without political boundaries, it suggests that the whole world, even those parts not directly ruled by Rome, is subject to the empire's influence. The mapping projects of this era illustrate the message of the Age of Diocletian: that the world has been restored under Roman domination.

Finally, although the Roman mapping projects of which we know have clear artistic and propagandist purposes, we should not forget that they also reflect the real interest of the Roman state in having an accurate image of the world.

Figure V (opposite)

This map copied from part of the *Forma Urbis Romae* depicts the heart of the city, showing the Theatre of Pompey, the Baths of Agrippa and the Theatre of Balbus, among other buildings.

CHAPTER 1

CAESAR'S HEIR: CIVIL WAR TO EMPIRE

By the time of Julius Caesar's assassination, in 44 BCE, the provinces ruled by Rome covered what – on a modern map – would be most of Spain and Portugal (to the west), as well as Syria, Israel and the southern shores of the Black Sea (to the east). To the north, Rome's sway was felt west of the Rhine, across France and Belgium, while on the African continent Roman power stretched across northern Libya, Tunisia and eastern Morocco. Rome's domination of the Mediterranean was absolute, as was its hold over the whole Italian peninsula: it was Julius Caesar himself who had, in the previous decade, conquered Italy's north (then known as Cisalpine Gaul).

The Roman world was undeniably *an* empire. But it was not yet *the* Empire as history would come to define it. Formally, it was still the Roman Republic, where – in normal times – two elected consuls were expected to exercise power for a year until the election of their successors, and where the senate acted as Rome's legislative council, advising on laws to be enacted by legislative assemblies. These constitutional structures had increasingly struggled to manage both the increasingly complex government of the empire and the ambitions of powerful men.

The ultimate failure of the system arose from its inability to manage the quarrel between the two most powerful of these men, Caesar and Pompey. As a result of the senate's refusal – at Pompey's behest – to honour the terms of an earlier agreement, Caesar crossed the Rubicon in January 49 BCE, at the head of the army that he had raised and was now largely paying with the spoils of his conquest of Gaul. His forces, more powerful than those deployed by the Roman state, vanquished Pompey in the ensuing civil war. He then imposed himself as Rome's 'dictator'.

Neither Caesar's coup nor his title was an innovation in Rome, and the concept of 'dictator' was generally understood as the temporary investing of one person with unusual powers in times of stress and crisis. For Caesar, that would now become an office he would hold on to. His decision to become 'dictator for life' capped a series of increasingly autocratic actions that had alienated a number of senators; they now feared Caesar had other designs: to re-establish a monarchy in Rome. On the 15th of March, some of those senators extinguished that threat, to the relief of others, although not all.

Word soon spread throughout the Roman lands of what would, through Shakespeare's reintervention, become history's most famous assassination – although the assassins called themselves 'liberators'. Hundreds of miles to the east, it reached the ears of the 18-year-old Gaius Octavius, generally referred to by historians of this period as Octavian. He was training in the province of Macedonia (northwestern Greece) for Caesar's planned invasion of the powerful Parthian Empire, which stretched from eastern Turkey to Afghanistan. As the great and the good of Rome decided how to align themselves amid the republic's violent and divided politics, the young Octavian now found himself pulled, by force of circumstance, centrestage.

Octavian came from an important family of the high-ranking Roman *equites* (equestrian) class. His late father had been a moderately successful senator, while his mother was Julius Caesar's niece. Most importantly, Octavian was named in Caesar's will as the dictator's adopted son and heir. With Julius Caesar dead, Octavian now took on the dictator's name, too – as Gaius Julius Caesar – and he was soon travelling westwards to Rome.

Upon his arrival in the city in April, the young Octavian found a state of chaos. Mark Antony, a distant cousin, was attempting to take control of the state, using his authority as Caesar's surviving colleague in the consulship. He had seized control of Caesar's papers, and when the senate declared that all Caesar's acts, as recorded in those papers, would have the force of law, Antony had even started inventing acts of Caesar. Ranged against Antony were not only Caesar's assassins, a powerful group within the state, but also Caesar's inner circle, a group of subordinates that included Caesar's financial team and former lieutenants on the path to high office. There were also members of the senate who, while not aligned with the assassins, either did not regret Caesar's murder or found Antony distasteful.

An uneasy truce prevailed, in which the assassins were pardoned. By early April, however, they were no longer in Rome. Of the three leading assassins, Brutus (Marcus Junius Brutus) and Cassius (Gaius Cassius Longinus) were sent abroad to take up minor duties, while Decimus Brutus took up the governorship of the province of Cisalpine Gaul ('Gaul on this side of the Alps'), roughly encompassing the Po Valley in northern Italy. However, Brutus and Cassius had grander ideas. Later in the summer of 44 BCE, they departed for the eastern Mediterranean, where they obtained the support of the garrisons of Macedonia and Syria, and so gained major military forces of their own.

In the meantime, Antony had been driven out of Rome. He responded by attempting a coup at the head of legions that had been brought back to Italy from the east, but it failed in the face of staunch opposition from Caesar's retired veterans and a mutiny in his own army. As the year 44 ended, Antony, at the head of his remaining soldiers, decided he would take Decimus Brutus's province by force. He led his four veteran legions into Cisalpine Gaul, at which point Decimus withdrew his three legions (one of new recruits) to Mutina (present-day Modena).

In Rome, the senate, eager to bring Antony to heel, placed the troops available to them under the command of the incoming consuls of 43 BCE, Aulus Hirtius and Gaius Vibius Pansa Caetronianus (better known simply as Pansa). These two men, deeply loyal to Caesar's memory, were now expected to cooperate with Octavian, who had been awarded the rank of *praetor*, an office second in authority to the consulship.

In early March 43 BCE, Hirtius and Octavian arrived in northern Italy, setting up camp at Bononia (Bologna) with their five veteran legions while they awaited Pansa's arrival with four newly raised legions. In theory, Pansa's troops would act as reserves for the veterans, since – according to a doctrine adhered to by Julius Caesar – new recruits were not thought to be battle-ready for several months. The wisdom of Caesar's doctrine would be confirmed by the events that followed Pansa's arrival in early April.

Figure 1

This statue of Augustus, once owned by his third wife, Livia Drusilla, captures her husband addressing his army, since he would have worn armour only in a military context. The image of the return of standards captured from earlier Roman generals by the Parthians commemorates one of Augustus's major diplomatic successes.

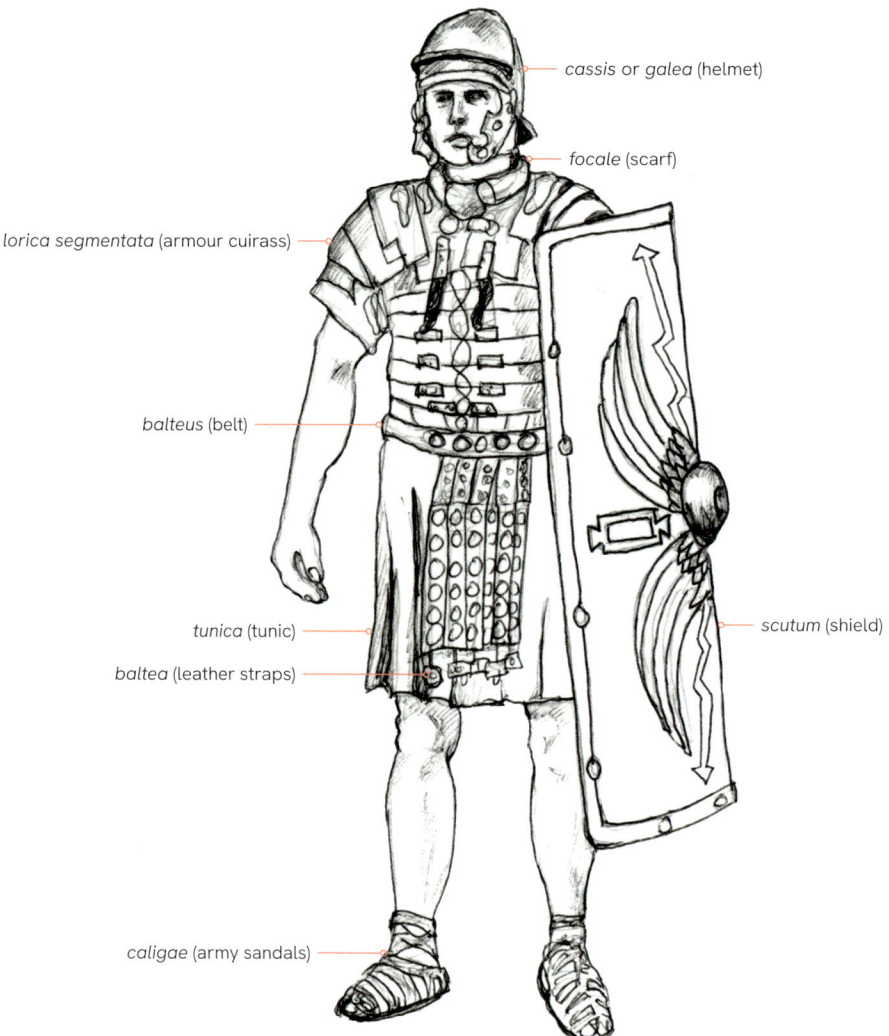

Figure II

A typical Roman legionary. A legion was formed of ten cohorts of heavily armed infantrymen like this one, whose equipment reflected the core tactics of the Roman army: to advance upon the enemy and engage at close quarters.

On the 14th of April, Antony, at the head of two legions, attacked Pansa at Forum Gallorum (Castelfranco Emilia). Initially, his attack was successful, as was to be expected in a conflict between veterans and new recruits, and Pansa himself was seriously wounded; however, a legion sent by Hirtius then attacked Antony's forces from behind as they pursued Pansa, near Mutina. Mark Antony withdrew to his camp with significant losses. A week later, on the 21st of April, Hirtius followed up by attacking Antony's camp near Mutina, in the process becoming a fatal victim of the battle, which was otherwise a victory. This conflict also brought the death, two days later, of Pansa, following his earlier injuries.

The demise of both consuls resulted in command of the senate's army passing to the 19-year-old Octavian, aided by the legions loyal to the ex-assassin Decimus. Together, they set off in pursuit of Antony, who had withdrawn from the area around Mutina. However, Octavian refused to speak to Decimus, who got the message that he was in grave danger if he stayed with the army. Instead, he fled to Gaul, hoping to rejoin the forces of

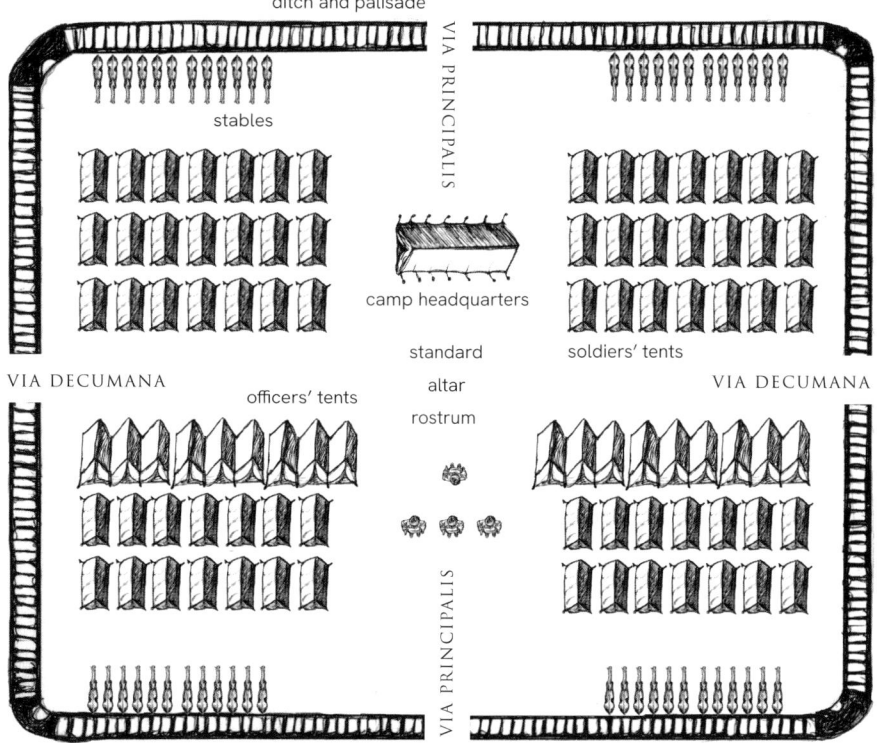

Figure III

The layout of a legion's typical marching camp. At the end of each day's march, legionaries would construct such a temporary camp surrounded by a trench (dug by soldiers), with the soil providing an earthwork behind, into which were planted the stakes that soldiers carried with them. The interior had two major pathways: the *via principalis* (the path where the senior officers encamped) and the *via decumana* (the east-west path). This layout also provided the model on which more permanent Roman bases were constructed.

the other assassins in the east. Decimus never made it, for he met his death at the hands of a Gallic chieftain.

Octavian now had an army of 12 legions. The troops were of varying quality, but Antony recognized that his force was no match for it and summoned assistance from various subordinates as he marched into southern Gaul, where Aemilius Lepidus, another of Julius Caesar's associates, held command. Antony convinced Lepidus's men to join him (while keeping Lepidus in titular command of his forces) and turned back to Italy, having raised the quantity of men at his disposal to 17 legions. In response, Octavian abandoned his pursuit, and the stage was set for the next transformation in political and military allegiances.

In the summer of 43 BCE, Octavian sent a band of soldiers to Rome demanding – unsuccessfully at first – that the senate award him one of the now-vacant consulships. It took the arrival of Octavian himself in Rome, at the head of his legions, to gain his wish. The other consulship went to Quintus Pedius, another of Julius Caesar's former generals (and another distant cousin of Octavian), who would serve as Octavian's agent in the city, passing a law declaring Caesar's assassins to be enemies of the state. Octavian now marched north again, encountering the forces of Antony and Lepidus near present-day Bologna.

Instead of engaging in battle, though, the troops urged reconciliation among their leaders – all of whom owed their positions in one way or another to Julius Caesar – so that they could take on the forces gathered by the assassins Brutus and Cassius. After a short period of negotiation,

Octavian, Antony and Lepidus reached an accommodation, agreeing they would be equal partners in the government of the Roman state as 'triumvirs for the restoration of the Republic'. (This was what historians refer to as Rome's Second Triumvirate, the First Triumvirate being the alliance agreed among Caesar, Pompey and the wealthy general Crassus in 59–55 BCE.) They would have power superior to that of all consuls, and their term would be for five years, with the possibility of renewal. The tribune Lucius Titius introduced the bill that formally created this board on the 27th of November.

The very next day, the triumvirs commenced decisive action against their political enemies and those complicit in the assassination of Julius Caesar. They issued 'proscription edicts', whereby any person whose name appeared on a list (the Latin verb for the process is *proscribere*) was to be sentenced to death, and their property confiscated by the state: effectively a cull of the ruling classes. The justification for such mass murder was that it was Julius Caesar's ill-advised mercy that had inadvertently brought about his assassination – and the triumvirs were not about to make the same mistake.

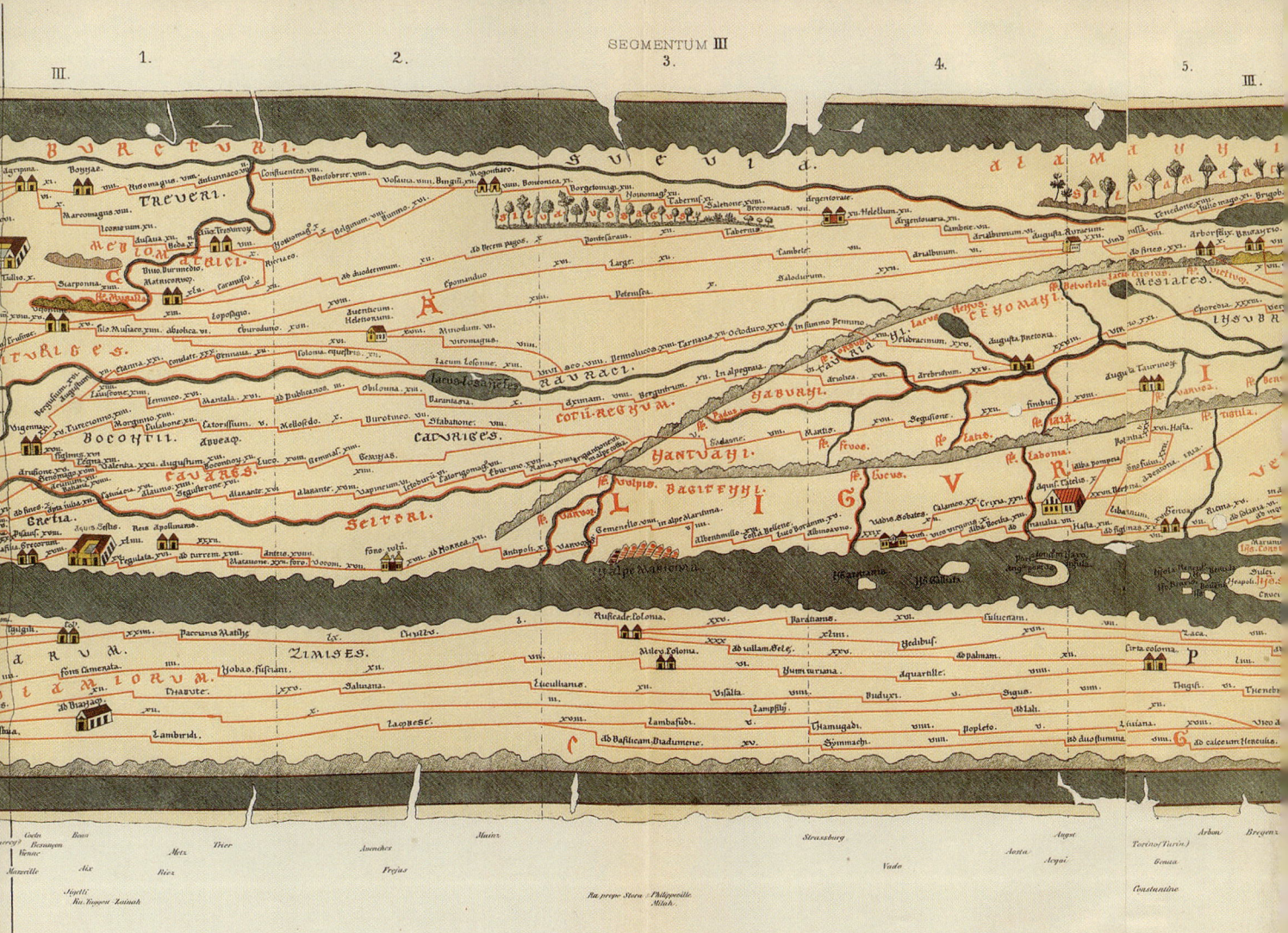

Three hundred senators were among the proscribed, as were some two thousand members of the next highest (and much larger) social order, the equestrians. The most prominent name was that of the great orator Marcus Tullius Cicero, who met his death on the 7th of December. As for the victims' property, it was allocated to pay for the vast army now accumulated under the triumvirs' command.

Of course, not all the triumvirs' enemies were close at hand. And so, while they agreed that Lepidus would remain in Italy, where he would also serve as consul, Antony and Octavian led their combined army of 19 legions against Brutus and Cassius, who had raised 17 legions of their own from the eastern provinces. The ensuing battles of the 3rd and 23rd of October, 42 BCE, would be the largest ever fought by Roman armies.

Figure IV

The *Tabula Peutingeriana* or *Peutinger Table* (see pages 16–17) depicts the Roman road system at the time of Augustus. The segment shown here stretches from Britain (an add-on to Agrippa's original map after the island's conquest in the 40s CE – the south of England is seen bisected by the River Thames) across the western provinces with the Rhone in the centre, through the islands of Corsica and Sardinia at right. The lower land mass represents North Africa.

THE BATTLE OF PHILIPPI

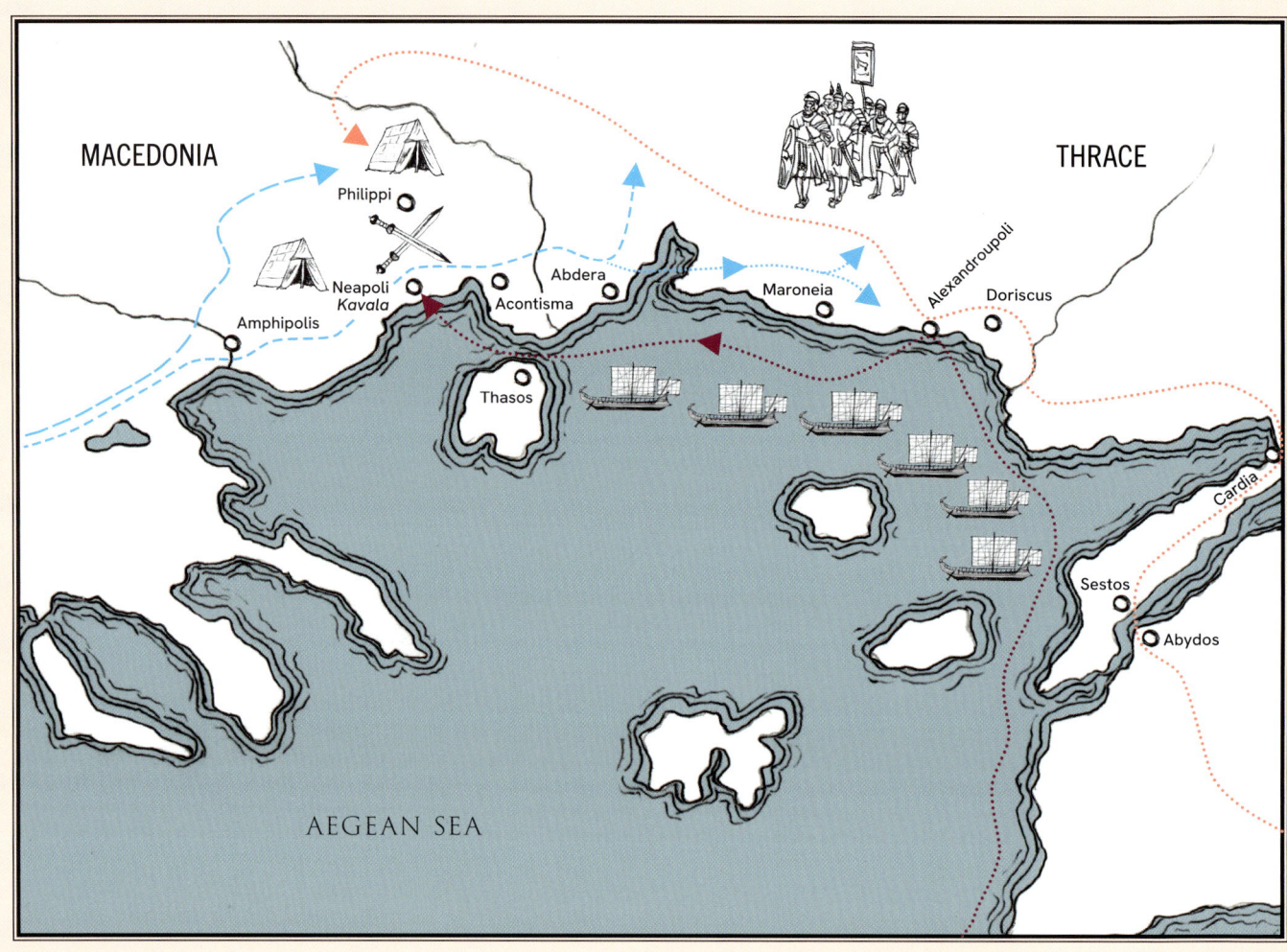

◄······ Army of Brutus and Cassius
◄······ Fleet of Tillus
◄── ── Army of Antony and Octavian
◄── ── Army of Norbanus and Decidius
◄······ Army of Decidius

In August 44 BCE Marcus Brutus, 'the noblest Roman of them all' (as Shakespeare has Mark Antony describe him), arrived in Athens five months after taking part in Caesar's assassination. He was technically governor of Crete, but in Athens he was able to gather a number of supporters and take over a large amount of money being shipped from the province of Asia to Rome. He then moved into the province of Macedonia, where he gathered recruits. They were drawn from among former soldiers loyal to Caesar's rival Pompey who had been settled there at the end of Caesar's war with Pompey, and from the legions gathered there for Caesar's planned invasion of Parthia. At the same time, Brutus's co-conspirator Cassius had taken control of the province of Syria, with its substantial garrison, and defeated the pro-Caesarian governor. Raising yet more money from the cities of the province of Asia (western Turkey) – which were greatly impoverished as a result – Brutus and Cassius joined forces in Greece. They had hopes that the Caesarian army, commanded by Antony and Octavian, would not be able to cross the Adriatic, which was controlled by their fleet and that of Pompey's son Sextus Pompey, who controlled Sicily. However, the assassins lost control of the sea when Queen Cleopatra of Egypt sent a fleet to support the Caesarians.

The army commanded by Antony and Octavian amounted to 19 legions, while that of Brutus and Cassius totalled 17 legions. The assassins drew up their forces at Philippi, at the northeastern edge of Macedonia, where they had a secure supply line. Their plan was that a shortage of supplies would disable the larger, and more experienced, army of Antony and Octavian. It might have worked, had not Antony's principal quality as a general been his exceptional boldness.

Brutus and Cassius each had his own camp on the hills overlooking the plain, while Antony and Octavian shared quarters on the other side of the plain. As one account of the battle puts it, 'The plain was well suited for fighting and the hill-tops for encampment.' Antony recognized the difficulty of the situation and began to dig entrenchments beyond Cassius's camp to cut off access to supplies. This forced the assassins to act. The fighting that took place in 42 BCE, on the 3rd of October, was actually two battles: one between Antony and Cassius, the other between Brutus and Octavian. Antony was thoroughly successful, defeating Cassius and overrunning his camp, while Brutus's men defeated Octavian and captured their enemy's camp. Octavian, who was said to have been ill when the battle started, hid in a nearby swamp.

The fighting also witnessed confusion, for the heavy dust that covered the battlefield prevented the generals from having a good view of what was happening. Cassius, who had fled into the hills beyond his camp and who believed that Brutus must also have suffered a defeat, took matters into his own hands: he committed suicide. As for Brutus, he halted the pursuit of Octavian's men once he had seized the camp, and withdrew to his own when he could not see how Cassius's forces were faring.

A further battle took place on the 23rd of October, and here the circumstances that led Brutus to fight, instead of waiting out his enemies' supply problems, are the stuff of legend. Allegedly, Brutus was convinced to commence battle by a vision of Caesar's ghost, as well as by bad intelligence and by grumbling among his soldiers that he was dragging out the war and disrespecting their courage. The battle began without the usual exchange of missile weapons, the two sides eschewing what the historian Appian called 'the usual movements and tactics of battles, but, coming to close combat with naked swords, they killed and were killed, seeking to break each other's ranks' (in *The Civil Wars*, IV, 128). Brutus's army was routed. He fled into the hills, where he, too, committed suicide.

Despite these resounding victories for the Caesarian forces, the standard of leadership in the campaign was generally poor. Only Cassius had held a significant independent command prior to Julius Caesar's murder. Brutus had served only a subordinate role under Pompey in 48 BCE. The 21-year-old Octavian was plainly just learning his way, while Antony displayed the combination of courage and carelessness that would be his ultimate undoing. Shakespeare's reading of the sources for the battle and the vision he creates in his *Julius Caesar* – of the assassins' defeat being the work of Caesar's ghost – has a great deal of merit, for it was their miscalculation that cost them the war.

Observers of the events of October of 42 BCE would have noticed Octavian's somewhat nervous disposition in the face of conflict; he was even sick in his tent during the first battle. It was this squeamishness, as well as the impact of his earliest experience of command in 43 BCE as a 19-year-old with minimal experience, that made him willing to delegate command to trusted subordinates.

In the aftermath of victory, Antony and Octavian were faced with the prospect of demobilizing an army they could not pay, despite all the penalties imposed on the proscribed senators and equestrians. A subtle administrative shift in the Triumvirate left Octavian to oversee the demobilization, as he was placed in control of Italy, Africa, Sicily and Sardinia, while Lepidus, who had overseen Italy, entered a temporary political limbo. Antony went on a tour of the eastern provinces and was beginning to build his own administrative structures – as well as a fateful relationship with Queen Cleopatra of Egypt.

The demobilization resulted in chaos and civil strife. Octavian resorted to mass confiscations in the style of that earlier dictator, Sulla: 18 cities had been selected, when the Triumvirate was formed, to suffer large-scale expropriations for veteran settlements. Leaders from central Italy, where most of the target cities lay, came to Rome to protest. Lucius Antonius, Antony's brother (and a consul for 41 BCE), encouraged them, declaring his interest in restoring the traditional government of the Republic – a scheme that would leave Lucius in charge as consul and Octavian without a position. His initiative collapsed when class solidarity drove the veterans into Octavian's arms. But a new force emerged to challenge Octavian in the shape of Sextus Pompey, son of Julius Caesar's old rival. With his control of Sicily and the assembly of a large fleet, he took in survivors from the assassins' forces. Octavian now had no fleet with which to contest the seas. Lepidus fled as the violence escalated, leaving Octavian to deal with Lucius. Open war broke out in the summer of 40 BCE. It resulted in the defeat of Lucius and the destruction of Perugia by Marcus Agrippa, who was emerging as Octavian's most trusted lieutenant. Lucius surrendered and was allowed to leave Italy.

Antony was furious at the turn of events. Interrupting his burgeoning affair with Cleopatra, he stormed west, now in alliance with Sextus Pompey. But when he reached Brundisium (present-day Brindisi), the troops there – still loyal to the concept of the Caesarian party – mutinied, demanding that Antony respect his alliance with Octavian. By the terms of a new settlement among the parties, Lepidus was stripped of almost all of his power and shipped off to Africa, while Antony agreed to marry Octavia, Octavian's recently widowed sister. Sextus Pompey, though, was left out in the cold. He responded by blockading Italy and causing serious food shortages in Rome, where the population was dependent upon imported grain. A fresh deal was struck in 39 BCE, this time at Miseno, on the Bay of Naples, recognizing Sextus as a partner to the triumvirs, ruling Sicily, Sardinia and Corsica along with other islands and a portion of the southern Peloponnese.

In 38 BCE Antony went east to participate in the war that had exploded with the Parthians. His departure from Italy had the effect of reopening hostilities between Octavian and Pompey, as the two went to war at sea.

Figure V

This image of a dying Gaul stresses both the heroic nature of Rome's enemies and the glory inherent in defeating them – a major theme in Julius Caesar's presentation of his conquest.

Octavian suffered a serious defeat off the coast of Calabria in 38 BCE and had to wait until 36 BCE, when, borrowing ships from Antony – after the Triumvirate was renewed for a further five years – he was able to confront Pompey once again. Agrippa, commanding Octavian's fleet, had learned from the experience of Julius Caesar's men in Gaul that lighter ships could be more effective than larger warships if they were equipped with grappling hooks fired from war machines. These tactics effectively converted a sea battle into a form of land battle, and Agrippa adopted them to destroy Sextus's fleet. It was the beginning of the end for Pompey's son. He fled east, where he was murdered by officials serving Antony.

While Octavian built up his naval power, Antony fought the Parthians. Having thoroughly reorganized Rome's eastern provinces – and given a good deal of Roman territory to Cleopatra in return for Egyptian logistical and financial support – he assembled a large army in Syria and was ready to fight by the summer of 38 BCE. Antony wrote to the Parthian king, Phraates IV, demanding that he return surviving prisoners from the Roman defeat at Carrhae (Harran, Turkey, in 53 BCE), as well as the standards taken in the battle, plus others lost after a subsequent Parthian assault on the eastern provinces. This was the first time that legionary standards were held up as important symbols of Roman power. But Phraates turned him down. In the summer of 36 BCE, Antony launched his invasion, using a plan originally developed by Julius Caesar. It envisaged a Roman army moving north from Syria into northwestern Turkey (then the kingdom of Armenia) before turning south along the River Tigris to seize major cities (in what is now northern Iraq) before descending on the Parthian capital at Ctesiphon (south of Baghdad today). This militarily sound scheme would be used successfully several times in future years, but in Antony's hands it failed. He left the invasion too late in the year and omitted to protect his supply and siege column. The result was a forced withdrawal, losing a couple more standards in the winter of 36 BCE.

While Cleopatra provided resources to revitalize Antony's army, he launched a propaganda campaign blaming the failure on Artavasdes II, the King of Armenia, because his outnumbered Armenian cavalry had not saved the supply and siege train. Now allied with the King of Media, in northern Iraq, Antony pursued his Armenian vendetta over the next two summers, finally taking Artavasdes prisoner in the summer of 34 BCE. The king's capture provided the occasion for a triumphal procession in Alexandria, at which Antony announced the reorganization of the eastern provinces, which also gifted more territory to Cleopatra. But that was not all. Antony announced his forthcoming divorce from Octavia and his marriage to Cleopatra, and, furthermore, asserted that Cleopatra's young son Caesarion (b. 47 BCE), whose legitimacy Caesar and his closest associates had vigorously denied, was Julius Caesar's biological child. A breach with Octavian was now inevitable.

The five-year term of the Triumvirate was due to end on the 1st of January, 32 BCE, and, moreover, two of Antony's friends were in line to take up the consulship. Octavian would have to take radical action if he were to preserve his power – and he did. According to the formalities, his power as a triumvir could lapse only if he crossed the *pomerium*, the sacred boundary of the city of Rome. When the 1st of January arrived and the consuls took up office within

Figure VI

Egyptian religion required a pharaoh as an intermediary between humans and the gods. For that reason, in the wake of Augustus's conquest of Egypt, Egyptian priests continued the tradition (that had begun with the Persian conquest in the sixth century BCE) of depicting their foreign rulers as pharaohs.

Figure VII (overleaf)

The portrait of Augustus expresses the qualities expected of the good ruler: humanity and responsibility. His calm gaze reflects the notion that his regime has brought tranquillity to the empire.

Figure VIII (page 36)

This portrait from Herculaneum has been identified as Cleopatra on the basis of its resemblance to portraits of the queen on her coins.

the city limits, Octavian did not attend the senate. The next day, a senate meeting was summoned outside the *pomerium*, where Octavian entered, at the head of an armed guard, to seat himself between the consuls, symbolically asserting his superior authority. He proceeded to read out a denunciation of Antony's relationship with Cleopatra. The new consuls were allowed to leave for Alexandria, as were other senators who felt a personal loyalty to Antony; but it was an effective declaration of war from Octavian, culminating at the Battle of Actium in September 31 BCE.

THERE WERE BRONZE FLEETS TO BE SEEN IN THE MIDDLE, ACTIAN BATTLES, AND YOU SEE THE WHOLE AREA DRAWN UP IN FEVERISH PREPARATION FOR WAR.

VIRGIL, *AENEID*, VIII, 675–93

THUS ANTONY AND CLEOPATRA, WHO HAD CAUSED MANY EVILS TO THE EGYPTIANS AND MANY TO THE ROMANS, MADE WAR AND MET THEIR DEATH IN THE MANNER I HAVE DESCRIBED; AND THEY WERE BOTH EMBALMED IN THE SAME FASHION AND BURIED IN THE SAME TOMB.

CASSIUS DIO

THE BATTLE OF ACTIUM

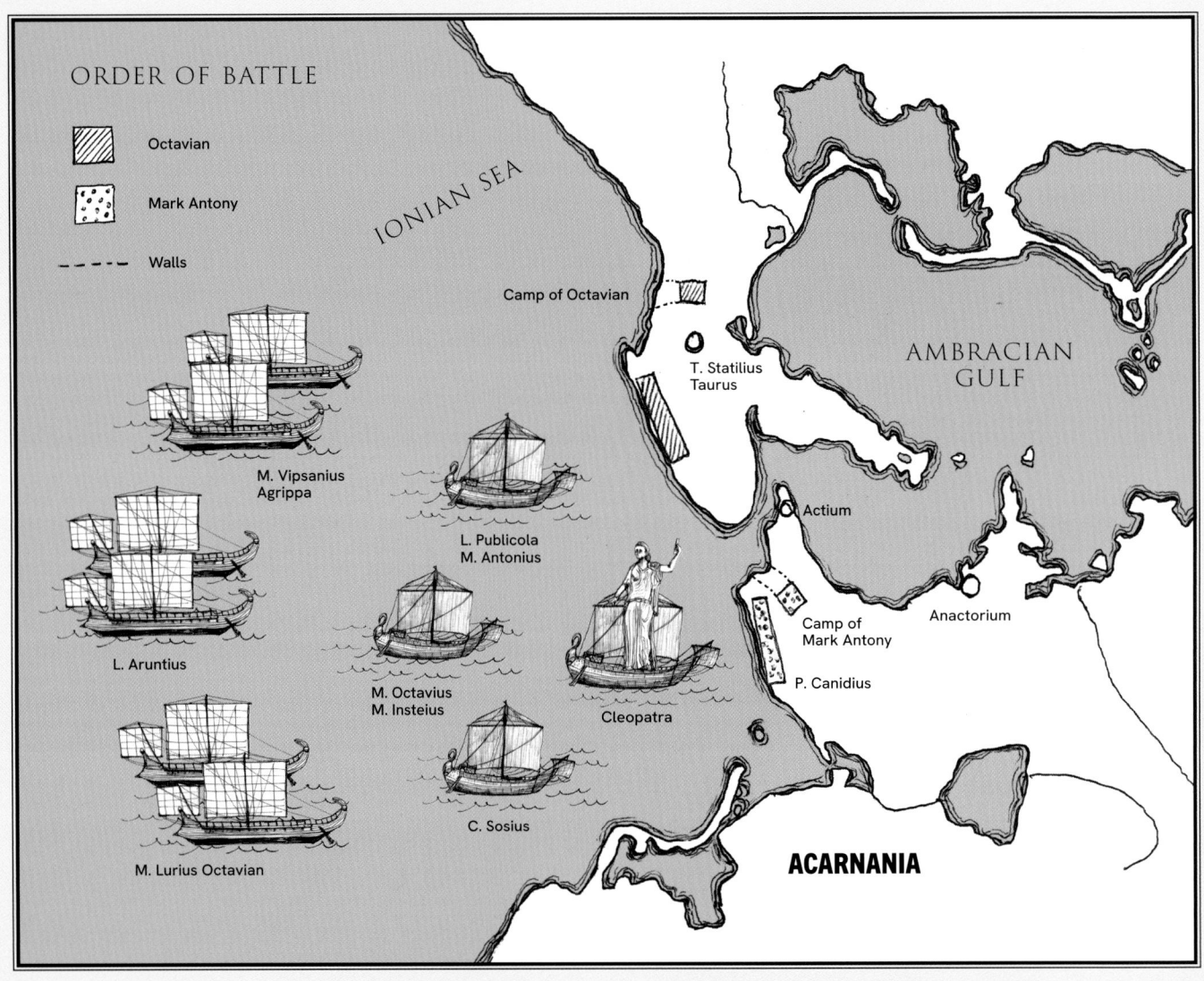

Mark Antony was erratic. At his best he could be clever, courageous and eloquent; at his worst brutal, vindictive and careless. Unfortunately for him, it was his worst qualities that were on display as the campaign against the forces of Octavian drew to a climax at Actium, on the eastern shores of Greece.

As had been the case during his unsuccessful attempt to invade the Parthian Empire a few years before, Antony failed to pay sufficient attention to logistics. His army and navy were very large by ancient standards, possibly numbering 60,000 men. That would have required approximately 55,000 kilograms (120,000 pounds) of food a day. Although he had tried to extract supplies from the cities of mainland Greece, the only way he could get enough food was if he controlled the sea lanes behind him, since overland transport in the age of the donkey would not bring in nearly enough supplies. But as Antony was settling in at Actium, which was intended to be his base for invading Italy, Octavian's admiral, Marcus Agrippa, had begun cutting his naval supply lines. The tide was turning against Antony as his supplies ran low.

Antony found himself unable to force a battle with Octavian's army, which had dug itself into a strong defensive position. Moreover, it became clear that Octavian also had a superior fleet. Antony's only long-term hope for continuing the larger struggle would be to evade the current predicament, so the purpose of the ensuing naval battle was to cover his escape with Cleopatra, whose continuing support would be critical to any future conflict.

Then the wind began to blow. For nearly a week, it was impossible to launch the ships. All the while, the situation in Antony's camp worsened.

Finally, on the 2nd of September, it was possible to set sail. Antony drew up his fleet so that the Egyptian squadron of 60 vessels was ranged behind the centre of his line. As the battle began on the wings of the fleet, a gap opened in the centre, allowing Cleopatra to sail away, followed by Antony. Unaware that they had been betrayed by their commander, Antony's men fought on against their better-fed and more experienced opponents.

The tactics of this battle in the Ionian Sea were dictated by the size of the ships. Antony's vessels were designed to fight at close quarters, to use their 'rams' to charge at their opponents or close with them and board. Octavian's lighter ships were designed to stand off and bombard their enemies with catapults. Fighting in the open water, Antony's heavy warships could get close enough to the lighter ships. The monument to the battle that Octavian would build at Nicopolis ('Victoryville') on the site of his camp contained rams of 35 enemy ships sunk in the battle, demonstrating that more than half of the vessels remaining after Antony and Cleopatra took off were destroyed. Antony and Cleopatra's surviving fleet, along with all Antony's legions, surrendered four days after the Battle of Actium.

Following Octavian's victory at Actium, he allowed Antony and Cleopatra to make good their escape to Egypt, while he took a slow trip through the eastern provinces, asserting his control and making arrangements with the allied kings of the region, all of whom had previously been Antony's people. It was not until July 30 BCE that Octavian reached Egypt and the couple's refuge in Alexandria. After a month of probing attacks around the city, Octavian launched a major assault. Even though Antony's forces resisted the first attack successfully, his supporters deserted him when the second assault was launched on the 1st of August. With his options closed, Antony committed suicide, followed nine days later by Queen Cleopatra herself.

Sixteen years after the assassination of his adoptive father, Octavian now ruled Rome's empire unchallenged. But Julius Caesar's rule had been brief. Could Octavian – Gaius Julius Caesar – achieve greater success and hold on to power?

IMPERATOR CAESAR AUGUSTUS

Summing up his achievements at the end of his life, Octavian wrote:

> *In my sixth and seventh consulships, after I had extinguished the civil wars, when I held power over everything through the consensus of all people, I transferred the Republic from my power to the control of the Roman senate and people. Because of this service of mine, I was named Augustus by a decree of the senate.*

The sixth and seventh consulships fell in 28/27 BCE. Octavian had remained in the east for two years after the capture of Alexandria. Upon returning to Italy, he surrendered his power as triumvir (the formal process to which he alludes above). He received the name 'Augustus', meaning 'extraordinary person', on the 19th of January, 27 BCE – a name that came to define not only him but also an era and the beginnings of what historians would call the Roman Empire, as distinct from the Roman Republic.

Augustus began to reshape the government of the state so as to avoid the errors of Julius Caesar, who had exercised close control over all aspects of the government, but in the process disrespected traditional offices of state. Indeed, it was frustration with that conduct that had largely inspired the conspiracy behind the assassination. By contrast, the system Augustus would develop left the day-to-day management of affairs in Rome and Italy in the hands of the traditional magistrates (*praetors*, consuls and so on) while he managed the major provinces, that is, those with armies.

In the document called *The Deeds of the Divine Augustus*, a summary of his life, Augustus listed the many benefactions he provided to the Roman people – games, distributions of food, construction projects, veteran settlements, gifts to the state treasury – as well as his various offices and finally the actions he took to expand the empire. He introduced this last

Figure IX (previous pages)

A first-century relief depicting the battle of Actium. The ship with the figurehead of a centaur with the head of Hercules is an allusion to Antony, who was viewed as being impetuous, like Hercules, and drunk like a centaur.

section of the work with the words: 'I expanded the frontiers of all the provinces of the Roman people where there are neighbouring nations that do not obey our *imperium*.' His would be an age of imperial expansion, beginning in the west, before moving on to settle the eastern frontier and launch major operations in Germany and the Balkans.

Before any expansion could take place, though, Augustus needed to reorganize the army into a force the state could afford. Once Antony's forces had surrendered, Augustus had roughly 55 legions, far more than the empire's tax base could support in the long term. He wrote that he released a large number of soldiers from service in the aftermath of the conquest of Egypt. These would have been men who had been enlisted during the 30s BCE, both by himself and by Antony, and the total would have amounted to nearly half of those under arms at Actium. Augustus retained 28 of those legions, and they were installed in the provinces according to perceived strategic need at the time: nine legions sent to Spain, three left in Egypt and four stationed in Syria. Africa had one legion, the provinces along the Rhine had six and the central European provinces probably another six.

The reorganization of the army implied a process for coherent strategic planning that had not been a feature of the government of the Roman Republic. Implicit in it was attention to a budget that controlled the size of the army, and terms of service that would enable the state to predict when it needed to provide to recruits the benefits promised on entry into service. Under reforms, funding for the army was detached from the traditional tax system (based on collection by independent corporations of public contractors) and placed in the hands of army commanders who reported to Augustus, and whose personal resources would be used to supplement those of the state.

In the absence of a formal long-term military staff, strategic planning depended on the emperor's work with experienced officials. There is an insight into this approach in a letter from Augustus to his then heir apparent, Tiberius, mentioning dining with men who had experience in the Balkans at a time when major campaigns were being planned. And of course, Augustus himself and his lieutenant, Agrippa, had already familiarized themselves with much of the empire during the civil wars. Additionally, some senators chose to advance their careers through military service, taking on in their early years additional provincial appointments that enabled them to take command of major armies once they achieved the consulship – an appointment requiring Augustus's support.

The disposition of the legions immediately following Actium suggests that Augustus's strategic priority was to complete the conquest of Hispania (Spain). Although Rome had established two provinces in Spain at the end of the third century BCE, taking over territory previously ruled by its rival, Carthage, it had never brought the entirety of the peninsula under direct control. War had broken out in northwestern Spain, the region still independent of Rome, in 29 BCE. With a large army at his back, Augustus entered the area to command operations in 26–24 BCE. The Spanish tribes avoided head-on conflict, preferring to wage a guerrilla war against the invaders. Augustus fell ill in the course of the operations, allegedly from

Figure X (overleaf)

The relief on the Altar of Peace, next to the mausoleum Augustus built as the last resting place for his family, represents the orderly Roman society that Augustus claimed to have established under the protection of the gods. This section depicts Roman priests to stress the centrality of religion to the Augustan project.

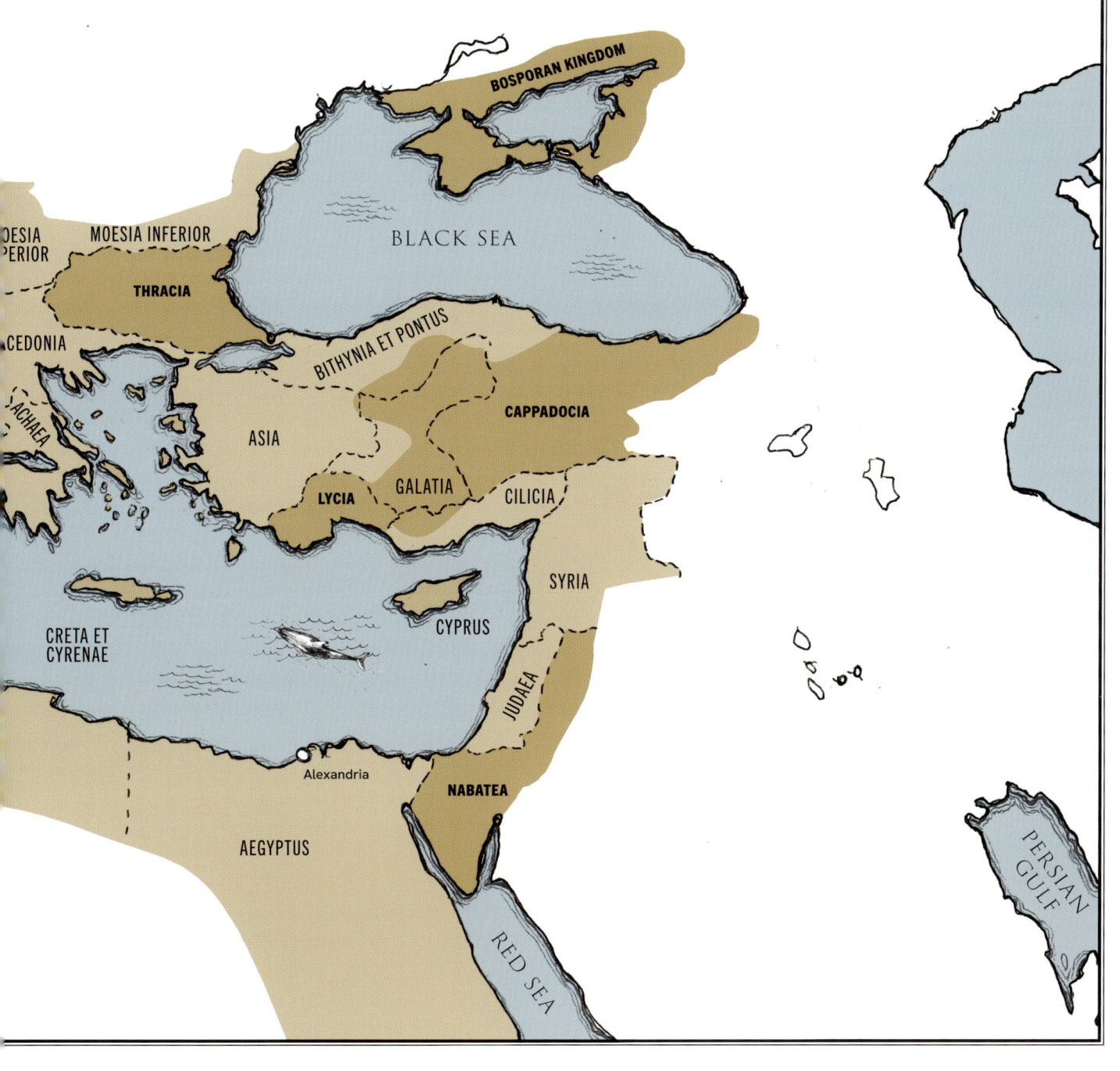

overwork, and returned to Rome claiming the job was done, but he turned down the offer of a 'triumph' – the traditional ceremony honouring a successful campaign commander. In fact, the campaigns in Spain would continue until 19 BCE, when the last of the Spanish tribes agreed to pay tribute to Rome in order to end the conflict.

There was also imperial expansion to the south and east. While he was completing his operations in Spain, Augustus instructed the governor of Egypt to lead expeditions into Sudan and Arabia. The first operation was in response to raids launched into Roman territory from that region (a continuation of a long-standing pattern of conflict). The motivation for the invasion of Arabia, which ended in failure, was the seizure of the peninsula's southwest (today's Yemen), which was the last stopping point outside the empire on the lucrative spice-trade route with India. Greater control of the route could have yielded a windfall for a treasury strained by the high cost of veteran settlement after Actium.

It was upon his return to Rome, in 23 BCE, that Augustus implemented constitutional change. Realizing that he could not continue to hold the consulship every year as he had since 31 BCE, he laid down that office, receiving instead a grant of *imperium maius* (greater power) in whatever province he should enter, accompanied by a grant of the power of a tribune, which allowed him to bring measures before the senate and legislation before the people. This combination of *imperium maius* with tribunician power would henceforth define his position, and those of his successors for several centuries to come. An important feature of both *imperium maius* and tribunician power was that they could be shared, and they usually were, throughout the rest of Augustus's life.

As Augustus entered his fourth decade, he faced a series of domestic crises. His nephew and designated heir, Marcellus, died, meaning that if the succession were to stay within the family, it would fall to the sons of his wife, Livia, by her prior marriage. Livia's elder son, Tiberius, was born in 42 BCE and could now be entrusted with titular commands to enhance his public image; her younger son, Drusus, born in 38 BCE, would soon be of an age to take up similar tasks.

It was Tiberius who played a significant public role in an extremely high-profile operation beginning in 22 BCE, shortly after Augustus quashed a rather inept assassination plot. While Augustus had been in Spain, a civil war had raged in the Parthian kingdom. The losing contender, Tiridates, had fled to Syria, where he had been received by the Roman administration. At some point, the son of King Phraates who had won the civil war also entered Roman territory. Given the fratricidal habits of his family, it looks as if Phraates had sent his son (whose name is unknown) to Roman territory for protection, although now he asked that both Tiridates and his son be handed over. Augustus denied the first of these requests, but agreed to the second if Phraates would return the standards taken at the Battle of Carrhae and any captives still alive. Phraates is said to have acquiesced, but by 22 BCE he still had not made good on the agreement. His failure to keep his promises gave Augustus the excuse to head east.

The expedition lasted four years and was more of a grand tour than a military operation. Neither Phraates nor Augustus was interested in

Figure XI

The surviving copy of *The Deeds of the Divine Augustus* – Augustus's account of his public life – from the temple honouring Augustus at Ankara, Turkey. The *Deeds* were originally inscribed on bronze tablets that were placed in front of his mausoleum at Rome.

full-scale war, and no effort was made on the Roman side to increase the garrison of Syria, which would have been necessary for an aggressive strike into Parthian territory. Augustus himself never reached the frontier on the Euphrates, spending most of his time in Athens or on the island of Samos. The situation was then complicated by events in Armenia, where a faction of the nobility hostile to King Artaxas asked Augustus to install the king's brother Tigranes in his place. Augustus agreed and entrusted the task to Tiberius.

A serious war with Parthia was quite possible at this point, but events in Armenia took a sudden and decisive turn in Rome's favour. Artaxas's enemies murdered him, and there was no domestic opposition to the installation of the brother as King Tigranes III. Phraates agreed to recognize Tigranes, and he returned the legionary standards to Augustus, along with the surviving prisoners. Tiberius himself crowned Tigranes King of Armenia. From these events it appears that for Phraates, the protection offered by alliance with Rome was more important than Armenia – although other Parthian monarchs would take a different view – and he delivered even more of his children to Augustus. The Roman emperor, in turn, could claim to have succeeded where Antony had failed and to have obtained recognition of Rome's superiority over Parthia. The ideological importance of the surrender of the standards can be inferred from the breastplate of the so-called Augustus of Prima Porta statue, as well as from Augustus's statement in *The Deeds of the Divine Augustus*:

> *I recovered many military standards lost by other generals from conquered peoples in Spain, Gaul and Dalmatia. I compelled the Parthians to return the standards and spoils of three Roman armies, and, as suppliants, to seek the friendship of the Roman people. I placed those standards in the inner shrine, which is in the temple of Mars the Avenger.*

The standard from Spain had been lost in 39 BCE, while the Balkan standards dated back to the civil war between Pompey and Caesar. The temple of Mars the Avenger was the centrepiece of Rome's new Forum, completed in 17 BCE. At the same time, the senate voted to expand the triumphal arch that had been erected in the Forum to commemorate the Battle of Actium, adding secondary arches alongside the main one, and inscribing a list of all triumphs celebrated from the earliest moments of Roman history (some of them imaginary) down to Augustus's own time. The triumph Augustus celebrated upon his return to Rome was therefore interpreted as the culmination of Roman history.

THE NORTHERN FRONTIERS

In the years after his return from the eastern provinces, Augustus concerned himself with domestic reform. In the meantime, action shifted from the empire's southern and eastern boundaries to the northern and central European zones. In western Europe, the boundary of the empire had been set by Julius Caesar on the Rhine. He had asserted, for ideological reasons, that the German lands, east of the Rhine, lacked the resources to make them worth conquering. In central-southern Europe, the Roman Empire's two border provinces were in the Balkans: Illyricum, which occupied the area of present-day Slovenia, Croatia, Serbia and Bosnia; and Macedonia, which covered northern Greece and what is now North Macedonia. To the east of Roman Macedonia lay the independent, but subordinate, kingdom of Thrace. Although there had been conflict with groups occupying Moesia and Pannonia (now Bulgaria and Hungary), there had been no effort to occupy these regions.

It is a sign of Augustus's lack of interest in central-southern Europe that repeated conflicts between the governors of Illyricum and Macedonia and the peoples along their northern borders had not elicited a plan to alter the status quo. The situation in Gaul and southern Germany had likewise remained static in the decade following the Battle of Actium. It was only after 20 BCE that Augustus decided to launch major campaigns to bring Germany, as far as the River Elbe, under direct Roman control, and to expand direct control in central Europe as far as the River Danube.

While the bulk of the Roman army was operating in Spain in the 20s BCE, the Roman military presence in Gaul was concentrated in three areas: the territory of the Remi in northern France; the area around Langres (in central France); and Aquitania, the region north of the Alps. These concentrations shifted gradually once the war in Spain finally ended, in 19 BCE, but it was in 16 BCE that a sudden disaster drew Augustus to the region. A coalition of Germanic tribes in the vicinity of what is now Cologne had massacred some Roman businessmen resident in their territory before crossing the Rhine and ravaging Roman Gaul, surprising the governor, Marcus Lollius, and snatching the standard of the Fifth Legion. Roman legions now began to be transferred from Spain to the troubled area, and Augustus spent the better part of 15 BCE along the Rhine, reforming the administration and dealing with the Germanic tribes, who asked for terms – which were granted, presumably once they had returned the standard they had taken.

While Augustus supervised the settlement of Gaul, there were two significant military operations in the Alps. The area known as Raetia occupied what are now the eastern cantons of Switzerland, as well as portions of Bavaria and Baden-Württemberg in Germany, while Noricum, to the east, occupied other parts of Bavaria and central Austria. The Raetians had a history of interfering with the passage from Italy into Gaul from the Aosta Valley through the mountains (later known as the St Bernard Pass), while raiders from Noricum tended to target their southern neighbours in Illyricum. Augustus assigned the subjugation of Raetia to Livia's children Tiberius and Drusus. They succeeded in their task by the end of 14 BCE. At roughly the same time, two tribes from Noricum raided the area around

Figure XII (overleaf)

Marcus Vipsanius Agrippa, Augustus's right-hand man and first husband of his daughter Julia. Agrippa's genuine military ability enabled the defeat of Sextus Pompey and the victory at Actium. His prominence underscores the crucial difference between Augustus's regime, where power was shared, and that of Julius Caesar, who was very clear that he alone was in control.

> HAPPILY FOR THE REPOSE OF MANKIND, THE MODERATE SYSTEM RECOMMENDED BY THE WISDOM OF AUGUSTUS WAS ADOPTED BY THE FEARS AND VICES OF HIS IMMEDIATE SUCCESSORS.
>
> — EDWARD GIBBON

present-day Trieste. Illyricum's governor, Publius Silius, drove them back to their lands, and Noricum was placed under Roman rule as a quasi-independent province; there would still be a King of Noricum, but there would also be a Roman governor of equestrian rank – the model for Roman regime in Judaea just over a decade later, when Jesus of Nazareth was born.

Despite such successes, the Roman armies had a demographic and financial problem. Most of the troops had been recruited in the immediate aftermath of Actium, on the standard terms of service at 16 years, which meant that Augustus now had to fund large-scale payments to retiring soldiers as well as recruit a new army. It would take several years to do the latter. In the interim, in 12 BCE, Augustus dedicated the Altar of Peace alongside the great family mausoleum he had constructed by the banks of the River Tiber.

In that same year, 12 BCE, Augustus suffered the loss of Marcus Agrippa. Agrippa had been Augustus's pre-eminent general since the years of the civil war, a man who was married to his daughter Julia, and father to Augustus's grandsons Gaius and Lucius, both under ten years of age. Augustus himself was now over 50, which was old by contemporary Roman standards. If the regime were to continue, new leadership had to be developed, and new credit gained for military success. Tiberius and Drusus were therefore given high-profile commands in Germany and the Balkans, although Augustus, surrounded by regional experts, still provided strategic direction in Rome for the campaigns.

Of these two conflicts, the Balkan war was the more important. That much is clear from the fact that the task had been assigned to Agrippa before his death, before being passed on to Tiberius, the senior heir apparent. Tiberius set out from Illyricum, following the line of the River Sava through what is now Bosnia and Serbia, while another Roman army advanced north out of Macedonia, taking in aid from the Scordisci, a group that had recently been raiding the Roman province. This war lasted four years, until Tiberius was able to proclaim victory and annex a new province, Pannonia, bounded to the south by the old provinces of Illyricum and Dalmatia, to the northwest by Noricum and to the north by the Danube.

Drusus's operations had involved wide-ranging raids into Germany following a reorganization of the Roman army into four legionary bases along the Rhine: at Fectio (Vechten), Vetera (Xanten), Novaesium (Neuss) and Mogontiacum (Mainz). The bases at Vechten, Xanten and Mainz each sat at the end of a Roman invasion route. Vechten, a naval base, was the departure point for Roman fleets accessing the Elbe and beyond, while Xanten sits at the mouth of the River Lippe, which leads into northern Germany, and Mainz lies at the intersection of the rivers Rhine and Main, the river that Roman armies could take into central Germany. For logistical reasons, there, as in the Balkans, Roman armies needed to operate near river lines to carry the supplies needed for extended operations.

The principal targets of Drusus's campaigns were the Chatti, a powerful confederation in the region of what is now Saxony, and the evidence from archaeology suggests that he had legions spend the winter north of the Rhine. It appears that operations in Germany were reasonably successful in this regard. Just outside what is now the town of Waldgirmes, in Hesse, the remains of a town designed on a Roman pattern have been discovered.

Figure XIII

When Agrippa died in 12 BCE, the two sons of Livia by her first marriage, Drusus (left) and Tiberius, were marked out as Augustus's likely successors. Both pursued active military careers. Drusus, however, died in 9 BCE, and Tiberius ruled as emperor from 14 until 36 CE.

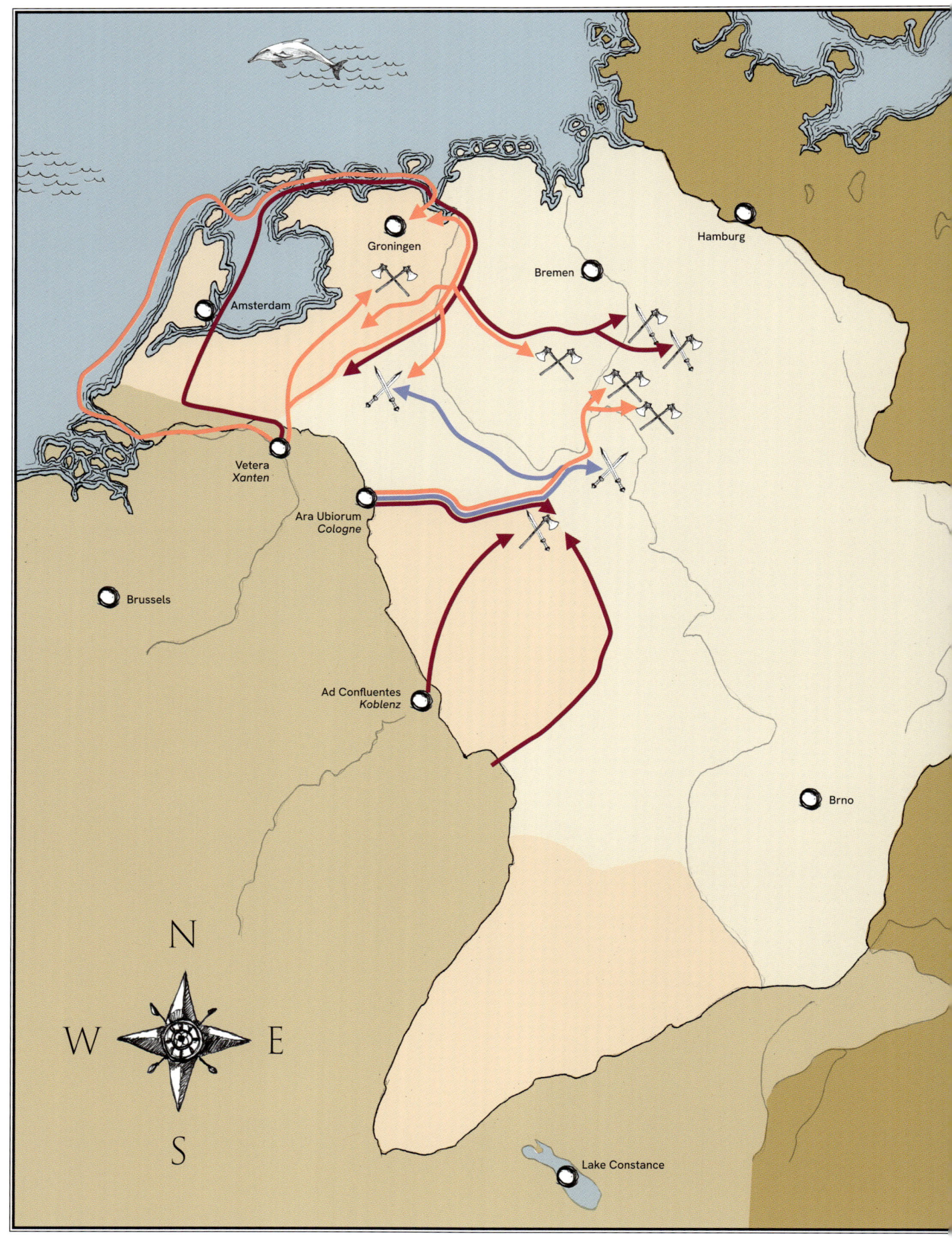

GERMAN CAMPAIGNS

- Germanicus advance: 14 CE
- Germanicus advance: 15 CE
- Germanicus advance: 16 CE
- Battle site 14 CE
- Battle site 15 CE
- Battle site 16 CE
- Roman Empire
- Germania pacified
- Hostile peoples
- Roman client state

In Germany, as elsewhere, the Roman strategy was to co-opt or create a local ruling group that would work in Rome's interests – not dissimilar to the situation regarding Armenia, where Rome hosted members of the Parthian ruling family. Leaders who appeared amenable to Roman rule would be recruited with bands of their followers to serve as auxiliaries to the legions. One such individual, from the Cherusci people (somewhat to the north of the main area of Drusus's operations), was Arminius, who, granted citizenship, was known thereafter as Julius Arminius.

Tiberius, too, travelled to Germany in 9 BCE, even though his new Balkan province of Pannonia was still taking shape (and would experience further conflict). The reason for the relocation was Drusus's untimely death after an accidental fall from his horse. Tiberius took over operations north of the Rhine for two years, allegedly with minimal losses, where, according to a contemporary, 'he subdued the country to the point of almost reducing it to the level of a tribute-paying province' and was presented to the public as an awesome warrior who impressed Rome's rivals:

> *One of the barbarians, older, tall and, as his clothing showed, of high rank, boarded a boat made from a cut-out log, as is typical among these people. Alone he steered this vessel into the middle of the river and asked safe passage to land on our bank and to see Caesar. His request was granted, and he brought his boat to the shore. After gazing upon Tiberius Caesar for some time he said, 'Our warriors are mad. When you're not here they worship you as a god, but when you are here, they fear your arms instead of accepting your offer of protection. But I, Caesar, thanks to your generous permission, have seen the gods I only used to hear about, and, in my whole life, I have not wished for or had a happier day.'*

Velleius Paterculus
Short History of Rome, II, 107, 1–2

By contrast, Tiberius later wrote that he felt he accomplished more through diplomacy than outright conflict in his dealings with the Germans. He returned to Rome in 7 BCE to celebrate a triumph and take up the consulship.

It was at this point, though, that Tiberius retreated in a huff to the island of Rhodes, a consequence of a huge argument with Augustus. The best guess as to the causes of this fight are Tiberius's troubled relationship with his wife (and Agrippa's widow), Julia, and the favour Augustus was showing to her children by Agrippa, Gaius and Lucius Caesar, to the relative exclusion of his own son, Drusus, by his previous wife.

Tiberius's withdrawal came at a difficult time for Augustus, who now had no family member to whom he could entrust a major operation; and trouble was brewing once again in Armenia. King Tigranes had died that year, and Augustus had ordered Tiberius, prior to his decamping to Rhodes, to replace Tigranes' successor, another Tigranes, with Ariobarzanes, who had been a hostage at Rome. Somehow this was achieved, but in 2 BCE Tigranes drove Ariobarzanes from the throne with help of Parthia.

The chaos in Armenia was matched by chaos in Parthia. Following almost immediately upon his successful support of Tigranes, King Phraates IV

Figure XIV

Lucius (left) and Gaius Caesar were the sons of Agrippa and Julia. Lucius died in 2 CE while returning from a campaign in Spain, and Gaius in 4 CE while on campaign in the eastern provinces.

was murdered by his wife, Thea Musa. She was once an Italian slave and actress, before being trafficked by Augustus to Phraates, whereupon he had fallen in love with her and made her his queen. After she killed Phraates, she ruled jointly with their son, also named Phraates. They were driven from the throne six years later, in 4 CE, by a cabal of Parthian nobility. Before that, however, Phraates V had a meeting with Augustus's grandson Gaius Caesar, who, at the age of 22, was now sent as the emperor's representative to the east, to resolve their differences over Armenia. The meeting was a dramatic moment, with a Parthian army assembled on the east bank of the Euphrates and a Roman army on the west. Phraates V dined with the Romans on the first night of the negotiation, Gaius with the Parthians on the second night. As a result, Gaius marched into Armenia to install a Roman candidate on the throne. Armenia, however, was to prove fatal to Gaius; supporting this candidate in the face of a revolt the next year, he was stabbed while negotiating with a rebel leader, and died a few months later.

With Gaius's death, there was a genuine dynastic crisis, for his brother had died two years previously. Augustus had lost both grandchildren. In 2 CE, he summoned Tiberius to Rome, where Julia was no longer resident. She was, by now, exiled to the island of Pandateria in the Adriatic for plotting in 2 BCE, along with several of her lovers, to kill Augustus; as for those lovers, they were invited to commit suicide or themselves be exiled. Faced with crisis, in 4 CE Augustus adopted Tiberius, thereby clarifying the succession, saying that he was doing so 'for the good of the state'. The state would very soon require Tiberius's considerable military skill.

> *Through the whole period of the German and Pannonian campaigns, none of those, either junior or senior to us in rank, experienced an illness without his health and safety sustained through the care of Tiberius Caesar. It was as if, despite the great burdens of all the other responsibilities he bore, this was the only matter for which he had time. There was a horse-drawn carriage for whoever needed one, and his litter was at everyone's disposal (I myself used it, as did others); at one moment his doctors were available; at another his cooking equipment, at another his bathing gear (as if this had been brought along for this purpose alone) were all made available to anyone who was ill.*
>
> Velleius Paterculus
> *Short History of Rome*, II, 114, 2

The year after his adoption, Tiberius was campaigning deep inside Germany, in the lands bordering those of the Cherusci, and setting up winter quarters there. But then chaos exploded elsewhere. One local response to the arrival of Roman power, and Roman interference, in a region was for formerly disparate groups to coalesce into a larger alliance. This process had led to the creation of a new state ruled by the Marcomanni tribe in what is now the southern area of the Czech Republic, under the leadership of a man named Maroboduus. The process through which his power increased is alluded to briefly by an author serving in the region at this time, who wrote that 'states and individuals revolting from us would find refuge with him.' In 6 CE Tiberius moved to launch an attack on

Figure XV

This cameo shows Tiberius as emperor, seated next to his mother, Livia. Germanicus, who was then Tiberius's heir apparent, approaches the emperor in the company of his wife, Agrippina, daughter of Agrippa and Julia.

Maroboduus, at the head of nearly half of the Roman army – 13 legions – when suddenly a massive revolt broke out in the recently conquered area of Pannonia.

Familiarity with Roman habits made this revolt especially dangerous. The author who described Maroboduus wrote that 'the Pannonians had knowledge of not only Roman discipline, but also of our language, which many of them could write, and of our military training.' An emergency levy was imposed in Italy, and troops were transferred to the Balkans from the east. Tiberius, now assisted by his nephew Germanicus, led the Roman army against the rebels, and by the summer of 9 CE the revolt was largely contained. But that is when disaster struck in Germany.

The winter camp that Tiberius had established in Germany was succeeded, at some point in the next couple of years, by a more formal base near Minden. The garrison there amounted to three legions, supported by a substantial force of auxiliaries. In the autumn of 9 CE, urged on by Julius Arminius, the current governor withdrew from Minden and headed for Xanten. But he walked into a trap. His army was destroyed in what became known as the Battle of the Teutoburg Forest.

THE BATTLE OF THE TEUTOBURG FOREST

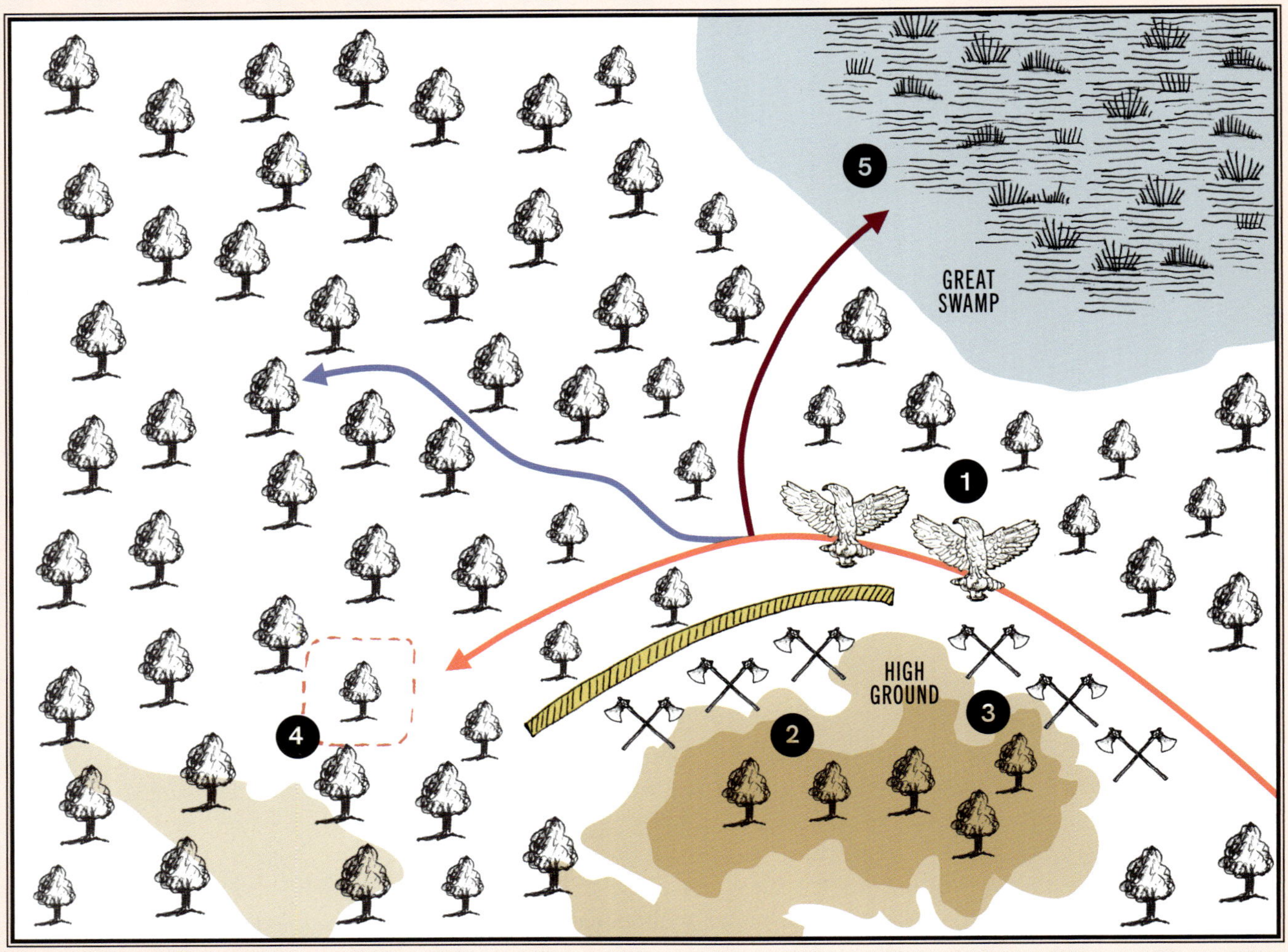

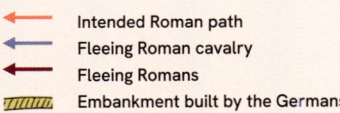
- Intended Roman path
- Fleeing Roman cavalry
- Fleeing Romans
- Embankment built by the Germans

1 The Roman column, made up of three legions, six infantry cohorts and three auxiliary cavalry wings (a total of some 20,000 men), stretched out in the forest for about 3.2 kilometres (2 miles).
2 Between 5,000 and 7,000 Germans behind the embankment, and a similar number in the forest.
3 Between 7,000 and 10,000 Germans on the eastern side of the high ground.
4 As a last and desperate defence, the Romans attempted to entrench themselves in a makeshift camp made of wagons.
5 Bewildered, many Romans fled north but died in the swamp.

Quinctilius Varus was an experienced provincial administrator with close connections to the imperial house. His second wife was a daughter of Agrippa, while his third wife was Augustus's grandniece. Before his appointment as governor in Germany, probably in 7 CE, he had been governor of Syria. The goal of his new, German assignment appears to have been to habituate the governing groups among the German communities along the Elbe to direct Roman government. His base was in the area of the present-day city of Minden.

As Varus was imposing Roman taxation and administering justice according to Roman legal practices, serious divisions emerged among members of the leadership group of the Cherusci, whose lands bordered the Elbe. Julius Arminius and his father, Sigimir, having previously been notable supporters of Roman endeavours, now abandoned their adherence to the imperial regime, splitting with Arminius's brother Flavus and his father-in-law Segestes, who would remain loyal to the Roman cause.

Arminius was sufficiently rich and accomplished to have been awarded equestrian status when he was given Roman citizenship in recognition for his service in previous years. He now assembled a coalition of German communities, while warning Varus that there would be rebellions in the region between his camp, at Minden, and the Rhine. This information convinced Varus to withdraw to the Rhine and into the trap – although the fact that he was still at Minden in September suggests he had initially planned to remain there for the winter, and further, that he required permission from Augustus to withdraw.

The battle that ensued, in the vicinity of Kalkriese, lasted for several days. The portion of the battle site that has been uncovered suggests that the Germans lined parts of Varus's anticipated route south with field fortifications from which they could attack his column. Varus, not expecting an attack, most likely organized his column in the standard Roman fashion, whereby each legion's baggage was placed behind the legion in the order of march, which would have made it impossible to launch a coherent response to the attackers. As one description of the action puts it:

they defended themselves against their attackers but suffered their heaviest losses when they did so. For, since they had to form their lines in a narrow space, so [that] the cavalry and infantry together might run down the enemy, they collided frequently with one another and with the trees.

The conflict along the route of the march lasted for four days, in persistently bad weather that hampered the Romans in using their bows and spears. As the days passed, the Romans became increasingly demoralized, so much so that the cavalry deserted the column and fled south to the Rhine on their own. The infantry moved on through the forests, now without the baggage they had abandoned after the first day's fighting. On the fourth day, the troops emerged from their camp and could no longer take the fight to the Germans. Years later, when a Roman army under Germanicus visited the site, they found that

Varus's first camp, with its broad sweep and measured spaces for officers and eagles, revealed the labours of three legions: then a half-ruined wall and shallow ditch showed where the survivors of the day's battle had taken cover. In the plain between were bleaching bones, scattered or in piles, where the men had fallen, as they fled or stood their ground.

Survivors of the action showed Germanicus where Varus had been wounded on that final day, and where he had taken his own life. Romans who surrendered had been slaughtered by their captors.

Arminius's plan of battle drew upon his experience of the way a Roman army fought. By attacking the Romans on the march, he avoided the sort of set-piece battle in which Roman soldiers excelled, and prevented them from launching coherent counterattacks until they were exhausted and their morale collapsed.

Augustus refused to accept the loss of Germany north of the Rhine. During his remaining years in power first Tiberius, then Germanicus sought to reverse the results of Varus's disaster. The best they could manage, however, was to maintain Rome's frontier along the Rhine. In the wake of the Pannonian emergency, there was no money to raise new legions to replace those that had been lost with Varus.

The Augustan monarchy – for that effectively was what Augustus's rule amounted to – was born of success in the civil wars. In Augustus's vision, expanding the reach of Roman power was a crucial aspect of his regime. In Germany, that project failed. Despite that, his success in other respects was remarkable. The borders along the Rhine and Danube would remain, with some adjustments, the borders of the Roman Empire into the fifth century CE, while his management of the relationship with Parthia enabled the development of Syria, along with a group of associated kingdoms that would ultimately be integrated into the empire as provinces in their own right. The ideology of victory supported the Augustan ideology of constitutionalism and service to the people; together, they served as the foundation of Rome's new imperial system, after 500 years of the Roman Republic.

Figure XVI

Germanicus Caesar, the son of Tiberius's brother, was adopted by Tiberius as heir apparent along with Tiberius's biological son Drusus. An able general, Germanicus died in Syria in 19 CE after negotiating a peace treaty with Parthia. The tension between him and Tiberius was such that Tiberius was rumoured to have conspired to kill him.

CHRONOLOGY 63 BCE–14 CE

BCE ← |70 |60 |50 |40

63 BCE
Birth of Gaius Octavius ('Octavian') to Atia and her husband, also called Gaius Octavius.

44 BCE
Assassination of Julius Caesar, with Octavian as designated heir; he begins using name 'Gaius Julius Caesar'. Battle of Philippi: Octavian and Antony defeat assassins Brutus and Cassius, who commit suicide.

43 BCE
Formation of the Second Triumvirate, consisting of Octavian, Antony and Lepidus.

36 BCE
Antony's failed invasion of the Parthian Empire. Octavian defeats Sextus Pompey.

34 BCE
Antony's marriage with Cleopatra announced. Final breach with Octavian.

31 BCE
Battle of Actium: Octavian's decisive defeat of Antony and Cleopatra.

30 BCE
Occupation of Alexandria, and suicides of Antony and Cleopatra. End of the civil war.

30 — 20 — 10 — 0 — 10 → CE

29 BCE
Octavian's return to Rome. Three triumphs celebrated: victories in central Europe (before the civil war), the victory at Actium and the conquest of Egypt.

27 BCE
Octavian's receipt of the name 'Augustus' and tribunician power.

26–25 BCE
Augustus's campaign in Spain.

23 BCE
Augustus's surrender of the consulship. Receipt of 'greater imperium' (*imperium maius*) and tribunician power for a five-year term. Death of Marcus Claudius Marcellus. Marriage of Agrippa to the widowed Julia. Marriage of Tiberius to Vipsania.

22 BCE
Detection of the Conspiracy of Murena to assassinate Augustus. Augustus's departure for the eastern provinces.

20 BCE
Royal succession in Armenia settled by Tiberius. Peace treaty with Parthia: military standards lost by Crassus and Antony are restored.

19 BCE
Augustus's return to Rome. Alleged conspiracy of Egnatius Rufus to assassinate Augustus exposed. Augustus's reform of the senate. Death of Virgil.

17 BCE
Celebration of the *saeculum*, commemorating seven centuries of Rome's existence. Introduction of moral legislation governing marriage and eligibility for senatorial offices.

16 BCE
German raids into Gaul, resulting in defeat of governor Lollius; Augustus governs from Lyons. Beginning of campaigns in the Alps and along the Danube, commanded by Tiberius and his brother Drusus.

12 BCE
Augustus's absorption of the role/title of *pontifex maximus*. Death of Agrippa. Marriage of Tiberius to the widowed Julia.

12–9 BCE
Drusus's campaigns in Germany. Tiberius's campaigns in central Europe.

9 BCE
Death of Drusus.

6 BCE
Withdrawal of Tiberius to Rhodes.

4 BCE
Death of Herod of Judaea.

2 BCE
Dispatch of Gaius Caesar east to deal with the Armenian royal succession. Conspiracy of Julia to assassinate Augustus detected. Julia exiled.

2 CE
Death of Lucius Caesar (younger brother of Gaius). Tiberius's return to Rome.

4 CE
Death of Gaius Caesar.

6 CE
Augustus creates permanent organization for Rome's grain supply. Regularization of retirement arrangements for the army. Rebellion in Danubian provinces. Detection of conspiracy of the younger Julia to assassinate Augustus, leading to her exile. Exile of the poet Ovid for promoting immorality. Governorship of Quirinius in Syria; most likely date for the birth of Jesus of Nazareth.

9 CE
Destruction of three legions, commanded by Quinctilius Varus, at the hands of German chieftain Arminius in the Teutoburg Forest. Germanicus, son of Drusus, given command of surviving Roman forces in Germany.

13 CE
Tiberius given powers equal to those of Augustus.

14 CE
Death of Augustus.

CHAPTER 2

MUTINIES, MURDERS AND COUPS: FROM TIBERIUS TO THE FLAVIANS

When Augustus passed away on the 19th of August, 14 CE, he was just shy of his 77th birthday. The first emperor had outlived not only his own generation, but also most people born in his children's generation. His stepson Tiberius, aged 56, was already old for the time, when average life expectancy for a Roman male was around 50. To him fell the imperial succession, which should have been straightforward.

Augustus had arranged for Tiberius to hold the same powers as himself in the provinces, and a senate meeting, convened after Augustus's elaborate funeral, conferred on Tiberius the few powers he did not already have in Rome. These brought him freedom from legal constraint, the right to introduce whatever legislation he wished to the senate, and more. Everything seemed to be going as Augustus had envisaged – until the armies on the Rhine and in Pannonia mutinied.

The rebellion in Pannonia stemmed from mismanagement on the part of the provincial governor, who had suspended standard drills for a period of mourning. As a result, the rank and file, freed from their usual duties, fell prey to the more disruptive and disgruntled among their number. Principal among their grievances was the extended term of service – 20 years instead of 16 – some had received in the surge of recruitment accompanying the beginning of the Pannonian campaigns.

The most memorable narrative of the life and times of Tiberius belongs to the greatest historian of Rome, Cornelius Tacitus, who was born about 30 years after Augustus's death. It is certainly not glowing, though, for Tacitus cast shadows on Tiberius's motivation and character, summarizing him as 'a ruler uninterested in expanding the empire'. His version of the Pannonian mutiny lays emphasis on complaints about lazy soldiers, but it also makes plain the mutual loathing between the troops and their unit commanders, the centurions. Tacitus, who was the son-in-law of a successful general, and who became a consul, shared with his class the generally negative view of the common soldier. However, his lack of sympathy did not prevent him from providing valuable insight into imperial military culture. He described, in the context of Pannonia, a collapse of military discipline in a system based on fear, which itself was a result of what a later senate decree called the 'military discipline instituted by the Divine Augustus'.

Figure I

The auxiliary cohorts, armed as here with spears and round shields, supported the more heavily armed legions. Being sent into combat ahead of the legions, they often bore the brunt of the fighting.

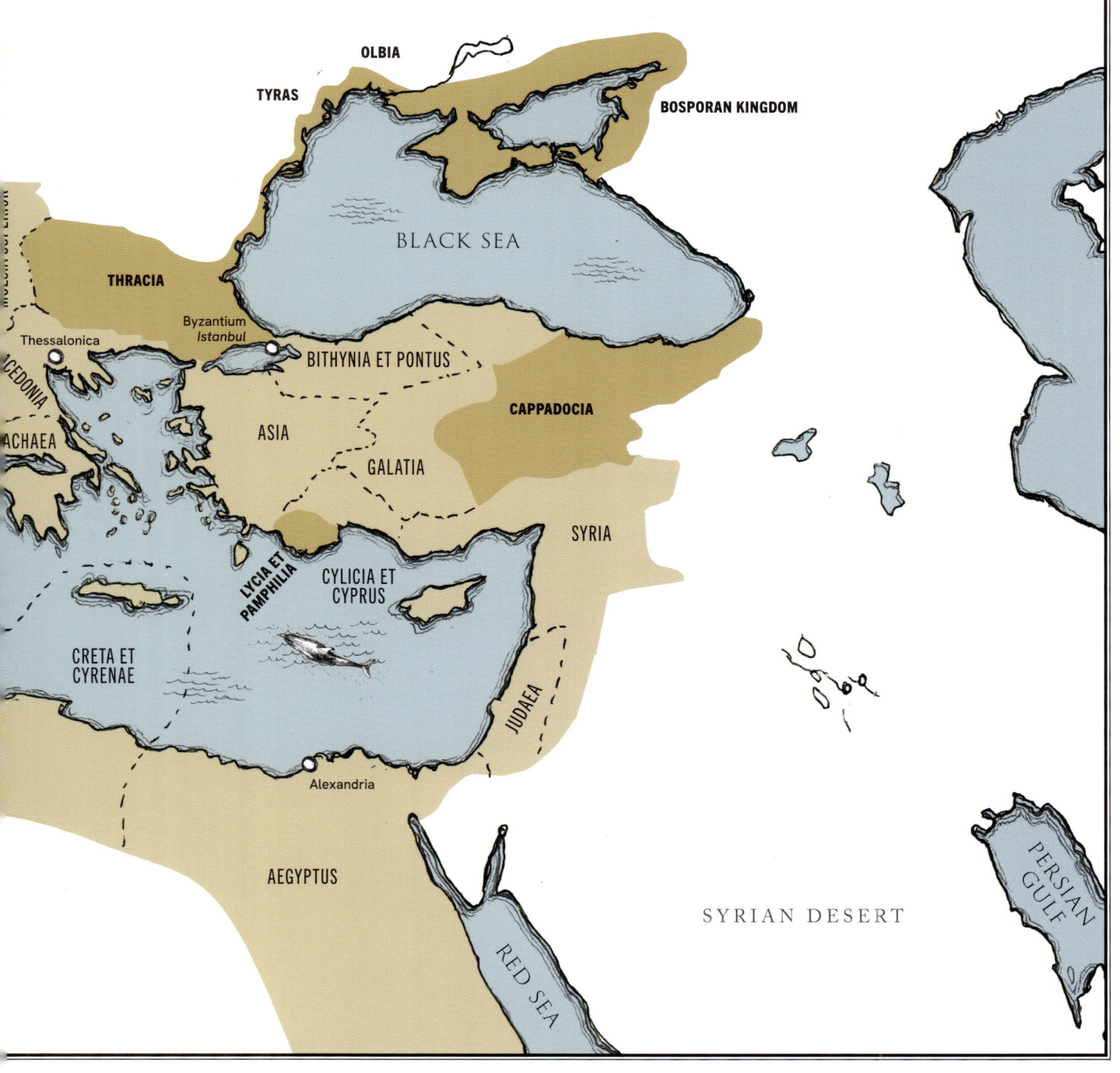

In the time of the Republic, Rome's armies had been community-based organizations, in which units drawn from allied states served under local leadership, while citizens, who were personally enrolled into units, elected their officers. But patterns of recruitment began to change, first in the recruitment wave of 14 BCE, then in the subsequent mass replacements of 2 CE. Now, troops were raised primarily from the provinces, while their centurions were largely members of the imperial elite, of the equestrian class, for whom service at this rank was just an early stage in an administrative career. As a result, there was little community of interest between the officers (who might be in post for only a year or so) and their men, generating an attitude to discipline that tended to be extremely brutal. Tacitus provides anecdotes suggesting just this.

The treatment that mutinous soldiers meted out, in their mutinies, mirrored the treatment they were used to receiving. More than that, soldiers subjected to routine harshness carried brutality into their treatment of subject peoples. This was true of the army Augustus now left to Tiberius, which would massacre populations in frontier zones, and whose soldiers were generally noted for their abuse of civilians. Indeed, it is the Roman military habit of forcing civilians to carry their baggage to which the Gospel of Matthew refers when, in the Sermon on the Mount, Jesus of Nazareth says, 'Whoever compels you to go one mile, go with him two' (Matthew 5:41).

Both of the mutinies now confronting Tiberius – in the German provinces and in Pannonia – ended more by accident than by design. In Pannonia, soldiers interpreted an eclipse of the moon as a prediction of their own future, after which the emperor's son Drusus, recently arrived in camp, talked them into abandoning their revolt. In Germany, a diplomatic speech by the emperor's adoptive son Germanicus restored the men's obedience; but subsequently he set up brutal punishments for the leading mutineers, bringing them one by one before the assembled legions, as their comrades cast judgment upon them. If the soldiers shouted 'guilty', they would cut the man apart. And, in the case of the mutinous legions at Xanten, the commander gathered the men he knew to be loyal and launched a surprise murderous attack on those held responsible for the revolt.

By all these means, order was restored. Germanicus now felt the best way to improve morale was to lead a raid into Germany (east of the Roman provinces), where he succeeded in surprising a band of Germans who had celebrated a rowdy festival, massacring them. He then moved further into Germany, slaughtering all those he encountered. In Tacitus's words, 'neither age nor gender brought mercy, while all structures, sacred and domestic, were destroyed, including the famous temple in those parts.' To Tacitus, this was an army held together by fear to inflict destruction.

More campaigns east of the Rhine took place in the summers of 15 and 16 CE. Their ostensible purpose was revenge for 'the treacherous defeat of a Roman army', that is, the crushing of the legions under Varus at the hands of Arminius at the Battle of the Teutoburg Forest in 9 CE. But, as so often when 'revenge' is the declared objective, actual strategic thinking (and attempting to reach a viable political settlement) took second place to killing.

Figure II

Agrippina, the wife of Germanicus (also the daughter of Julia and Agrippa, and thus Augustus's granddaughter), was a powerful, strong-willed woman who was often at odds with Tiberius.

Figure III

Roman warships, such as these depicted at the House of the Vettii, Pompeii, were designed for service in the Mediterranean. They had to be handled with caution in the rougher northern seas to which they were exposed when supporting Roman operations in Germany.

There were three major German groups in the area of present-day Germany now occupied by portions of the states of Hesse, Lower Saxony and Hanover. This was where Varus had been attempting to establish Roman control. It was dominated by the Cherusci to the south, the Chatti to the north and the Angivarii in between. Germanicus opened the campaign by joining his general Aulus Caecina, with four legions, to ravage the land of the Chatti, who fled before him. He then proceeded into the eastern territory of the Cherusci to rescue Segestes, father-in-law to Arminius, who was still loyal to Rome; he had kidnapped his daughter but was now being besieged by Arminius. Caecina succeeded, bringing Segestes, along with his pregnant daughter Thusnelda, back to Roman territory, where she gave birth to a son. In the second part of the summer of 15 CE, Germanicus loaded the other half of his army on to a fleet of ships that sailed from Vechten down the River Ems. The united forces then visited the site of Varus's disaster, collecting the bones of the fallen for burial and erecting a funeral mound on the site of the army's final collapse.

The return home, however, was nearly as disastrous as Varus's earlier defeat. A storm wrecked Germanicus's fleet, while Caecina was ambushed in a marshy area on his way south. Arminius again commanded the Germans, calling to them that they had caught a new Varus and another army in the same trap – terrain in which a Roman army could not draw itself up in its accustomed formation. Caecina himself is said to have had a dream in which

the bloody figure of Varus appeared before him. But he did not prove as unfortunate as Varus, and Arminius lost control of his over-eager followers. While Arminius wanted to hold back until the Romans were again marching through swampy ground, his followers thought their enemies were already badly beaten and tried to swarm the Roman camp. Caecina anticipated their attack, and as the Germans poured over the walls, they found the Roman army drawn up for battle. A slaughter ensued, this time of the disorganized Germans. Caecina led his army back to Xanten, where Agrippina, Germanicus's wife, greeted them as they crossed the Rhine.

During the winter of 15 CE, fresh recruits arrived from the Gallic and Spanish provinces to make up the losses from the summer's campaign. A new campaign was planned for the coming summer, along with a fresh fleet to transport the army to the heart of Arminius's territory.

> *Now in his third year of campaigning he [Germanicus] reflected on invasion routes in light of what had been successes or failures[;] he noted that the Germans were routed in set-piece battles on open ground, and that they were aided by woods, swamps, the short summer and early winter, [that] his men suffered less from wounds than [from] long marches and shortages of weapons ... and [that] long baggage trains offered opportunities for ambushes and were difficult to defend.*

Tacitus, *Annals*, 2.5

Sailing again from Vechten along the Ems, Germanicus disembarked and advanced towards the River Weser in the territory of the Cherusci. Reaching the Weser, he marched down the east bank until he encountered a German army, again commanded by Arminius, holding the west bank at Idistaviso, near the present-day city of Minden. On the first day of the conflict, Germanicus forced his way across the river. That night the Germans retaliated by attacking his camp, but with no success. The scene was set for the decisive encounter.

Germanicus drew up his army with archers preceding the cohorts of auxiliary infantry, which were lined up in front of the legions. This was precisely the sort of battle Arminius had avoided in past years, and the result now was a crushing defeat for his men. The Roman auxiliaries, with supporting cavalry, broke the German ranks before the legions made contact – and the slaughter of Germans continued from midday until dusk.

Additional German forces rallied to Arminius's support, intending to ambush the Romans on their return, and building earthworks along the Roman line of march. But the Romans were prepared to deal with what had, by now, become familiar German tactics. Germanicus kept his army in good order, attacking the earthworks with his auxiliaries and artillery before sending the legions forwards to overwhelm the defences. 'The Germans were no less brave than our men,' wrote Tacitus, 'but they were defeated by the style of fighting and weapons.' Crammed together in a narrow space, the Germans could not use their long spears, while the Romans, deploying their short swords, slaughtered the enemy. The Germans dispersed and fled.

Germanicus sent half of his victorious army home by land. They were luckier than the rest, who, loaded on to ships, struck disaster in the North Sea, where a storm scattered the fleet and brought heavy losses.

> *The liberator, without doubt, of Germany, Arminius did not contend with the Roman people in their early days, as had other leaders and kings, with the empire at its height. His record in battle was uneven, but he never lost a war. He lived for thirty-seven years, was king for twelve of them, and is celebrated to this day in the songs of the barbarians.*

Tacitus, *Annals*, 2.89

At the end of 16 CE Tiberius recalled Germanicus from Germany in order to send him east, where a crisis over the succession to the throne of Armenia threatened to erupt into a full-blown conflict with Parthia. The emperor would order no more offensive actions across the Rhine, leaving the frontier as Germanicus had left it. It would remain there for the better part of the next century. In any case, time was running out for Germanicus, who, after ensuring a peaceful settlement and installing a pro-Roman candidate on Armenia's throne, died in 19 CE. Within four years Drusus was dead too, leaving Tiberius himself – now in his sixties – too old to personally lead an army into battle. The emperor spent the remaining decade of his life in self-imposed exile on the island of Capri.

Tiberius's detachment from government during his final years had the effect of strengthening Rome's emergent bureaucracy, which now proved capable of the day-to-day running of the empire. This, and a general peace pervading the central Mediterranean, facilitated the smooth incorporation of local aristocracies into the Roman system, the protection of their interests and a rise in overall prosperity. The spread of Roman power at this time – largely unsupervised by the imperial palace – can be attributed to bureaucrats whose self-interest guaranteed orderly solutions to local problems.

CALIGULA

The growth of a professional bureaucracy in Rome had another fortuitous consequence: it meant that the empire's government could survive the extremely unstable characters who would govern the empire after Tiberius's death in 37 CE. The first of these was Gaius, the youngest son of Germanicus, whose two older brothers and mother, Agrippina, had died in prison after having been charged with conspiracy against Tiberius. Gaius was born in 12 CE. Along with his three sisters, he was raised on Capri, which was far from a healthy environment. Suspicions swirled around Gaius: that he enjoyed incestuous relationships with his siblings (especially his younger sister, Julia), that he was mentally unstable, and that he showed an excessive interest in autocratic power unrestrained by a senate, stimulated by playmates who were the children of Parthian and other eastern monarchs. Despite all these drawbacks, Gaius was the imperial candidate backed by the commander of the Praetorian Guard.

Augustus had created the Guard as a garrison for Italy, and initially its 12 cohorts, each numbering 1,000 men, were scattered around the central part of the Italian peninsula. When Augustus died, the Guard's prefect, Aelius Sejanus, advised Tiberius to concentrate the force in a new camp, the remains of which now lie in the vicinity of Rome's Termini railway station. Sejanus went on to dominate the day-to-day government of Rome when Tiberius moved to Capri; and it was he who charged Gaius's brothers with treason against Tiberius – although it was rumoured that he was, himself, preparing to eliminate the emperor. Whether a plotter or not, Sejanus was removed from his considerable power in 31 CE at the hands of Tiberius's agent Sutorius Macro; execution swiftly followed. Macro, who had led what was, in effect, Rome's police and fire department (another Augustan creation), now took over as Praetorian prefect in Sejanus's place – and was now Rome's emperor-maker.

Tiberius had intended that there should be two co-heirs, including his grandson Gemellus, son of Drusus. In the arrangement that emerged, Gemellus was made secondary heir. But his cousin Gaius – popularly known as 'Caligula' (little boot), the nickname given him by his father's soldiers during the German campaign – received all the powers of Tiberius by decree of the senate and voted into law by the Roman people. And soon the potential challengers disappeared. Gemellus had a fatal accident; shortly afterwards, Macro was charged with treason and killed. Caligula would be his own man.

As his own man, Emperor Caligula would earn military glory, or so he thought, especially as his relationship with the senate deteriorated. From late 39 until mid-40 CE he travelled to Germany, where he executed the

Figure IV
Tiberius anointed Caligula as one of his successors, even though the emperor doubted the younger man's mental stability. It was rumoured that Caligula's relationship with his three sisters was excessively close.

long-serving governor of Germania Superior – that is, 'Upper Germany', higher up the Rhine (and so the more southern German zone) – on a charge of conspiracy, and led some minor raids across the Rhine. While there, he received a son of the British ruler Cunobelin, who held power over the Trinovantes and Catuvellauni of southeastern England; vying with his brothers for the succession, he appears to have interested Caligula in the conquest of Britain (Britannia). Before returning to Rome to claim a triumph in the late summer of 40 CE, Caligula began to develop the naval infrastructure needed for any conquest.

Caligula never realized his invasion plans, for, before anything could happen, he was murdered on the 24th of January, 41 CE. The perpetrators were members of the Praetorian Guard, some senior palace officials and a few senators, who were disgusted by their emperor's cruelty and who might have felt personally threatened by his erratic behavior.

The conspirators understood that they would need an emperor of their own, so they selected the last surviving male relative of Augustus, who happened to be the younger brother of the late Germanicus. Claudius was not obviously imperial material; he had a pronounced stammer and a club foot, which was why both Augustus and Tiberius had denied him a place in public life. Augustus was also on record as thinking Claudius dimwitted. But that verdict is unfair. Claudius had been a friend of the historian Livy, and was actually an extremely learned man. It was Caligula, interested in reversing many of Tiberius's policies, who had brought Claudius out of the shadows, making him his fellow consul when Caligula succeeded Tiberius. In the event, the support of the Praetorian Guard, along with some timely diplomacy by a member of the ruling house of Judaea (who had been a hostage on Capri and had come to know Claudius), ensured that the senate would pass the legislation – despite some hesitation – to make Claudius emperor.

CLAUDIUS AND THE CONQUEST OF BRITAIN

Once Claudius was installed, an attempted rebellion by the governor of Dalmatia at the beginning of 42 CE helped to convince him that he needed military glory of his own. He was already fascinated by Julius Caesar, some of whose proposed domestic projects he set out to complete, and now Claudius chose Britain as a suitable venue for displaying his martial talents. To command the expedition, Claudius appointed Aulus Plautius, a loyal general with no obvious connections to the old nobility, and therefore not someone likely to claim the imperial throne in the event of extraordinary success. The naval bases and fleet that Caligula had begun to create would now be ready to support the invasion. And there was one other propitious factor: continuing political chaos in Britain. One of the major British kingdoms – that of the Atrebates, centred at Silchester (near present-day Basingstoke, Hampshire) – fell victim to the sons of Cunobelin, and its king, Verica, fled to Gaul, where he encouraged a Roman invasion. The divisions among the Britons made it plausible that a relatively small force (for Plautius had only four legions at his disposal) might be successful.

CONQUEST OF BRITAIN

The Romans' implicit strategy was to align with those Britons alienated from the house of Cunobelin. It does not seem that there was a well-developed plan to take over the entire island, or even a clearly defined objective other than to grab enough land to form a province and allow Claudius to claim his triumph.

It was not all plain sailing, however. The invasion, in 43 CE, was almost halted before it could begin, when the troops, fearful of the unknown, refused to board the fleet. The revolt was calmed by Narcissus, a powerful bureaucrat in the Claudian administration (despite being a freed slave), enabling Plautius's force to set sail and land near what today is Richborough, on the Kent coast. From there, Plautius moved inland towards Camulodunum (Colchester), the centre of Cunobelin's kingdom.

All the time, Plautius appears to have been in touch with Claudius, who moved to Gaul, allegedly bringing elephants with him to add an element of the spectacular to his eventual appearance on the British battlefield, at the Battle of Colchester. That battle ended the first phase of the campaign, after which Plautius divided his forces, dispatching a legion under Vespasian (the future emperor) to campaign around what is now Chichester while he led the other legions in pursuit of Cunobelin's son Caratacus, who rallied opposition to Rome in the communities of central Britain and Wales.

A critical feature of the Roman occupation was the willingness of British leadership groups to come to terms with Rome, rather than fight. Togidumnus (or Cogidubnus), ruler of the Atrebates, plainly decided to side with Rome and built an impressive villa for himself at Fishbourne, near Chichester; the Iceni, based in Norfolk and parts of Cambridgeshire and Suffolk, also came to terms with the Romans. Caratacus's resistance finally ended when he was turned over to the Romans by Cartimandua, queen of the Brigantes in northern Britain, in 51 CE. Thereafter, the land of the Brigantes marked the northern edge of the region directly controlled by the Romans, while a veteran settlement was established at Colchester and London began to develop as a hub for trade between Britain and the mainland.

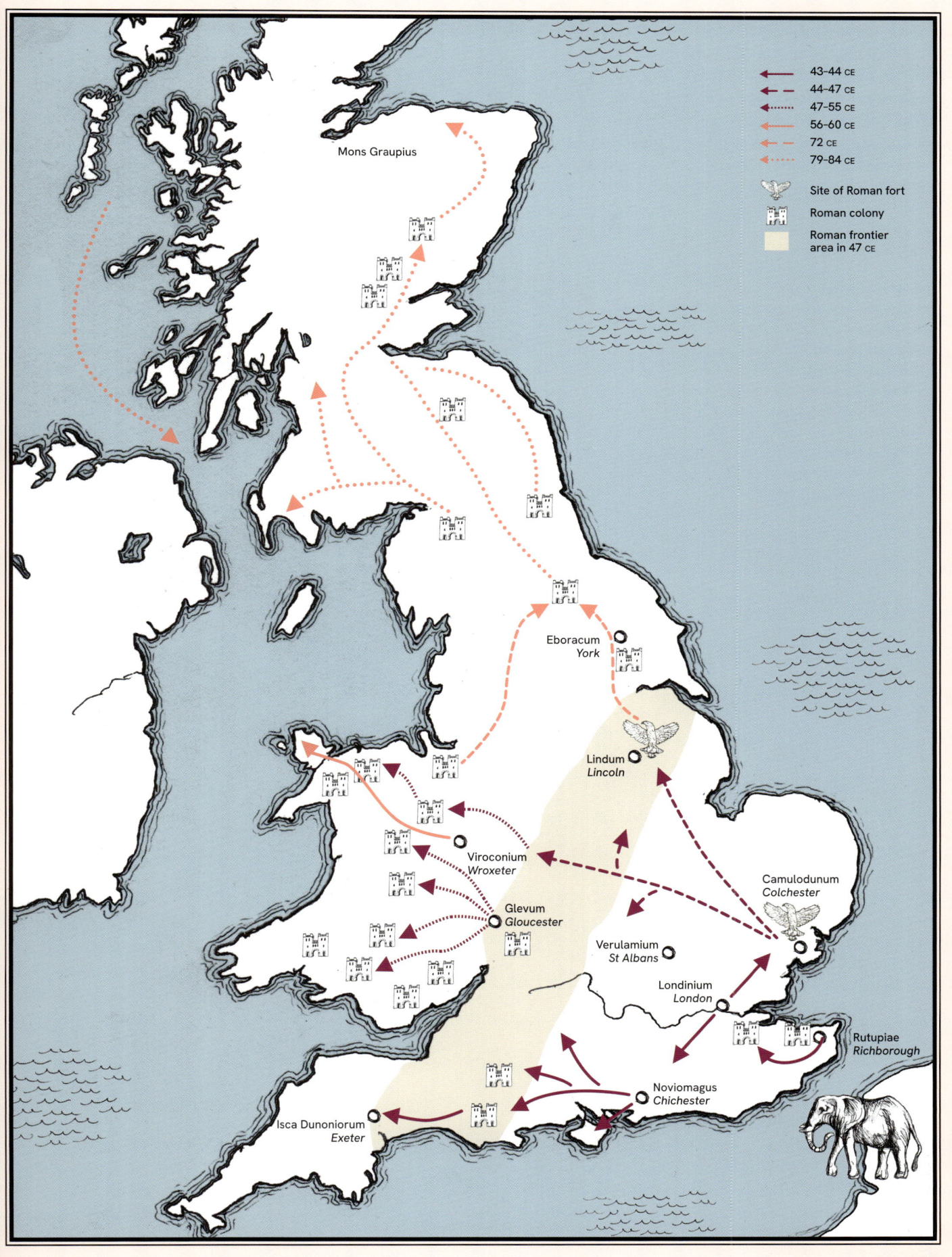

Claudius departed Britain almost immediately after the battle and the surrender of the Catuvellauni, celebrating a triumph when he returned to Rome. Plautius remained in Britain until 47 CE, as, quite likely, did Flavius Vespasianus (Vespasian), who was commanding the Second Legion *Augusta*. A first-generation senator, Vespasian had earned a poor reputation for his egregious flattery of Caligula; now, by contrast, he showed himself to be an excellent officer. Having played a significant role in the preparations for the Battle of Colchester, he was dispatched to southern Britain, capturing the Isle of Wight, defeating two 'very strong peoples', and taking 20 British towns. Also significant for Rome's conquest was the development of relationships with British ruling houses who wished to have nothing to do with Cunobelin's aggressive children. Togidumnus, based around Noviomagus Reginorum (present-day Chichester), was one such; another was Cartimandua, Queen of the Brigantes, who ultimately played a significant role in turning Cunobelin's son Caratacus over to the Romans, while Prasutagus, ruler of the Iceni (the northern neighbours of the Trinovantes), formed a strong connection with the imperial authorities. It was in the context of these arrangements that the Romans founded a settlement for retired veterans at Colchester and developed the city of London, which rapidly became a significant base and node for trade between Britain and the continent.

Plautius's immediate successors established the new province's initial frontiers at the border with Wales (whose inhabitants, the Silures, lived in scattered settlements and were difficult for the Romans to manage), and along the border of the Brigantes (whose realm was centred on what is now Yorkshire). With the conquest of Britain, the Roman Empire under Claudius had clearly expanded. Nevertheless, Tacitus, our best guide to these years, did not think highly of the emperor, seeing him as a passive figure, the figurehead for senior officials (almost all of whom were freed slaves who had grown up in the palace) and for his wives, especially the last one, Agrippina. Since she was his niece, the daughter of Grammaticus, the senate had to pass a bill declaring that the marriage would not constitute incest. She brought with her to the palace her son from a previous marriage: Nero.

Whether Agrippina really fed Claudius poisoned mushrooms to ensure Nero's succession – a story prevalent at the time – is uncertain. What is known for sure is that she controlled the palace bureaucracy and essentially ran the imperial government for the first 'golden years' of her son's reign following Claudius's death in 54 CE.

There was change, too, in Britain, where, four years into Nero's reign, a new governor arrived in the shape of Suetonius Paulinus, a man who had gained a substantial reputation for his campaigns in North Africa under Claudius. He adopted a more aggressive stance against the Silures, while also seeking to stamp out druidism, which Claudius had declared to be an illegal religion. In the summer of 60 CE Paulinus took the fight to the centre of druidic practice, on the isle of Mona (today's Anglesey) off the northwestern coast of Wales, destroying the druids' stronghold there with two legions. But at the same time Paulinus nearly lost his province, for in the east of Britain a major revolt took form under Boudicca, Queen of the Iceni.

Figure V

Flavius Vespasian came from a non-traditional background. His father was not a member of the senate, but Vespasian gained a powerful reputation as a warrior during Claudius's invasion of Britain. He later achieved a loose connection with the imperial court and was regarded by some as a sycophant. Tacitus wrote that Vespasian was the only man who ever became better once he was emperor.

Figure VI

Thomas Thornycroft's brilliant statue of Boudicca and her daughters, erected in 1902 (after the sculptor's death) at the western end of Westminster Bridge in London, is now a symbol of British resistance to tyranny. The location is somewhat ironic since Boudicca destroyed London, which was an important centre of Roman occupation at the time of her rebellion.

BOUDICCA'S REVOLT

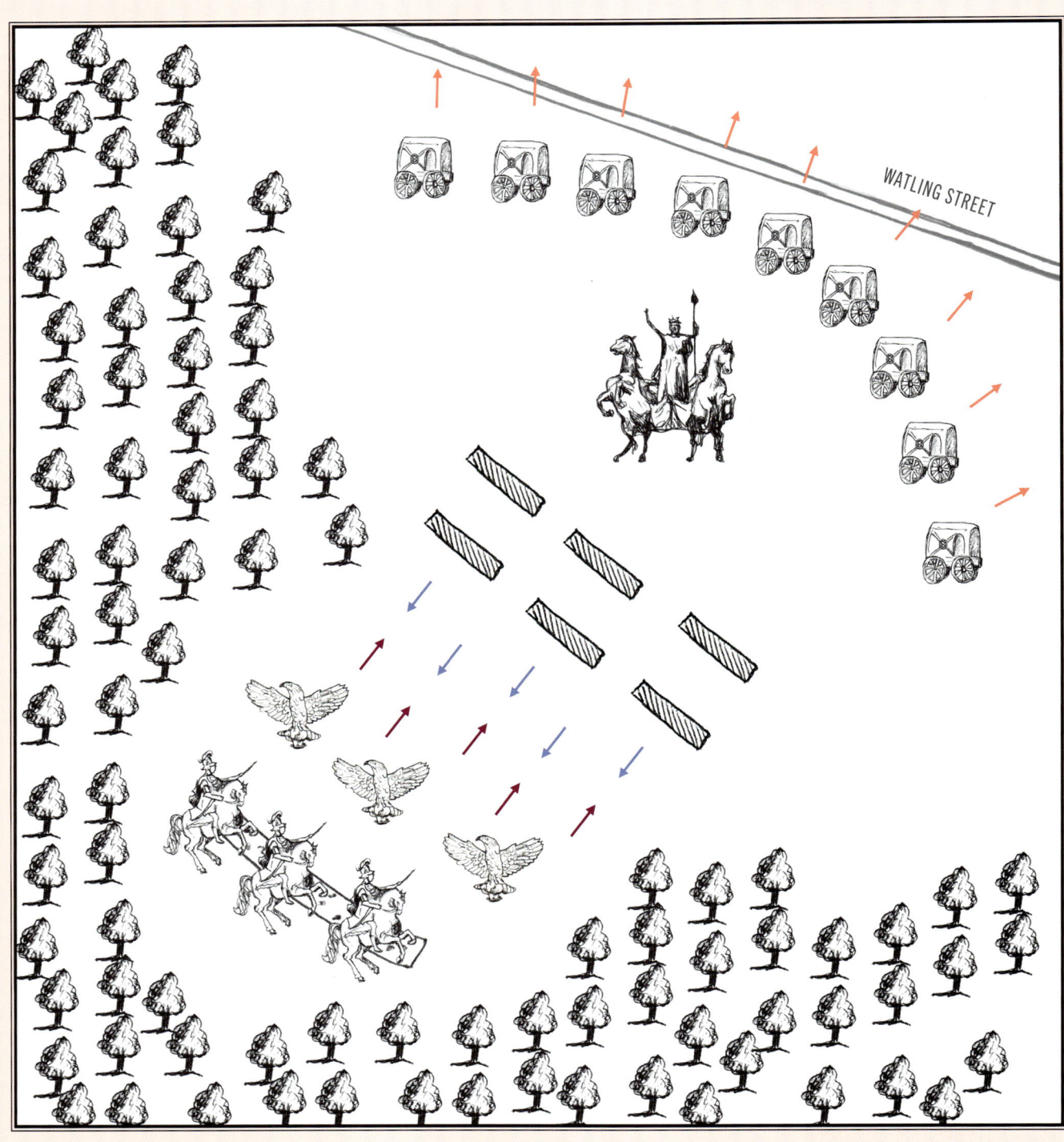

← Britons attack with 50,000 soldiers
← Romans attack with 15,000 soldiers
← Britons escape
▨ Embankment

While Paulinus was in Wales in 60 CE, looking to stamp out the druids, atrocities perpetrated by his Roman colleagues generated a crisis in the province of Britannia. Prasutagus, King of the Iceni and a Roman ally, died, leaving his personal property to Emperor Nero. Decianus Catus, the Roman treasury administrator, who was operating out of Colchester, completely overstepped his authority, stripping the other Iceni leaders of their estates. Worse, his men raped Prasutagus's daughters and flogged his widow, Boudicca. Such abuse might have been sufficient in itself to spark a revolt, but in this case, it also intensified the festering resentment of veterans settled at Colchester and fuelled unrest stemming from the activities of those who had moved to Britain and were transforming the economy. These immigrants included agents of Nero's former tutor Seneca, who had chosen this moment to call in extensive loans he had made to British leaders. As trouble brewed, Catus fled to Gaul.

Boudicca was a formidable character, described in one source as

very tall, and of terrifying appearance, in the glance of her eye most fierce, and her voice was strong; a great mass of red hair fell to her hips; around her neck was a large golden necklace; and she wore a tunic of diverse colours over which a thick mantle was fastened with a brooch.

Cassius Dio, *Roman History*, 62.2

She now set out to eliminate not only all traces of Roman culture, but also those Britons who had accommodated themselves to Rome's ways. The Trinovantes rose in support of her, joining the Iceni in the destruction of Colchester, routing a column sent to defend the city by the commander of the Ninth Legion, before incinerating the emerging Roman settlement at London, where the intensity of the fires would become all too evident in the archaeological record. And that was not all. Verulamium (present-day St Albans) was reduced, too. Tacitus, who was probably summarizing Paulinus's memoirs at this point, wrote that the rebellious Britons 'did not take captives or sell hostages or engage in the other business of warfare; they hastened to slit throats, hand, burn, crucify, as if avenging in advance the retribution that was to follow.'

For all the destruction it caused, Boudicca's army was not large, limited as it was to warriors from the Iceni and Trinovantes. When Paulinus, who had returned ahead of his army to see what had been unfolding, was rejoined by the two legions back from Anglesey, he was able to give battle and destroy her forces. Boudicca, again according to Paulinus, poisoned herself after the battle.

Paulinus continued to campaign throughout the winter, inflicting huge damage on the lands of his enemies. The slaughter went on until a new imperial agent in the province, Classicianus – a Briton who had risen rapidly in the imperial service – complained to Nero's court. Subsequent investigations backed up Classicianus's view, and Paulinus was ordered to cease his campaign of retribution.

THE EMPIRE UNDER NERO

It took years for Britain to recover from the destructive effects of Boudicca's revolt. Britain was not, however, the only trouble spot in the empire. There was conflict and murder at the heart of the imperial family, for a start, as the relationship between Nero and his mother collapsed after the emperor began an affair with Acte, an influential freed slave of whom Agrippina disapproved. In 59 CE Nero took drastic action and tried to kill his mother by sending her across the Bay of Naples, from her villa, in an unseaworthy boat, which fell apart. But Agrippina was strong enough to swim ashore. At this point, Nero lost all patience and sent members of the imperial guard to murder her.

By this time, a crisis was also threatened by events on the empire's eastern borders, where disputes over the Armenian kingdom had once again been calling Rome's relations with Parthia into question. In the closing years of Claudius's reign, Mithridates, the ruler of Iberia (in what is now eastern Georgia), had engineered a coup in Armenia, placing his son on the throne. But he, too, was overthrown within the year by a cabal of Armenian nobles. They invited Vologaeses, King of Parthia, to provide a new king, which he did, naming his brother Tiridates. The Roman administrators in the region feared to act without instructions from Rome, which they did not receive.

When Nero succeeded to the imperial throne, his advisers decided on a more proactive approach, selecting Domitius Corbulo to take command in the east, giving him considerable authority to deal with the Parthians as he saw fit. In reputation he rivalled Paulinus, on account of his aggressive campaigns in Germany – which Claudius had curtailed for fear Corbulo would become too popular. Nero's advisers ensured that Corbulo could not become too powerful by splitting the command of the eastern army between him, as governor of Cappadocia, and the governor of Syria.

Figure VII

This representation of a Parthian prisoner wearing cap and trousers stresses the central Asian, nomadic heritage of the Parthian dynasty as the Romans sought to depict their most settled rivals as 'barbarians'.

Corbulo arrived in his new command at the beginning of 55 CE. After arranging a truce with Parthia, whose king was distracted by internal rebellion, Corbulo invaded Armenia in 58 CE, having spent considerable time the previous year getting troops who had never seen active service into fighting shape. Advancing across the border from Cappadocia, he captured the Armenian capital, Artashat, burning it to the ground and driving Tiridates into exile. He then moved southwest towards Armenia's other major urban centre, Tigranocerta, and installed a Roman-raised Cappadocian on the Armenian throne: Tigranes VI. Corbulo ensured that he had support from the Armenian nobility and other allied kings in the region before withdrawing to Syria, where he now added that province's governorship to his Cappadocian appointment.

The barbarians varied in their response according to their circumstances[;] some submitted, others fled their homes into the hills, some even hid themselves in caves with their families. The Roman commander varied his responses accordingly. He was lenient to those who surrendered, he pursued those who fled and, as for those in hiding, he stuffed the entrances and exits of caves with bushes and branches which he set alight. Corbulo sent the Iberians against the Mardi, experienced brigands, protected from invaders by mountains, who had attacked him as he marched past their territory, and punished their hostile audacity without loss of Roman blood.

Tacitus, *Annals*, 14.23.2

Peace then reigned until, in 62 CE, the Armenian nobility told Vologaeses that he could not abandon Armenia or his usurped brother, prompting a failed Parthian invasion of Armenia. Tigranes VI withdrew to Tigranocerta, which the Parthians lacked the technological and logistical capacity to capture. However, following fruitless negotiation by Parthian ambassadors in Rome, Vologaeses prepared a fresh attack – and this time managed to humiliate the foolish new governor of Cappadocia, Caesennius Paetus, who led a single, understrength legion into Armenia, mishandled the situation and ended up besieged in his camp by the Parthians. Paetus wrote to Corbulo, begging to be rescued; but before Corbulo could arrive from Syria, Paetus surrendered to the Parthians and withdrew from Armenia.

The upshot of Paetus's disgrace was that Corbulo was given more troops and supreme command over Rome's eastern provinces. But he also understood that he could probably achieve everything he required without risking his men's lives. Vologaeses was, likewise, interested in avoiding the risk of full-scale conflict with Rome, and therefore, during the opening months of 65 CE, he joined Corbulo at an elaborately stage-managed negotiating session. There, the usurped Tiridates agreed that the price for regaining the throne would be to receive it from Emperor Nero in person, in Rome. Corbulo agreed to Vologaeses' request that at no time on his journey would Tiridates be subjected to public signs of subjugation. The process of negotiation revealed that the two superpowers in the Near East realized that, with resources evenly balanced between them, threats of violence were best followed by genuine negotiation.

Figure VIII (overleaf)

The artist who produced this portrait of Nero emphasizes the artistic side of the emperor, who prided himself on his abilities as a performer.

HE OFTEN ADMITTED THAT HE WAS HAUNTED BY HIS MOTHER'S GHOST ... HE EVEN HAD RITES PERFORMED ... TO SUMMON HER GHOST AND APPEASE HER. AND WHEN HE MADE HIS TRIP TO GREECE, HE DID NOT DARE TO PARTICIPATE IN THE ELEUSINIAN MYSTERIES WHERE THE HERALD PROCLAIMS THAT THE IMPIOUS AND CRIMINALS MUST LEAVE.

SUETONIUS, *LIFE OF NERO*
(*LIVES OF THE CAESARS*), 34:4

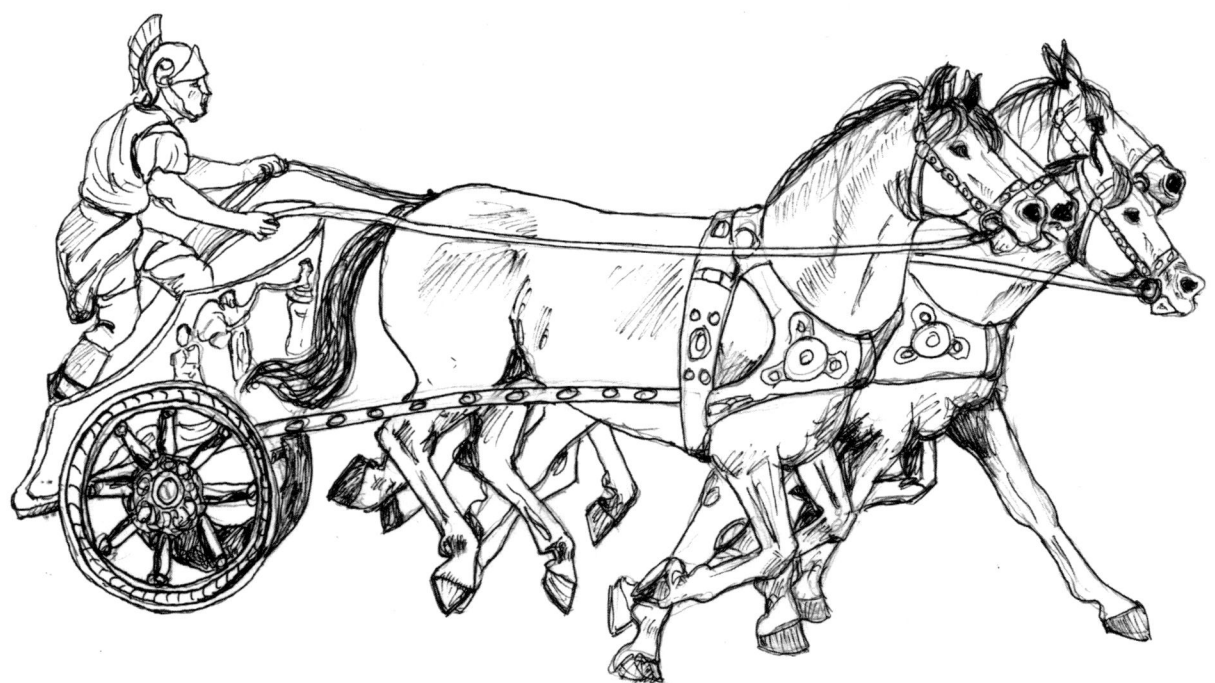

Figure IX

In Rome's most popular entertainment, chariots would typically race seven laps around the track in the Circus Maximus. Accidents were common and many charioteers, even some of the most famous, died on the track.

Tiridates's journey took eight months overland, at enormous cost to the Roman state. He met Nero at Naples, then participated in a massive display of gladiatorial action and beast hunts at Pozzuoli, where Tiridates showed off his skill as an archer, shooting animals from the imperial box. A few days later, in Rome – a city that Nero was transforming in his image, following a disastrous fire the previous year – Tiridates formally received his crown from Nero. For Nero, the display of power was an important win, since it enabled him to bury the memory of a major aristocratic conspiracy to eliminate him from the throne a few months previously.

No sooner had Tiridates headed home than Nero resumed his pattern of self-destructive self-indulgence. The empire's actual government remained in the hands of his palace staff, along with those of the Praetorian prefect, Ofonius Tigellinus. He now accompanied the emperor on an expedition to Greece in 67 CE, while his colleague Nymphidius Sabinus remained in Rome.

As Nero moved east, he ordered all the public festivals of the Greek world to be celebrated during his stay; he would become an Olympic champion in chariot racing, despite falling out of his chariot. But there was business that needed attention beyond the partying. A revolt was breaking out in Judaea, and Nero had become deeply suspicious of Corbulo, with whom he had next to no personal contact, but whose designs upon the throne he had been told to suspect. Summoning Corbulo to Greece, Nero ordered his assassination as soon as he disembarked. Seeing the fate that awaited him, Corbulo chose suicide. His death did nothing to solve the events now unravelling in Judaea, where Corbulo's successor badly botched the management of the situation around Jerusalem. The attempt to rescue the situation involved sending Vespasian – who had close contacts with the court through his long-term mistress, the freed slave Antonia Caenis – to take charge. Vespasian would take over both an expanded army, reinforced with troops from the Balkan legions, and Corbulo's connections, which would prove crucial to his actions in the years to come. In the meantime frustration with Nero's irrational conduct reached a boiling point.

Shortly after his 'competition' at Olympia, Nero received word of trouble in Rome, to which he returned in early 68 CE. That spring, the governor of southern Gaul, Julius Vindex, raised an army from among the people of his province and announced his hostility to Nero. He wrote to Sulpicius Galba, who was governor in northern Spain and from an ancient noble family, offering to support him as the next emperor. Galba, in turn, declared his loyalty to the senate and people of Rome, and prepared to join Vindex. However, further news from Gaul revealed that the provincial army of Germania Superior had defeated Vindex, who had committed suicide, but that the victorious army had tried to proclaim its own general, Verginius Rufus, emperor. Rufus instead declared his support for Galba.

The key to what happened next was the disloyalty of the Praetorian Guard, which had been corrupted by Sabinus and now exerted 'artful pressure', deserting Nero. On the 9th of June, 68 CE, Nero found himself deserted in his palace. He fled to the house of one of his freedmen outside Rome. There, when he heard men coming to arrest him, he killed himself. His last words were: 'What an artist dies with me.'

Nero was the first Roman emperor not to visit a military province. Indeed, his overt lack of interest in military affairs and his perceived (or actual) ill-treatment of senior generals were crucial factors in the failure of his regime. His demise represented the end of the Augustan line, and it raised a crucial question: What now qualified a man to be Rome's emperor?

Figure X

Roman armies deployed sophisticated machinery, such as this mobile battering ram, to shatter the defences of cities. Even the strongest defensive positions could not withstand a Roman assault.

THE JUDAEAN REVOLT AND THE DESTRUCTION OF JERUSALEM

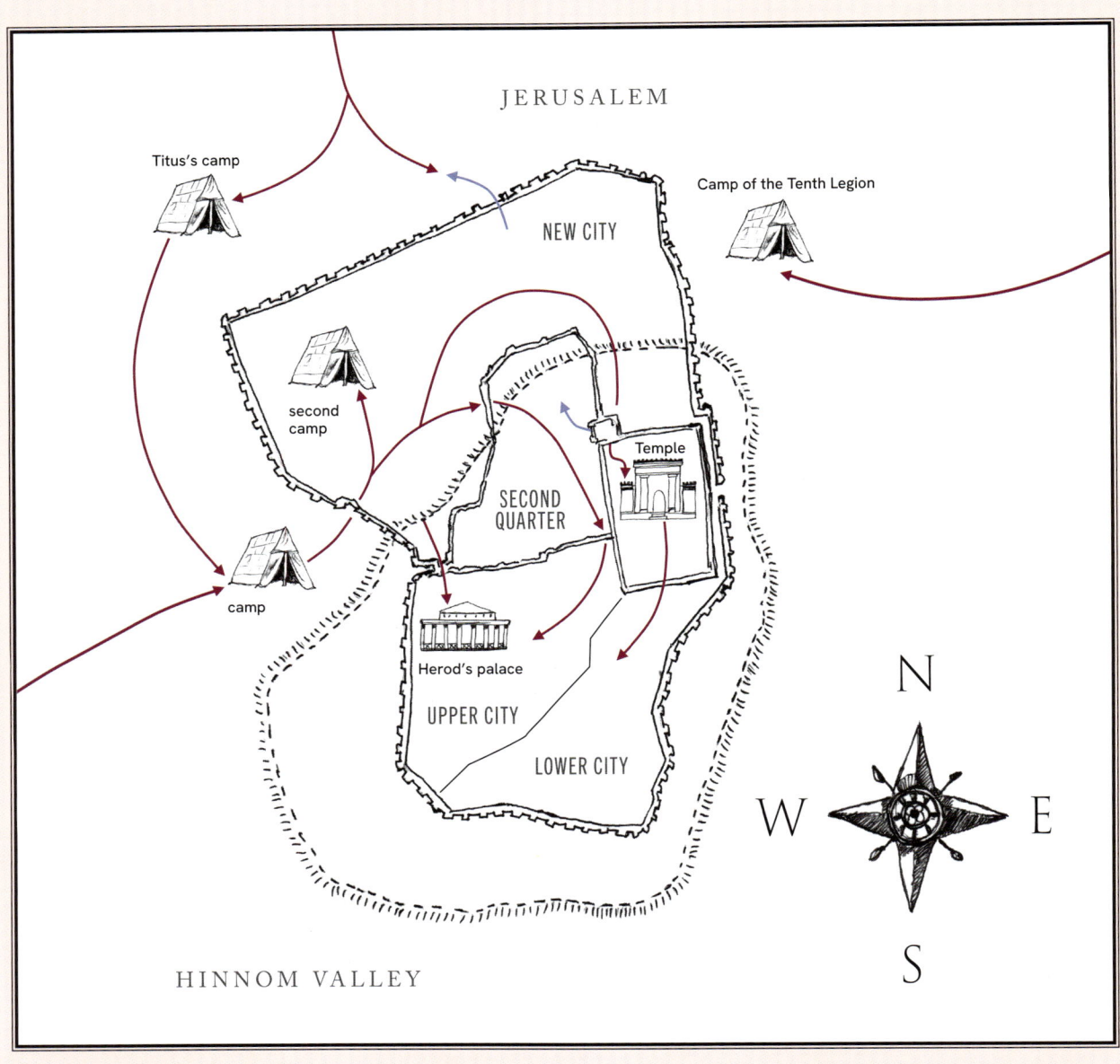

The revolt that broke out in Judaea during the spring of 66 CE, and which ended with the destruction of the rebels holding out at Masada in 73 or 74 CE, has some similarities with Boudicca's rebellion in Britain (see pages 86–87). The root cause of both uprisings was the breakdown in relations between the local ruling class and the Roman authorities, in the wake of Roman administrative failings. And the resulting struggles mingled civil war with rebellion.

The trouble in Judaea began when the Roman procurator, Gessius Florus, seized treasure from the Temple treasury in Jerusalem. As his guard marched through the city with their loot, a riot broke out, forcing Florus to flee to his capital, Caesarea, on the coast. The local dynast (a descendant of Herod) tried to calm matters but was driven out of Jerusalem by more extreme actors, urging revolt. Soon, they seized the royal palace of Masada. After several months of conflict, during which the rebels strengthened their position in Jerusalem, the governor of Syria, Cestius Gallus, intervened with a substantial force drawn from his provincial garrison; but his overconfidence mingled with his incompetence. When he realized he could not take Jerusalem, he began to withdraw, at which point he was ambushed and suffered severe losses. A rebel administration – albeit one often divided against itself – took over the bulk of Judaea.

Nero learned of Gallus's defeat while he was in Greece. He dispatched Vespasian to take command of an army that included two legions from Egypt and detachments from the Danubian garrison. Arriving in early 67 CE, Vespasian campaigned effectively throughout Judaea, recovering Galilee from a rebel force commanded by Josephus, who would become the most important historian of Judaism in antiquity. Presented as a captive to Vespasian, he predicted that Vespasian would be emperor. The thought might already have crossed Vespasian's mind. At any rate, he kept Josephus with him as an adviser and personal prophet.

In March 68 CE Vespasian's connection with the opposition to Nero became obvious when he stopped campaigning on the very day that the governor of Gaul (Vindex) declared his revolt against the emperor; news could not travel that fast, so Vespasian clearly had advance knowledge of the revolt's timing. Operations in Judaea would remain on hold until 70 CE, when Vespasian's son Titus took command and moved on Jerusalem with an army consisting of four legions and numerous units of auxiliaries contributed by allied kings. He arrived a few days before Passover.

Jerusalem in that era stood on two hills divided by a ravine running from north to south. The lower, eastern hill held the 'Lower City' and the western hill the 'Upper City', which bordered a 'New City' to the north. Titus began his assault in early May by battering his way into the New City. He then began constructing four ramps (one for each legion) against the wall of the Upper City. When the defenders set fire to these ramps, Titus surrounded the city with a wall to starve the defenders while he constructed new ramps. The rebel leaders kept the food in the city for themselves and their troops, while the unfortunate civilian population was reduced to cannibalism. In June, Titus fought his way into the Upper City, and the surviving defenders withdrew into the Temple and the Lower City. On the 30th of August Titus stormed and destroyed the Jewish Temple; a month later he completed the conquest and destruction of the Lower City.

The capture of Jerusalem transformed the nature of Judaism. Sacrificial worship in the absence of the Temple was no longer possible, prompting a shift in the practice of the faith to prayer, synagogue gatherings and study of the Torah. For Vespasian, the destruction of Jerusalem, coming hard on the heels of the defeated revolt in Germany, enabled him to claim that – as the man who had restored the empire's security – he was truly Rome's legitimate emperor.

THE YEAR OF THE FOUR EMPERORS: 69 CE

When Nero committed suicide, the senate voted that Galba should be his successor. The qualification he claimed for the throne was simply his willingness to oppose the legitimacy of his predecessor's regime. In the months of Galba's slow journey to Rome, Nymphidius Sabinus acted as de facto emperor, sending his erstwhile colleague Tigellinus into retirement. When Sabinus learned that Galba intended to replace him as Praetorian prefect, he entered the Praetorian camp seeking to be proclaimed emperor instead. Rather than do that, his own Guard murdered him.

Galba, in taking his time getting to Rome, sowed the seeds of his own destruction. He replaced Verginius Rufus as governor of Germania Superior and acquiesced in the assassination of the governor of Germania Inferior ('Lower Germany', further down the Rhine and thus the more northern zone). Of the two new governors, while Aulus Vitellius (in Germania Superior) was the ambitious son of the most powerful Claudian-era senator, Hordeonius Flaccus (in Germania Inferior) was a nonentity. What Galba failed to do was reward the legions of Germania Superior for their desertion of Nero, while the legions of the other German province, which had been slower to abandon Nero, suspected that Galba would treat them poorly. In the meantime, another Roman governor, Salvius Otho (in Lusitania: now Portugal), was ingratiating himself with the Praetorian escort sent to Galba after Nero's death. In late September or early October 68 CE, when Galba finally reached Rome, he dismissed some troops who had been signed up under Nero. Moreover, noting that Nero had emptied the treasury through his extravagance, he refused to pay the bribe that Sabinus had promised the Praetorian Guard for deserting Nero.

Galba's primary political virtue, in the eyes of ambitious people around him, was that, being without a son and heir, he surely needed an alliance to secure his regime by adopting a suitable successor. However, he failed to do this, thereby alienating Otho, who thought that his early adherence to Galba's cause made him successor material. At the same time, Aulus Vitellius was conspiring with the generals in both German provinces to be proclaimed emperor. He would have eight legions at his disposal. On the 1st of January, 69 CE, when the legions were expected to renew their oath of loyalty to the reigning emperor, those of Germania Superior refused to do so and proclaimed Vitellius emperor. The legions of Germania Inferior swiftly followed suit.

When news of the German events reached Rome, on the 9th of January, Galba decided he needed to name an heir. Being an intense social snob, he chose not a man with experience of public life but rather Piso Licinianus, a descendant of Pompey and Crassus, Julius Caesar's partners in the First Triumvirate. A furious Otho immediately suborned the Praetorian Guard to support a coup, and within days, on the 15th of January, another emperor was dead, after the Guard killed Galba – and, for good measure, Piso. The senate proclaimed Otho emperor. It was now time to assemble an army that could resist the anticipated invasion from Germany.

Vitellius managed to manoeuvre a significant strike force of around 20,000 men across the Alps in early April, commanded by two of his subordinates from Germany, Aulus Caecina and Fabius Valens. After some skirmishing in the Po Valley, the rival armies confronted each other, somewhat by accident, near what is now the village of Calvatone, where Otho's men were defeated after a hard fight. This lost battle was hardly decisive, since reinforcements for Otho were on their way, but his will was broken. After meeting with his senior officials, Emperor Otho killed himself.

The path appeared open for Vitellius to claim the imperial throne, which he would do with a display of respect for constitutional norms. He did not advertise himself as emperor until May, when the imperial powers were conferred on him by statute. But, well before then, he had dealt his regime a fatal blow. Although he had forgiven Otho's generals, including Suetonius Paulinus and Verginius Rufus, who confessed to having betrayed their emperor through poor handling of their men, he ordered the execution of the most strongly pro-Othonian centurions in the legions from Moesia that had supported Otho. How he could have known who those were, or determined the truth of the charges against them, is unclear, and the difference between his treatment of junior and senior officials was lost on no one. Similarly, his decision to cashier Otho's Praetorian Guard and replace it with men drafted in from the northern legions gave the impression that men were suffering in inverse relation to their importance.

The executions had the effect of alienating the Danubian forces. Elements of the three legions that had reached northern Italy put on a brief anti-Vitellius demonstration before returning to their camps to listen to another imperial claimant, Vespasian, who had arranged his own acclamations, first in Alexandria on the 1st of July, then again, two days later, in Palestine. By the end of the week, the garrison of Syria was showing its support for Vespasian's cause.

In fact, Vespasian had been laying the groundwork for his coup for several months, coming to an understanding with Mucianus, the governor of Syria, that they would act together, and spreading stories of miraculous events so that he could be seen as the choice of the gods, rather than just another usurper. Nevertheless, Vespasian was expecting more trouble than actually materialized. While Mucianus led the Syrian legions west and Titus took charge of suppressing the Judaean revolt, Vespasian headed to Alexandria to control the departure of grain ships to Rome in the event of a long struggle. This measure would prove unnecessary. The disgruntled Danubian legions took his side, while relations among Vitellius's generals collapsed, creating an impossible command situation for his army.

In early August 69 CE commanders of the Balkan legions met at Poetovio, Pannonia (Ptuj, Slovenia), to discuss letters that had arrived from Vespasian. The provincial governors – appointed by Otho – allowed Antonius Primus, a man with a somewhat disreputable past, and Cornelius Fuscus, an imperial procurator, to drive the agenda. They secured support for Vespasian and prepared to invade Italy without waiting for the rapidly advancing Mucianus. Primus wanted to get there before Vitellius could gather reinforcements from the German legions.

When news that the Balkan legions were on the march reached Vitellius in September, the defence of Italy began to disintegrate. Aulus Caecina contacted Primus; on the 12th of October one of Rome's two major fleets, based at Ravenna, declared its loyalty to Vespasian; on the 18th of October Caecina tried to make his two legions follow suit but was arrested and placed in custody at Cremona. Six days later Primus's troops encountered Caecina's former army very close to Calvatone, where, after a desperate night-long struggle, they defeated the Vitellian forces:

> *Fortune favoured neither side until, with night well advanced, the rising moon revealed and deceived the battlelines. It favored the Flavians, shining from behind, since on their side the shadows of men and horses were exaggerated, and the weapons of the enemy fell short …; the Vitellians, on the other hand, were shining in the moonlight in their faces and, unaware, they were offering clear targets to those hurling weapons from their concealed positions.*

Tacitus, *Histories*, 3.23

Caecina negotiated their surrender at Cremona, which Primus then sacked. Fabius Valens took flight. He would later be captured and executed, while Caecina, having effectively switched sides, would survive and thrive for some time in Vespasian's court.

After the forces of Mucianus caught up with those of Primus, they moved on Rome, against a now defenceless Vitellius, who was left with only his hand-picked Praetorian Guard. He tried to negotiate his abdication with Flavius Sabinus, Vespasian's older brother, but his Guard – with nothing to lose – refused to acquiesce. As a result, Sabinus and Vespasian's younger son, Domitian, took a small band of men to seize Rome's Capitoline Hill, but they held out for only a day before the Guard stormed the defences, burning the great Temple of Capitoline Jupiter as they did so. Sabinus was killed and Domitian went into hiding. That brief fight-back only postponed the inevitable. On the 20th of December, the pro-Vespasian forces fought their way into Rome, and Vitellius was killed by a mob.

After months of civil war, Vespasian became Rome's fourth emperor of the year 69 CE. He would prove more durable than his three predecessors.

THE FLAVIANS

The reign of Vespasian heralded a new, Flavian ruling dynasty. By contrast with the turbulent contestations and coups of 69 CE, Vespasian was succeeded (in 79 CE) by his eldest son, Titus, who was in turn followed (in 81 CE) by Titus's younger brother Domitian, who ruled until 96 CE. But the new regime immediately faced a number of provincial crises. For a start, there was the continuing revolt in Judaea, as well as trouble on the Rhine. The area south of the Rhine's mouth was home to the Batavians, a tribe that prided itself on its militarism and which, along with tribes to its immediate south, had provided numerous auxiliary units to the Roman army. The contacts made between these groups' leaders during the British campaigns under Nero had facilitated the development of a network that Vespasian would now have to deal with.

Figure XI

Titus, Vespasian's elder son and an able general, is shown here on the arch that bears his name, on the Via Sacra a little west of the Colosseum in Rome. It commemorates his capture of Jerusalem in 70 CE.

FLAVIAN MONUMENTS AND THE COLOSSEUM

It was Emperor Vespasian who gave Rome some of its most striking monuments, not least the enormous edifice of the Colosseum, a temple to such entertainments as gladiatorial combat and wild animal hunts, and a stage for imperial pomp. First, though, he had to deal with what Nero had done to the fabric of the city.

In the wake of the great fire that devastated Rome in 64 CE, Nero had turned much of the central part of the city into what he called his *Domus Aurea* (Golden House), a vast palatial home for himself. As a sign of his devotion to the Roman people, Vespasian set about tearing down Nero's vanity project and constructing, instead, monuments commemorating the suppression of the revolt in Judaea – although he had no interest in commemorating the recent civil war. The most famous of these monuments, today, is the Temple of Peace, to the southeast of the Forum, constructed on the site of an artificial lake in the Domus Aurea.

Work began on the Colosseum – originally referred to as the 'Flavian Amphitheatre', after Vespasian's dynasty – in 72 CE, and it was completed eight years later. Its familiar name derives from the colossal statue whose remains can still be seen to the east of it, and which was originally a statue of Nero, until Vespasian replaced Nero's head with that of the Roman sun god. The emperor's eldest son, Titus, presided over its opening with a massive series of gladiatorial combats and beast hunts, during the course of which some 9,000 animals were killed.

As can be seen today, the Colosseum stands nearly 50 metres (165 feet) high, while the arena covers an area of more than 3,000 square metres (32,000 square feet). Spectators were seated in four sections, of which the lowest one, filled with wooden seats, was designated for members of Rome's upper classes. The next two sections were made up of large marble steps, while the top section was of wood. In all, the Colosseum accommodated about 65,000 people, who entered through the 76 marble entryways that are visible today. The vast majority of spectators were men; women (and slaves) were allowed only into the highest section. The elaborate underground chambers that can be seen today date from a little later, and were constructed under Domitian, to enable props and animals to be hoisted up through the floor of the amphitheatre.

The Colosseum remained in active use for public spectacles into the fifth century CE, and its centrality to Rome's urban plan, even today, is palpable. There is a sense in which the building symbolizes the city, encapsulated in the much-quoted lines ascribed to the eighth-century scholar Bede: 'As long as the Colosseum stands, Rome shall stand.'

A decade after the Colosseum's completion, Emperor Domitian added to his dynasty's monuments in Rome with the Arch of Titus, constructed on the Via Sacra (Sacred Way) as it enters the Forum from the southeast. Its decoration, recalling Titus's triumph in Judaea, depicts the treasures from the Temple at Jerusalem, the most significant of which, the seven-branched Menorah, was then stored in the Temple of Peace.

Figures XII and XIII (overleaf)

The Colosseum in Rome, begun under Vespasian and dedicated by Titus, celebrated the capture of Jerusalem. The space below the floor of the arena was used to store equipment and participants that could be hoisted into the arena as needed.

The revolt had taken shape while Vitellius ruled, and its leaders derived essentially from the Roman administration. The one-eyed Julius Civilis, a Batavian, had been arrested for conspiracy under Nero before being released by Galba, and was then in contact with Antonius Primus in August or September 69 CE, urging rebellion against Vitellius. He was fond of comparing himself with Rome's great Carthaginian enemy, Hannibal. Julius Sabinus, another rebel leader, claimed to be descended from a bastard fathered by Julius Caesar. Yet another leader, Julius Classicus, is recorded on a writing tablet from London as commanding an auxiliary unit in the immediate aftermath of Boudicca's revolt. Their revolt, unlike Boudicca's, was not so much anti-Roman as 'alternative Roman'. Civilis's evident hope, in the chaos of the civil war, was to establish an independent enclave straddling the mouth of the Rhine, which he could rule on his own; and that seems to have been Classicus's notion as well.

Civilis was helped by Hordeonius Flaccus, governor of Germania Inferior and a previously reluctant Vitellius supporter-turned-aspiring ally of Vespasian. Since his men remained loyal to those comrades who had gone south with Vitellius, his way of aiding Vespasian was to allow Civilis to build up his strength without interruption. This Civilis did, linking units of his fellow Batavians with people from north of the border. When Hordeonius heard that the pro-Vespasian forces had taken Rome, he tried to have his men swear loyalty to Vespasian. Instead, they killed him.

Hordeonius's assassination gave Civilis the excuse to continue attacking the legions in Germania Inferior, scoring a couple of notable successes. He captured Xanten, which was defended by two depleted legions who were massacred. Classicus, who dressed as a Roman emperor, took over three more legions – the garrison of Germania Superior – after the assassination of their pro-Vitellian commander. In the spring of 70 CE the rebels controlled a fair portion of the Rhine frontier.

While Vespasian remained in the east, Mucianus, faced with constructing a new government in Italy, sent Vespasian's son-in-law Petilius Cerialis, governor-designate of Britain, to deal with the situation. Except for his connection with Vespasian, Cerialis was not an obvious choice for a major command. He was noted for his rashness, manifested when a column he had sent to relieve Colchester during Boudicca's revolt was ambushed with heavy losses; and in the recent fighting he had advanced too eagerly on Rome at the head of a cavalry detachment, which had also lost many men.

Cerialis set out with an army made up of troops from Vitellius's army, Antonius's Balkan legions and a legion from Spain. Taking advantage of his superior numbers and displaying some diplomatic skill, he managed to recover the garrison of Germania Superior, and by the end of the summer had pretty much restored the situation on the Rhine. He went on to Britain, while Mucianus moved into Gaul, where he organized the shifting of legions between the Balkan and Rhine armies so as to rebuild the latter and remove Vitellians from their home bases. Henceforth, it became standard practice to deploy auxiliary units anywhere but in their home provinces. Of the leaders of the revolt, Classicus was killed, while Civilis and Veleda made off into the German forests.

Figure XIV

The tombstone of the Roman centurion Marcus Favonius Facilis, dating from 43-63 CE, is one of the earliest Roman sculptures to survive from Britain. The accompanying inscription tells us that the monument was erected by two of Facilis's freed slaves, a reminder that centurions were people of some means.

THE ERUPTION OF VESUVIUS

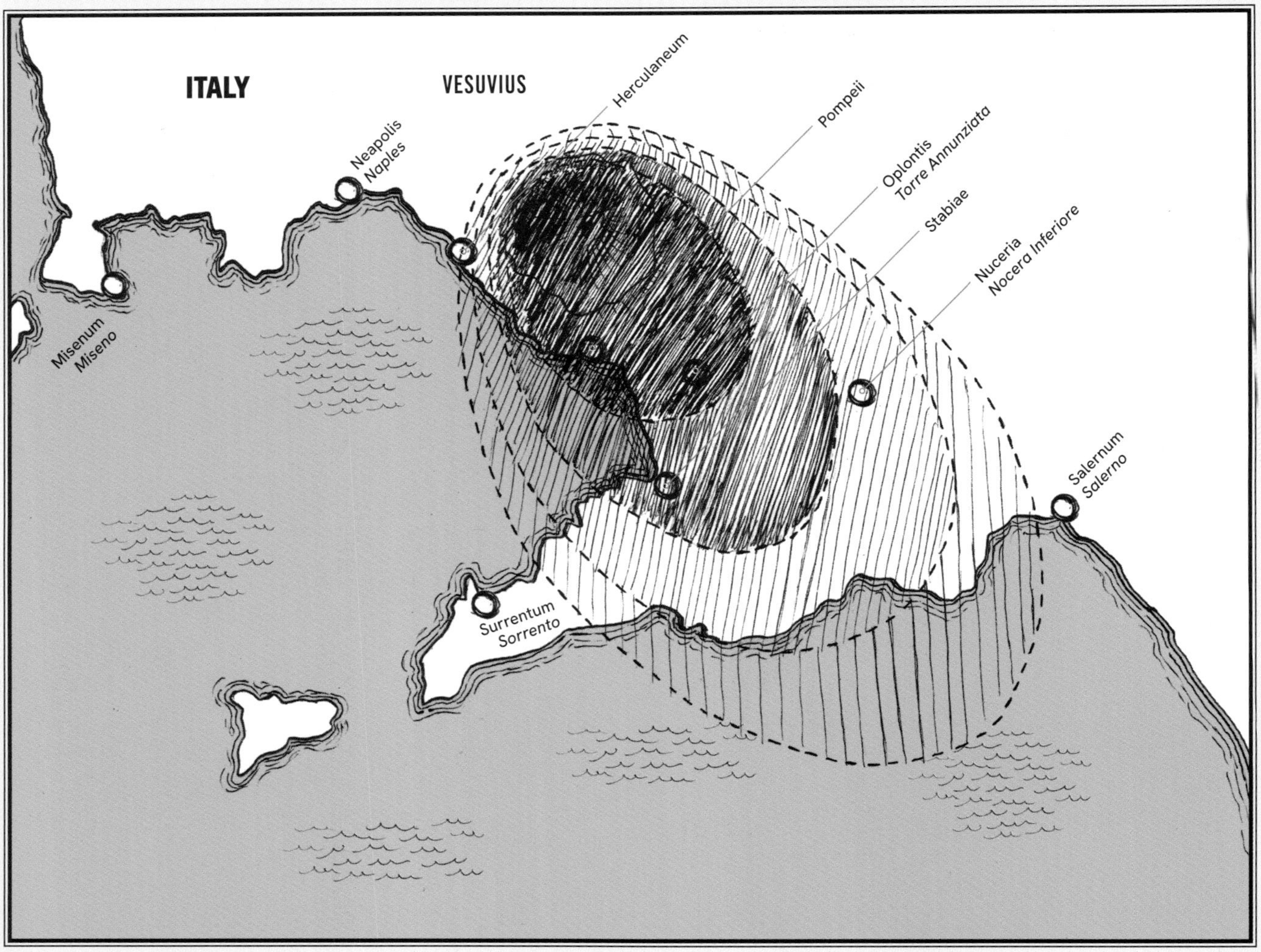

Distance from eruption:

 30 kilometres (20 miles)

 25 kilometres (15 miles)

 17 kilometres (10 miles)

 10 kilometres (6 miles)

Figure XV (opposite, left)

The House of the Vettii in Pompeii was owned by two prominent freedmen. The painting shown here depicts a sacred serpent and a pair of *lares* (household gods) on either side of the homeowner.

Figure XVI (opposite, right)

The House of the Papyri in Herculaneum housed an immense library, including volumes of Epicurean philosophy once owned by Caesar's father-in-law.

It was on the 24th of October, or possibly November, 79 CE that the volcano of Vesuvius blew up, about 225 kilometres (140 miles) south of Rome. Our dating for the month comes from remains discovered at Pompeii, one of the two cities – along with Herculaneum – that were devastated that day. Years later the consul and author Pliny the Younger wrote up his eyewitness account for Tacitus, describing how:

> *Around noon my mother pointed out to him [Pliny's uncle Pliny the Elder] a cloud of enormous size and shape … The cloud was rising from a mountain, it was unclear to us gazing from afar which it was, we later learned it was Vesuvius. Its appearance can best be described as looking like a pine tree, for[,] carried up to a great height as if on a tree trunk, it began to spread out branches. This was because, I think, it was driven by a recent blast, then, wearing out, as if defeated by its own weight, it spread out far and wide.*

Herculaneum, lying about 6.5 kilometres (4 miles) from the crater, was destroyed by a wave of volcanic gas and lava, while Pompeii, about 8 kilometres (5 miles) from the volcano, was buried in pumice as its people were killed by sulphurous gases. The site was then buried in volcanic ash.

What constituted a disaster for the populations of these cities was a gift to history, for the eruption captured Pompeii and Herculaneum in time, preserving them as the most vivid and direct encounters with daily life in the ancient world. Interest in the two sites – and some very unscientific archaeology – dates from at least the eighteenth century, when treasure-hunters began bringing antiquities to the surface. (There is even some evidence of digging on the site in antiquity.) More scientifically orientated excavations began in the eighteenth century, inspiring such works of fiction as Edward Bulwer-Lytton's *Last Days of Pompeii* (1834) and enabling the modern world to begin to glimpse first-century life in imperial Italy as lived across all social classes.

The so-called House of the Papyri at Herculaneum was home to members of Rome's most prominent families, the Calpurnii Pisones, while such buildings as the House of the Vettii and the House of the Faun in Pompeii reveal how well-off families lived. At the other end of the scale, the bakery of Modestus, the laundry of Stephanus and the *thermopolium* (restaurant) of Vetutius Placidus reveal the lives of people whose experience is generally absent from the literary record, because of its focus on the rich and powerful.

Major military operations under Vespasian and Titus were thereafter concentrated in Britain, where Cerialis and his immediate successor, Frontinus, completed the conquest of Wales and began to concentrate their troops in Yorkshire. Frontinus's successor, arriving in 77 CE, was Julius Agricola, who, like Cerialis, had previous experience in Britain. Undaunted, he undertook a series of campaigns to bring the whole of the island under Roman control. He remained in office until 85 CE, and even occupied Scotland briefly, establishing a line of military bases north of the Firth of Forth, including the well-excavated fortress at Inchtuthil, and won a major victory at a site known in Roman sources as Mons Graupius, but not matched with any modern location to date. He also sent his fleet on the first voyage taken by a Roman fleet around the north of Scotland. All these endeavours earned him a great deal of publicity, a fact that did not sit well with Emperor Domitian; Agricola was recalled in 85 CE but permitted to live out an honourable retirement until his death at the age of 93.

Agricola's career is well known thanks to the biography composed by Tacitus, who was his son-in-law. It makes clear that one problem in Domitian's relations with Agricola was the fact that the former's military record was less than stellar. After a successful German expedition, which enabled him to extend the frontier across the Rhine in the early 80s (to link it more firmly with the Danubian frontier), Domitian suffered a series of defeats in central Europe. A new power had arisen north of the Danube – the kingdom of the Dacians – which was now ruled by Decebelus, a leader who united the warring peoples north of the border and began raiding Roman territory, destroying one Roman army in 85 and another in 86 CE.

Domitian had better luck in 88 CE, when one of his generals vanquished the Dacians at Tapae, near Sarmizegetusa (in present-day Romania), thereby setting up an opportunity for the emperor to take the field a year later and celebrate a triumph. But in 92 CE Domitian was badly defeated, again by Decebelus. The emperor negotiated a peace settlement that he tried to present as a triumph, possibly damaging his prestige as much as did the lost battle. Defeats in war could be survived; blatant lies were less forgivable.

Meanwhile, in the imperial palace, the rising tension was now reaching breaking point. First, Domitian targeted one of his cousins, Flavius Clemens; then, in 95 CE, he executed Epaphroditus, a freedman who had been a powerful member of the household since the reign of Nero. By this time the palace staff had had enough. When the Praetorian prefects agreed to support them, they murdered Domitian in his private quarters on the 28th of September, 96 CE.

It was the end of Rome's second imperial dynasty. In place of the Flavians, an elderly senator named Cocceius Nerva was proclaimed Rome's new emperor.

ROBBERS OF THE WORLD, HAVING RUN OUT OF LAND TO PLUNDER, THEY LOOKED TO THE SEA[;] IF THE ENEMY ARE WEALTHY, THEY ARE AVARICIOUS, IF THE ENEMY ARE POOR, THEY ARE KEEN FOR GLORY[;] NEITHER THE EAST NOR THE WEST HAVE BEEN ABLE TO SATISFY THEM. ALONE OF ALL MEN, THEY SEEK POVERTY AND WEALTH WITH EQUAL DESIRE. THEY GIVE THE FALSE NAME OF EMPIRE TO THEFT, SLAUGHTER, AND RAPE. THEY MAKE A WASTELAND AND CALL IT PEACE.

SCOTTISH CHIEFTAIN CALGACUS, DESCRIBING THE ROMANS, QUOTED IN TACITUS, *AGRICOLA*, 30.4–5

CHAPTER 3

EXPANSIONISTS AND CONSOLIDATORS: FROM TRAJAN TO MARCUS AURELIUS

The elderly new Emperor Nerva was a survivor. He had been close to Nero, but also to Vespasian. Now, if he was to survive in his new role, he needed help. Like Galba, he had no children, and that was not his only difficulty, for the Praetorian Guard resented the way in which he had been imposed on them from within the palace. The Praetorian prefect compelled Nerva immediately to execute the men connected with Domitian's assassination. Ideally, Nerva needed sufficient force at his disposal to overawe the Guard, and it just so happened that this was delivered to him in the shape of Ulpius Trajan, governor of Upper Germany, and the four legions at his disposal.

Trajan's family was relatively new on the scene. His father, born in Spain, was the first member of the family to achieve senatorial office; he had also been one of Vespasian's leading generals. In the summer of 97 CE Nerva adopted Trajan, who nevertheless remained in Germany. He was still there, in Colonia Agrippinensis (Cologne), when Nerva's brief rule concluded with the emperor's death on the 28th of January, 98 CE. Trajan heard about his own accession to the imperial throne from his nephew Hadrian, who had been dispatched from Rome to bring him the news. Secure enough in his position to feel no immediate need to go to Rome, Trajan took off for the Danube, having first summoned to his headquarters the Praetorians who had rebelled against Nerva. They never returned to Rome.

It was not until the autumn of 99 CE that Trajan himself journeyed to the imperial capital, there to be reunited with his wife, Pompeia Plotina, a woman notable for her intellect and simple lifestyle, and one whom Trajan must have loved deeply, since they remained married despite being unable to have children. Another powerful figure in Trajan's palace was to be his sister Ulpia Marciana, whose granddaughter Sabina was married to Hadrian. Plotina's friendship with Marciana was underscored by the fact that they would both soon receive the title *Augusta*, which was thereby redefined to mean 'leading lady' rather than 'Madame Empress'. In such ways, the new regime presented itself to the public as a family business.

Trajan's claim to fame was his extensive military service, but he understood that as emperor he must build a relationship with the Roman people. Just as Vespasian had constructed the Colosseum to show his appreciation of the people's pleasure in watching gladiators, so now Trajan looked to Rome's other big entertainment genre: chariot racing. One of his first acts after returning to the capital was therefore to enhance the Circus Maximus, adding new rows of marble seating to Rome's most venerable entertainment venue.

Figure 1

The representations of Trajan on his column in Rome (see page 121) stress his ability to work with his subordinates, as shown here.

EXPANSIONISTS AND CONSOLIDATORS

IMP CAESAR
TRAIANVS G[...]
DACICVS PO[NTIFEX MAXIMVS]
NIC POTESTA[...]
IMP VI [...]
IIS QVI IN A VIG[...]
DR IEREO PEE[...]
CLASSE PRAETO[RIA...]
SVB Q MARCIO T[VRBONE...]
NOMINA SVBSC[RIPTA...]

Figure II

Upon retirement from service, members of the fleet and auxiliary cohorts at Misenum received Roman citizenship for themselves and any children they had, as well as exemption from personal taxes. The diploma consisted of a pair of bronze tablets hinged together, giving the rights granted to the veteran and the names of seven witnesses.

Hints of Trajan's manner of government can be gleaned from his correspondence with Pliny the Younger, who was by now a senior senator. The emperor comes across as a thoughtful man, with respect for precedent. He plainly sought to define his own place in the tradition of 'good' emperors (as listed, very conveniently, in the decree that had granted Vespasian imperial power).

Pliny gives us a glimpse of Trajan's worldview when he describes an occasion on which he joined the emperor for a business weekend in the country. There is no hint of the allegation made a century later by the historian Cassius Dio – on good information, he claimed – of an imperial fondness for drink and sex with boys. True, Dio qualified the assertion by saying that Trajan had never caused harm to anyone as a result; it was generally assumed that debauchery and cruelty went hand in hand. But Pliny wrote instead of his own pleasure at witnessing the emperor's 'justice and dignity' and Trajan's modesty in private. Pliny was advising Trajan on a legal case involving an official, a freed slave. Trajan was 'under suspicion' because he had a financial interest in the outcome, so, when he made a judgment against his official, he wanted to make it plain to people like Pliny that he was not Nero. In other words, his freedmen were not all-powerful, as Nero's had been, so people should not be fearful when they found themselves entangled with the emperor's subordinates.

> *You ought not to worry, my dearest Pliny, about that matter about which you decided to consult me since you know my practice very well; that loyalty to my person is not obtained through people's fear or apprehension or by charges of treason. Forget that side of the issue, which I would not hear even if it was supported by actual evidence; but an account should be produced of all the work done under the supervision of [the Greek orator and writer] Dio Cocceianus, as the public interest demands, and Dio has not objected, nor should he.*

Trajan in Pliny, *Letters*, 10.22

Other sides to Trajan are evoked in later letters, written when Pliny was governor of Bithynia, northern Turkey, in which he asked the emperor for direction. That correspondence suggests that Trajan (or the staff members to whom he must have delegated some of these responses) had an intense interest in detail and in the fiscal well-being of subject communities, as well as a genuine sense of fairness.

THE CONQUEST OF DACIA AND EASTWARD EXPANSION

Fairness should not be confused with weakness, and Trajan was still a militaryman. Even as he introduced himself to the Roman people, he had his eye on the barbarian kingdom of Dacia (encompassing much of present-day Romania and portions of neighbouring countries). He had visited the Roman provinces bordering Dacia before arriving in Rome, and now he provoked conflict with the Dacian king, Decebelus, by cutting the Roman subsidies that Domitian had agreed to give him at the end of the war Rome had lost in 92 CE. Decebelus – who probably depended on the distribution of Roman gold to keep his followers onside – retaliated by invading Roman territory. Trajan, most likely anticipating trouble, had posted some experienced commanders in the area: men from families that had not been part of the traditional aristocracy but who had risen to prominence through service to the state, and who formed what was essentially Trajan's war cabinet in the region.

Trajan took the field in the summer of 101 CE, leading an army of some 75,000 men from the boundary of the Roman province of Upper Moesia (in what is now central Hungary) and heading for Decebelus's capital at Sarmizegetusa (now in south-central Romania). On the way, he won a decisive victory at Tapae, near the Iron Gates gorge of the Danube, on what is now Romania's border with Serbia. Decebelus was unable to mount an effective resistance, so this First Dacian War concluded the next year with his making agreements: to surrender weapons, war engines and deserters; to keep the same friends and enemies as the Romans; to stop recruiting soldiers of his own from within imperial territory; and to allow Roman soldiers to be garrisoned in his territory.

The terms of this peace treaty put Decebelus's regime under great stress. In 105 CE, he attempted to relieve the situation by attacking Roman territory, treacherously seizing a senior official and demanding that Trajan withdraw Roman forces from his realm. Once again, the emperor – now determined to bring an end to the Dacian kingdom – took command of the Roman forces, which were reinforced by the formation of two new legions. His invasion of Dacia began in the spring of 106 CE, with the Dacians resorting to guerrilla warfare since they could not hope to challenge the Roman army in a conventional battle. The pursuit of Decebelus continued into the autumn as the Romans established bases throughout the region (using a tactic they had employed earlier to take control of Wales). Victory in this Second Dacian War was declared in September 106 CE, when a Roman cavalryman, Tiberius Claudius Maximus, presented Decebelus's head to the emperor. The Dacian king had taken his own life.

Trajan now transformed the Dacian kingdom into a Roman province. A monument sprang up at Adamclisi, the site of a great Roman victory in the First War, depicting a trophy and scenes from the conflict stressing the army's role in upholding the traditional virtues of the Roman people. And with victory in Dacia, Trajan turned his attention once again to the city of Rome, where another monument would soon be raised. Trajan had already shown a taste for magnificence in his redesign of the Circus Maximus. Now, he

Figure III

Trajan was the first emperor to be descended from a provincial family (in his case, from Spain). He was regarded by later generations as Rome's best emperor, the *optimus princeps*.

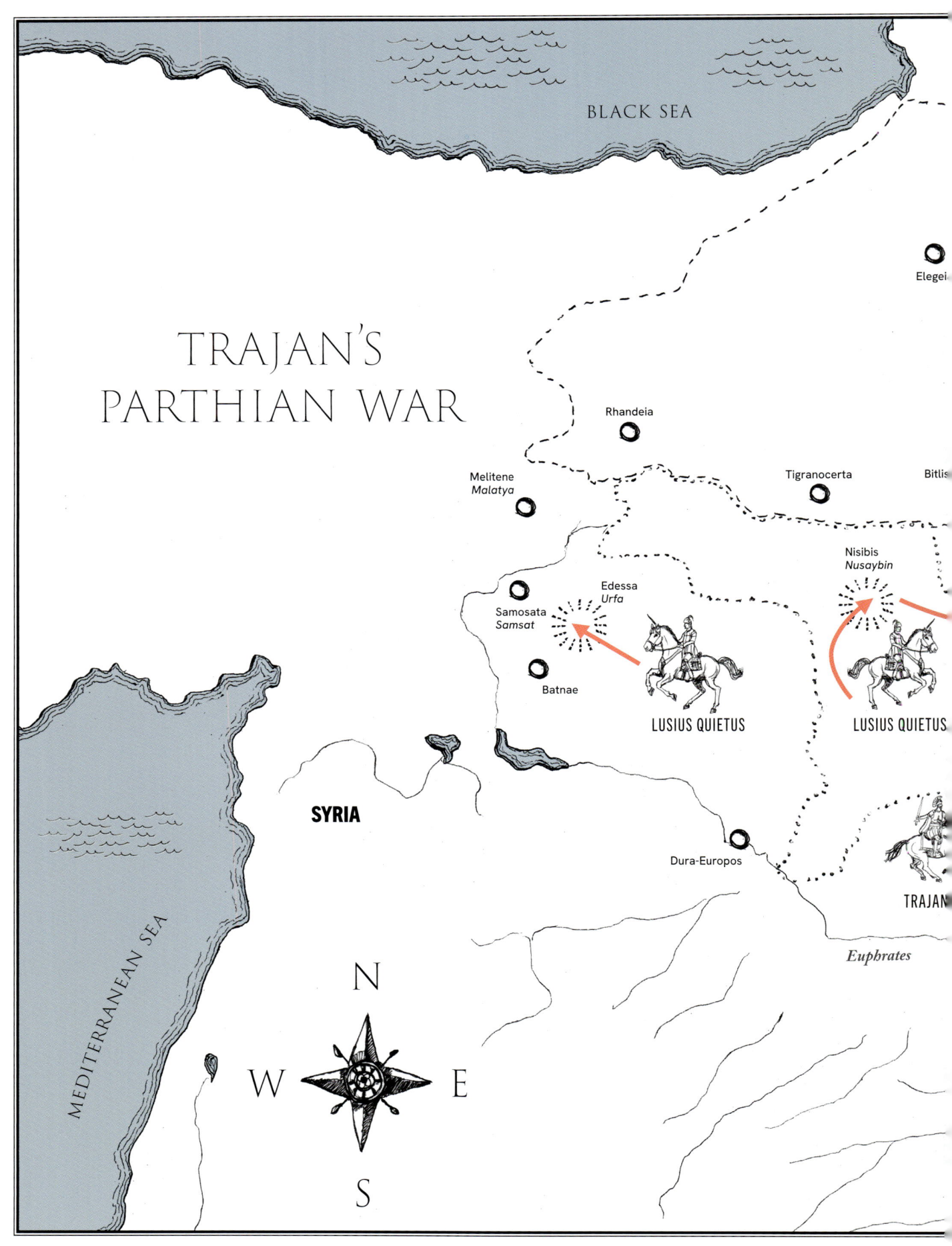

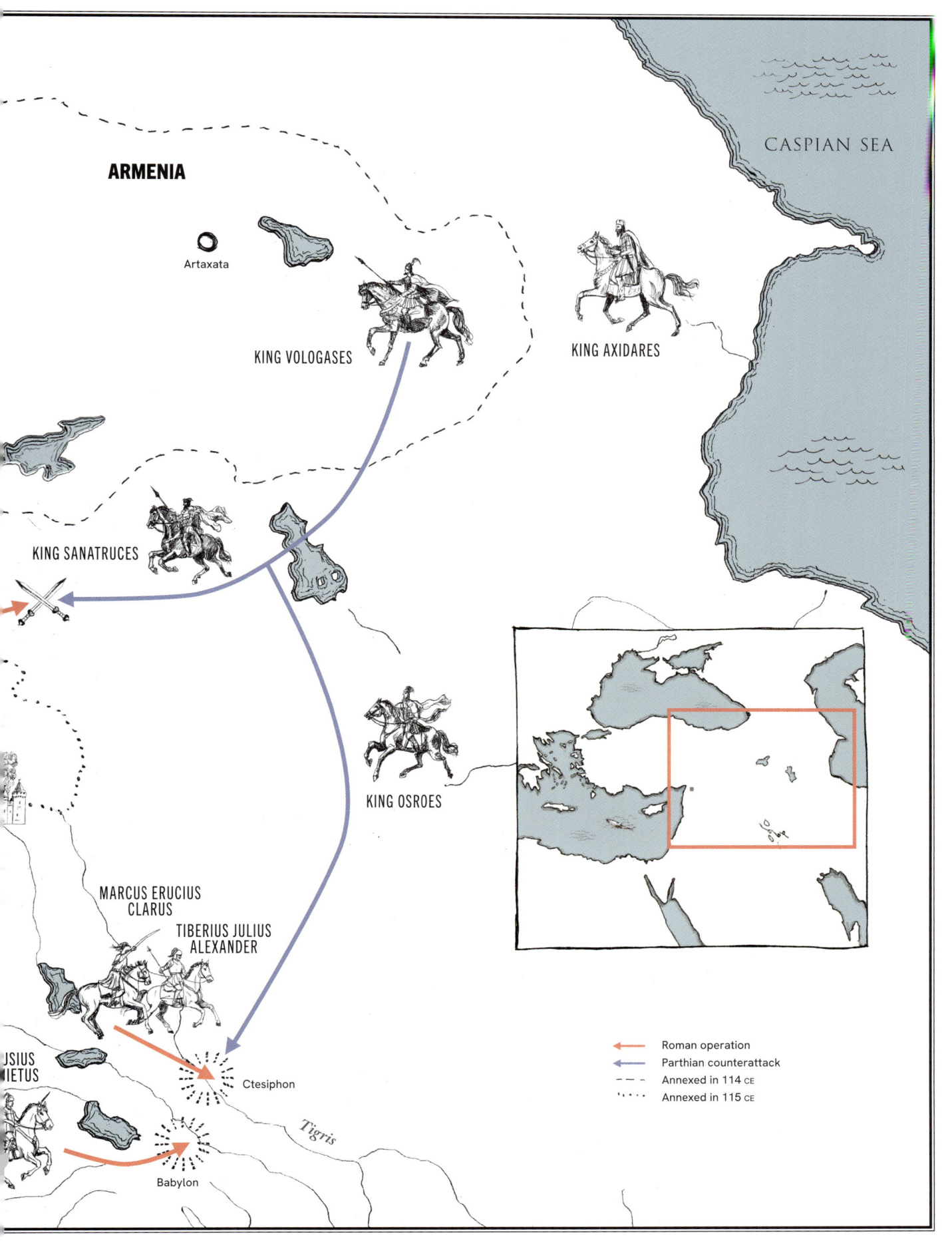

Figure IV

Trajan's Forum was constructed with the spoils of the Dacian wars. It consists of two sections; the first comprises the Basilica Ulpia, the Temple of the Divine Trajan and two libraries (one Greek, the other Latin) bordering Trajan's column (completed 113 CE). The second (southern) section consists of a large piazza entered through a triumphal arch that celebrated the victory over Dacia.

planned something much more spectacular: a new forum, of which a great column celebrating the Dacian victory was to be the centrepiece. Far bigger than the forums of earlier emperors, the new structure was entered from the northern end through a ceremonial gateway leading into a piazza, where the column was flanked by public libraries – one for Greek, the other for Latin – beside a massive basilica. South of the basilica was another large piazza, entered through a triumphal arch supporting a statue of Trajan in his chariot. The piazza itself, with semicircular buildings (exedrae) to east and west, had as its centrepiece a huge statue of a mounted Trajan.

As the Forum was being completed, Trajan further asserted the centrality of his family to the empire by deifying his sister Marciana, who died in 112 CE. She was the first imperial sister to receive such honours, and, for all his civility, Trajan evidently expected people to acknowledge a difference between their families and his own. Plotina remained, meanwhile, immensely powerful in the palace, where she nurtured the career of Hadrian.

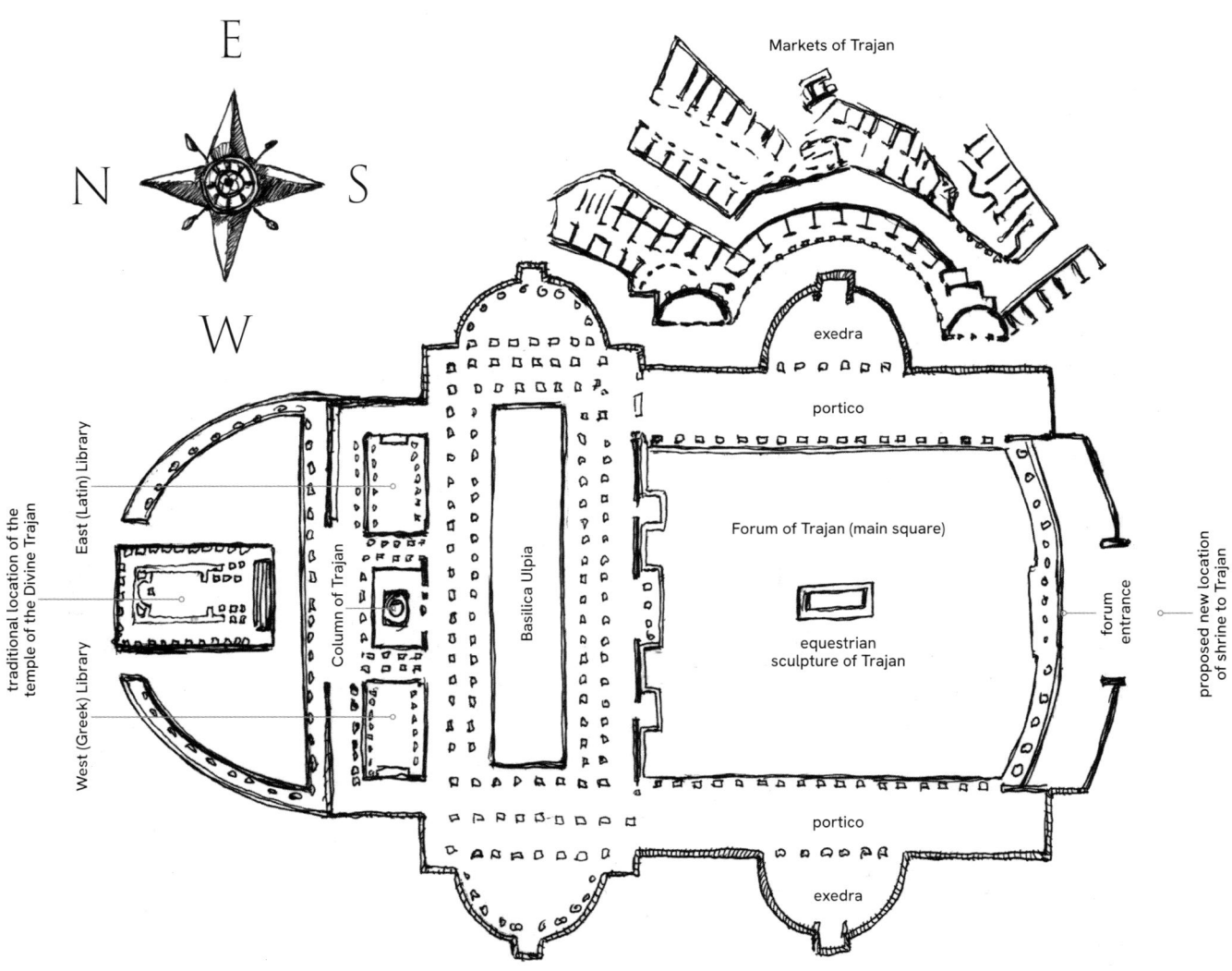

TRAJAN'S COLUMN

Today, visitors to Rome can see an eloquent sculpted interpretation of Trajan's Dacian wars in the column constructed, by 113 CE, at the centre of the great forum built by Trajan. As the column's frieze spirals upwards, its scenes (155 in all) depict the Roman army conducting an orderly march through enemy territory. The army's diversity is prominent. There are traditional legionaries in their heavy armor, supported by auxiliary troops from around the empire, who would have retained their own tactics. Men from eastern zones, such as that around Palmyra, supplied mounted archers, while slingers were recruited from the Balearic Islands, and cavalry from North Africa. Enemy civilians are portrayed as being driven from their homes but not slaughtered. The emperor is shown, surrounded by his staff, rewarding his men, dealing with ambassadors and prisoners, and bringing aid to his soldiers in need. The Roman army is also depicted as constructing a new world in Dacia, to bring Roman-style civilization to the new province. The defeated Decebelus is seen variously hiding in the woods, surrendering and finally committing suicide at the end of the Second Dacian War, all the consequence of his treacherous attacks on Roman garrisons.

Imperial expansion was under way not only north of the Danube, but also in the Middle East. As the Dacian wars were ending, Cornelius Palma, governor of Syria, annexed the Nabataean kingdom of Arabia (roughly present-day Jordan). This was a logical conclusion to the process Vespasian had initiated, to turn eastern client kingdoms into actual provinces. It also gave Rome greater control over a region along the lucrative trade route for spices from southern Arabia.

One aspect of the elimination of the Nabataean kingdom, and the progressive absorption of other eastern client kingdoms, was the direct military recruitment of local auxiliaries, especially archers and mounted archers (as depicted on Trajan's Column), to provide the heavily armed infantrymen of Roman legions with tactical flexibility. No fewer than six cavalry units appear to have been incorporated from the Nabataean army after the annexation in 106 CE. These auxiliaries were organized in a variety of ways. They could be deployed in *alae* (wings) of roughly 500 cavalry, in mixed units of infantry and cavalry, or in cohorts of infantry. From the reign of Vespasian onwards, it had become increasingly common to mix infantry and cavalry in the same unit of roughly 1,000 men. The terms of service for these auxiliaries were longer than those for soldiers in the legions – 20 years rather than 16 – at the end of which the men were granted citizenship. Officers for auxiliaries were typically figures of importance in the district from which the unit was recruited. For units stationed at a distance from their homelands, it was not uncommon for the next generation of recruits to be drawn from the immediate area but trained according to the style of the original unit.

In 113 CE, Trajan himself was in Syria as yet another quarrel with Parthia brewed over the Armenian succession. Three years earlier, the Parthian 'king of kings', Osroes, had crowned the new Armenian king, Axidares, without consulting Rome's emperor. Although evidently Rome and Parthia had agreed on Axidares' accession, it was a point of pride that the Armenian king should not formally succeed until he had received his crown from Rome. The issue seems to have been festering when, in 112 CE, Trajan named Hadrian titular commander-in-chief over the eastern provinces, and Osroes tried to appease Rome by replacing Axidares with his own nephew Parthamasiris. Trajan was not appeased. Thus, in 113 CE he arrived in the Syrian province having assembled an army of some 80,000 men, by drawing detachments from the Danubian forces to join the eastern garrison. The massive preparations were in anticipation of adopting the strategy dating back to the invasion of Parthia planned by Julius Caesar, just before his assassination,

Figure V (left)

Roman standards were of two sorts. The *signum*, or eagle (left), served for cohorts and legions, while banners or *vexilla* (right) were used for detached units (often quite large) from a legion, or for cavalry units.

Figure VI (opposite)

This relief from Ephesus commemorating a later war between Rome and Parthia – that won by the Romans under Marcus Aurelius – presents the struggle between the two sides as an enactment of the eternal struggle between the forces of civilization and barbarism.

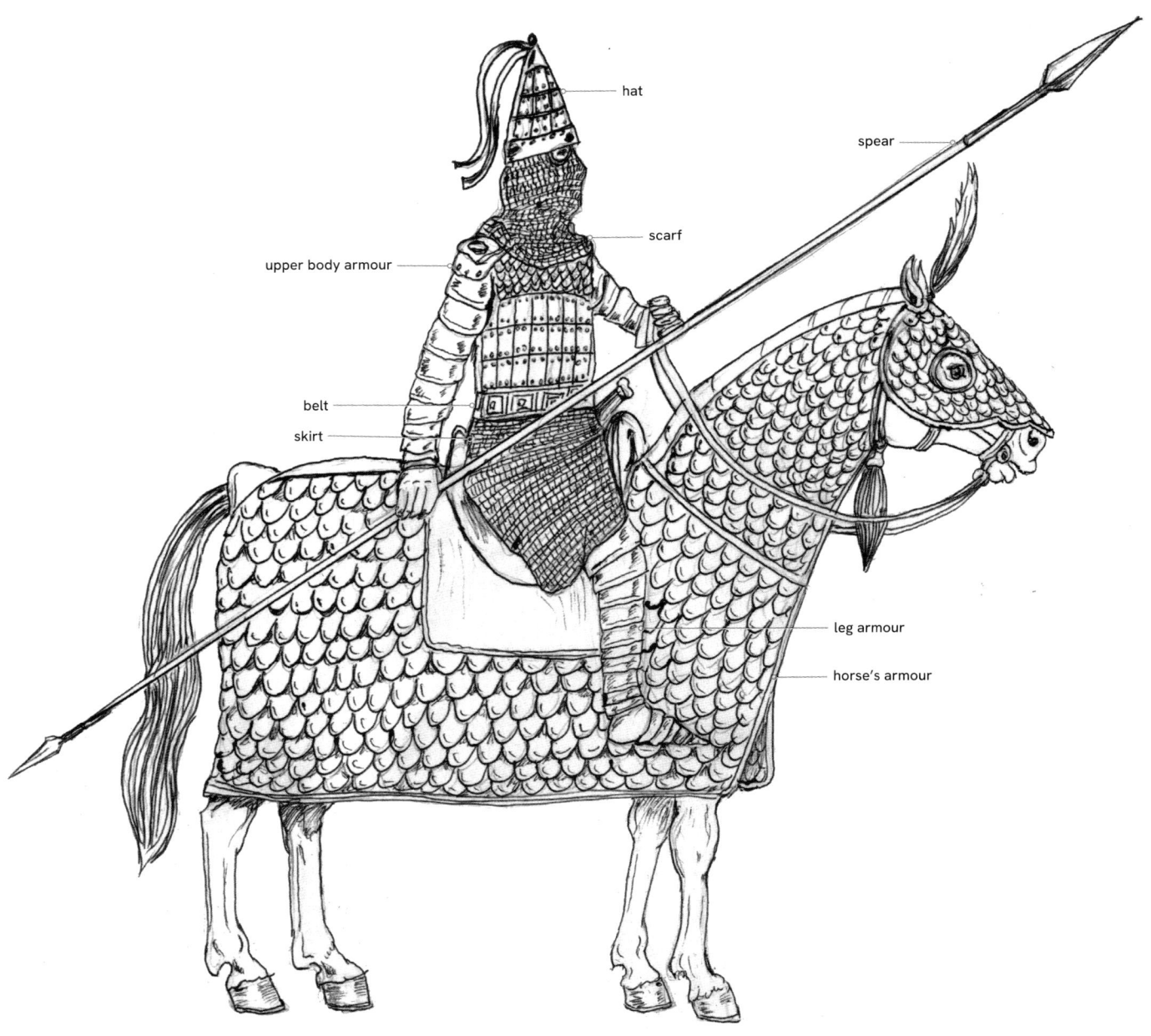

which would open the action in Armenia and proceed south along the Tigris into what is now northern Iraq. The theory was that the terrain would make it difficult for the Parthians to make effective use of their most effective troops, the cavalry. Trajan had plainly decided that the dance in which the two empires had engaged for more than a century needed some new steps.

By the end of 114 CE Trajan's armies had occupied Armenia, and when Parthamasiris submitted to him in the hope of retaining his throne, Trajan sent him back to Parthia instead. Armenia would now become a Roman province. In the meantime, civil war broke out in Parthia. The next year, Trajan took advantage of the situation and advanced further into Parthia's empire, bringing his troops into northern Mesopotamia, where he turned the kingdom of Osrhoene into a Roman province before proceeding into

Figure VII

The most effective troops mustered by the Parthians were their heavily armed lancers or cataphracts.

Adiabene (roughly the Kurdish zone in present-day Iraq). In 116 CE Trajan led an elaborate expedition down the Euphrates before crossing Mesopotamia to the Parthian capital at Ctesiphon (south of what is now Baghdad). Osroes had retreated to the Zagros mountains. The region through which Trajan had campaigned would become a new Roman province of Mesopotamia. Moving on from Ctesiphon, Trajan journeyed to the kingdom of Mesene (also known, from the Greek, as Characene), at the mouths of the Tigris and Euphrates rivers. At this point, he learned that his plans for reconstructing the eastern frontier had fallen apart.

The prospect of Roman occupation had disturbed networks existing since the Parthian kingdom had come into being, and now, finally, the Parthians got their own house in order sufficiently to mount a resistance. At the same time, thanks to an earthquake at Antioch in 115 CE – which had nearly killed Trajan himself – the Jewish populations of Egypt and Palestine were fuelled by Messianic visions of the end of Roman rule. In late 115 CE a massive Jewish revolt broke out across the region, from Syria to Egypt. A year later Abgar, the ruler of Osrhoene, declared his antipathy for the Roman regime and defeated a Roman column commanded by the man whom Trajan had left as governor of Mesopotamia. When Trajan tried and failed to capture the Mesopotamian city of Hatra, he gave up, abandoning the territory he had occupied in 115 CE. The emperor left Lusius Quietus – a North African tribal chieftain who had become one of his most trusted subordinates – to avenge the defeat in Osrhoene and then to massacre the Jews of Palestine. Trajan also made a deal with a new Parthian client king in Mesopotamia, Parthamaspates, who formally acknowledged Roman superiority in return for the Roman withdrawal from his kingdom. With that, the emperor prepared to return to Italy. He would never make it. On the 8th or 9th of August, 117 CE, Trajan died at Selinus in Cilicia, with Plotina at his side.

HADRIAN'S IMPERIAL PEACE

Trajan had come to his deathbed without having named an heir. The obvious candidate from within the family was Hadrian, but at the same time, Trajan had promoted many senior officials who might think themselves qualified for the job. It was even said that Plotina had a freedman slip into Trajan's bed after he had died, pretending to be the emperor so as to give the necessary order for Hadrian's adoption. That may be a tall tale, but Plotina did sign Trajan's final letters to the senate. Her ally was the Praetorian prefect, Publius Acilius Attianus. At issue was whether the palace would continue the practice of choosing the new emperor, or whether the choice might be left to the senate or a cabal of generals in a case where the previous emperor had not spoken. It does seem that Trajan had not made up his mind – and that some senior officers did not think the role should go to Hadrian. But none of that changed the course of events. Within weeks of taking office as Rome's new emperor in 117 CE, Hadrian executed four of Trajan's most senior officers, including Lusius Quietus, who had evidently been opposed to his succession.

While honouring Trajan's memory, Hadrian rapidly made it clear that he would be his own man. Over the course of a long reign, he would visit all Rome's provinces and set in motion a more formal definition of the empire's frontiers. The period of expansion was at an end. The frontiers would, instead, form the walls of a fortress protecting the 'civilized' world from barbarians. It is perhaps not accidental that Tacitus, completing his *Annals* in the early years of Hadrian's reign, would recall Augustus's advice that the empire should be contained within fixed boundaries.

Hadrian's first act as emperor was to bring a formal end to the war with Parthia. This he did through a treaty with Osroes, who had been reinstated as king by the Parthian nobility in place of Parthamaspates (his son). Under its terms, Rome renounced the province of Armenia, which once again became an independent kingdom with a Parthian prince as king, albeit one whom the Romans would pre-approve. Hadrian then departed for the west.

Hadrian spent his first couple of imperial years at Rome, establishing his administration, before departing, in 121 CE, for the German provinces, spending the winter at Mainz. He was accompanied by his senior staff, including the biographer Suetonius, who served as his secretary, and his wife, Sabina. While in Germany he inspected the frontier that stretched, north of the Rhine, from Mainz to the headwaters of the Danube, defining the northern frontier of Raetia. There, he decided to replace the existing fortifications, comprising a series of watchtowers, with a continuous wooden barrier, perhaps 3 metres (10 feet) high, to create a clear boundary between 'civilization' and 'barbarism'.

A year later, Hadrian moved on to Britain, becoming the first emperor to visit the province since Claudius's brief epiphany in 43 CE. There had been serious conflict there in recent years, including the near annihilation of one of the garrison legions, the Ninth, based around York. The province's northern frontier was now defined by a series of fortresses and watch posts between the River Tyne and the Solway Firth, after the more northerly fortresses established by Agricola had been abandoned at some point under Trajan. The military situation was resolved with the transfer of a legion from Germany, while Hadrian now planned an even more spectacular frontier line in the form of the great stone wall that would cross the entire island and come, in time, to bear his name. It was while Hadrian was in Britain, planning new edifices, that it appears his relationship with Sabina collapsed. He dismissed officials who, he felt, had too much sympathy for her – including Suetonius.

Figure VIII

Trajan's nephew Hadrian was notable for changing the clean-shaven imperial style. He wore a beard as a statement of his affection for Greek culture.

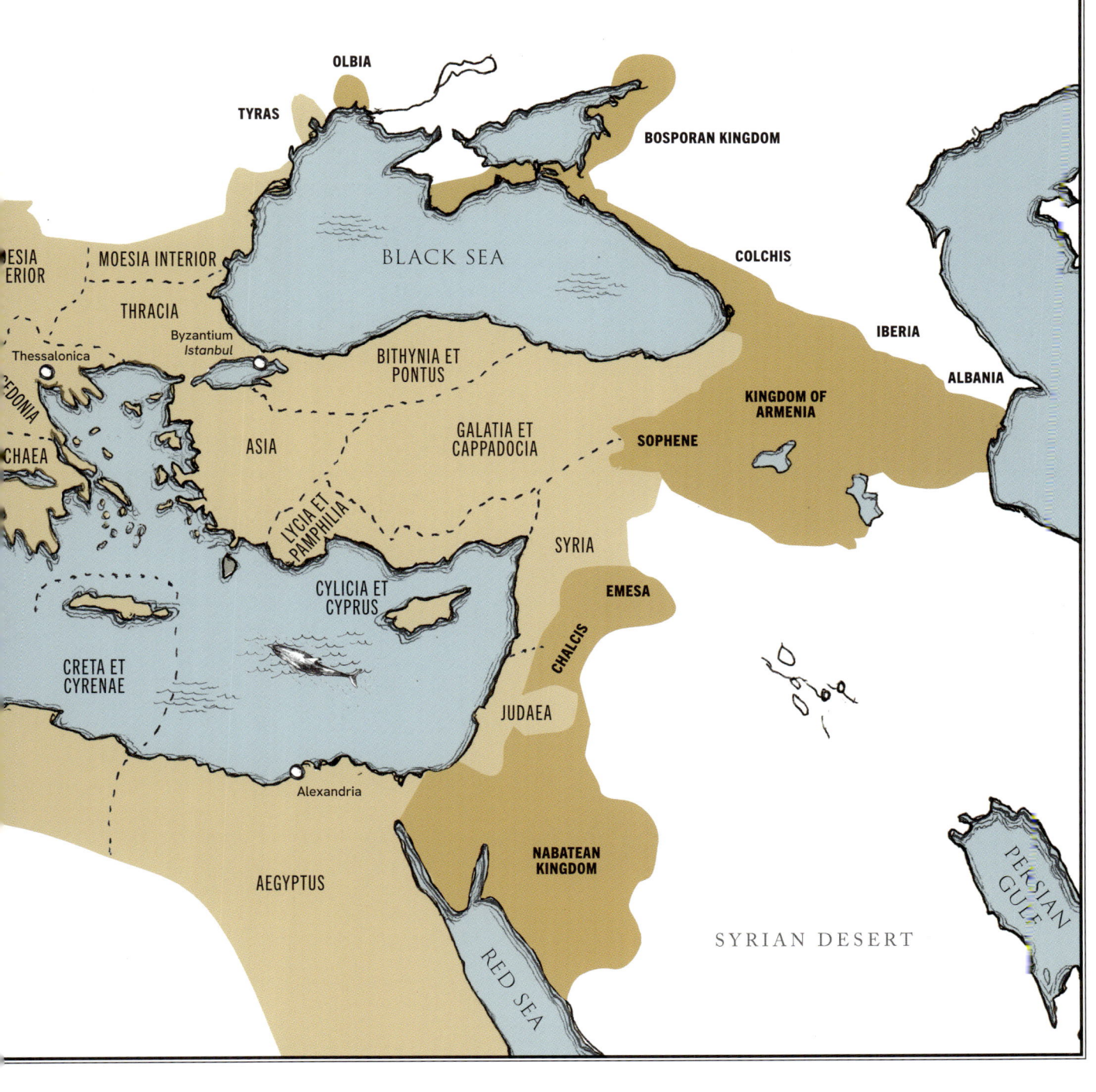

HADRIAN'S WALL

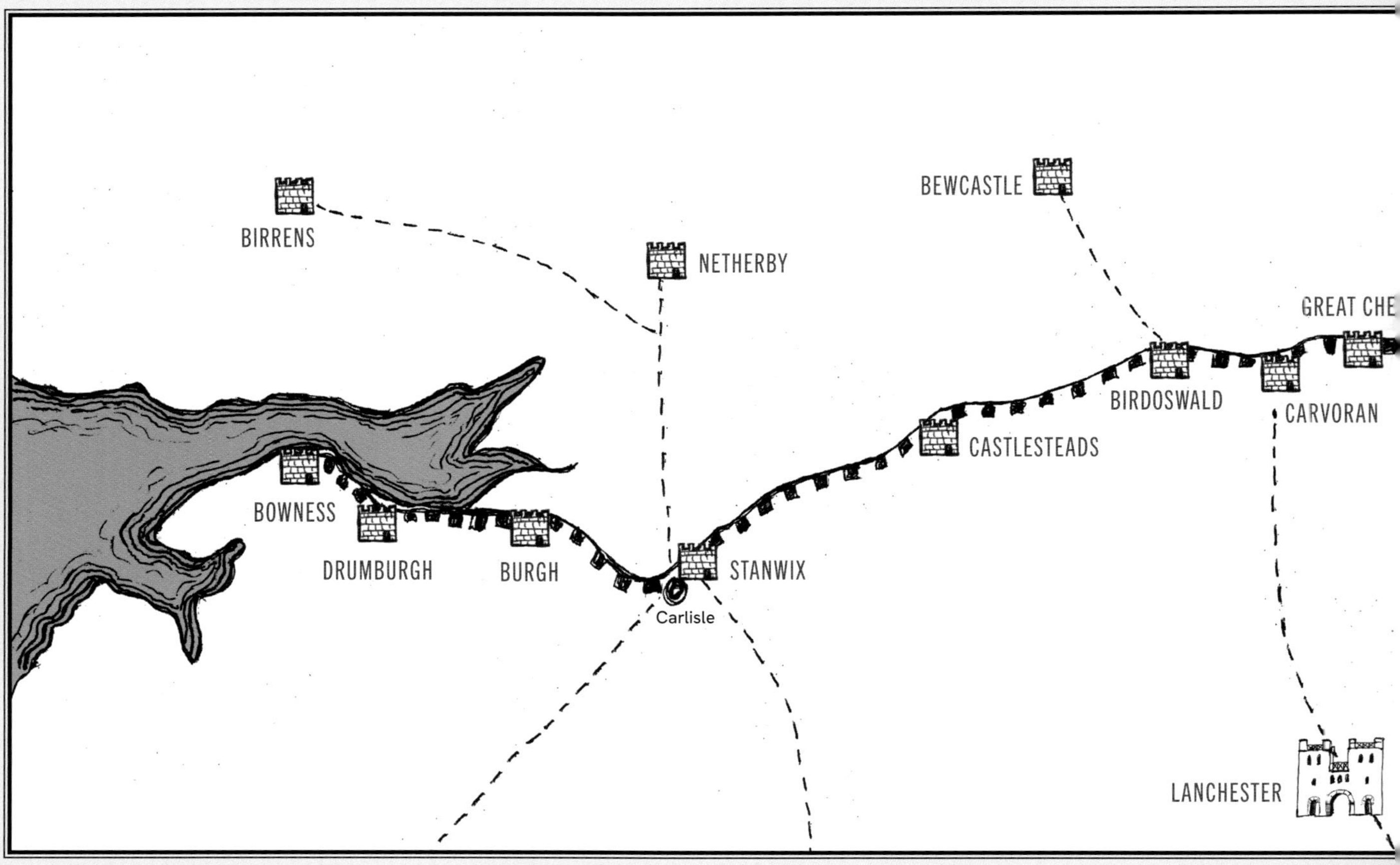

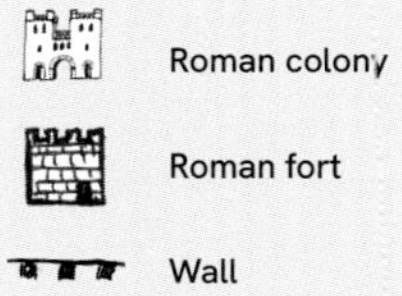

 Roman colony

 Roman fort

Wall

Extending 118 kilometres (73 miles) from one side of England to the other, Hadrian's Wall remains one of the most dramatic symbols of Roman power. It replaced a line of seven forts, located at intervals of a day's march (roughly 22 kilometres/14 miles), which housed auxiliary units, and which were constructed between Wallsend and the Solway Firth.

In its original form, Hadrian's new wall stood 4.5 metres (15 feet) high behind a ditch and had 80 'milecastles', mostly small fortlets, each of which could hold a dozen men (sometimes including a cavalryman). Between the milecastles there were turrets, which stood 9 metres (30 feet) high and numbered 158 in total, each holding a couple of men. These turrets, with no cooking facilities, were plainly observation posts manned from the milecastles.

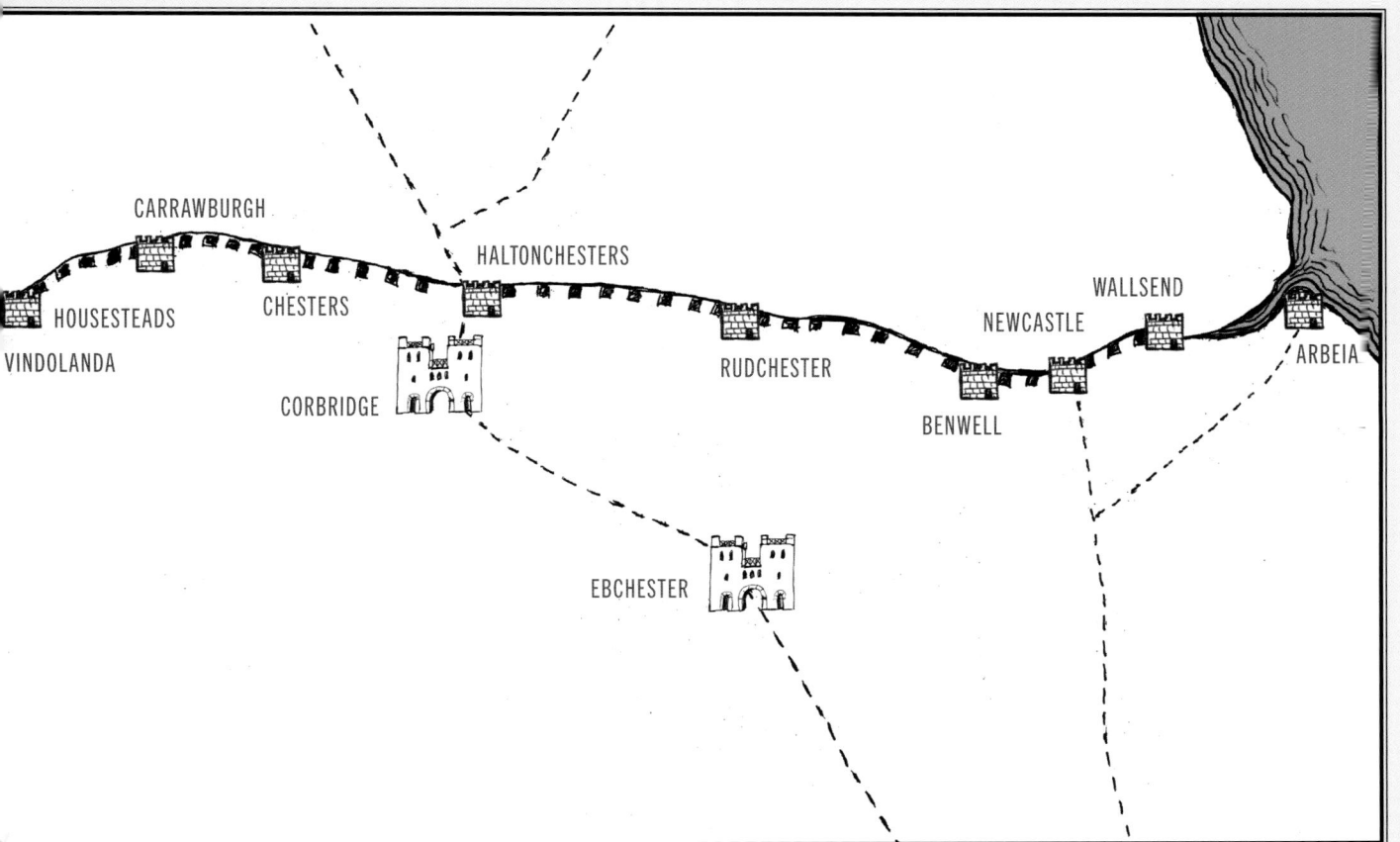

A change in the design as the wall was being built added 15 forts at roughly 8-kilometre (5-mile) intervals, of which the best-known is the one at Housesteads. It includes a headquarters building with a hospital, housing for a commanding officer, granaries, barracks buildings and a latrine. As was standard with frontier settlements at this time, civilian settlements developed in the immediate vicinity of the forts to provide basic infrastructure, food, clothing and – often – partners for the soldiers, who tended to retire in the places where they served, and raise families there.

It was an impressive undertaking. But what was the point? The 'Aelian Wall' – as it was known in antiquity – could not stop a determined invasion from the north; yet there is no reason to think that this was ever its purpose, or that its aim was purely military. In practical terms, the wall controlled the movements of people in a time of peace, offered security against random acts of violence, and provided a focal point for the development of a frontier society made up of immigrants from various parts of the empire, as well as indigenous peoples. It also divided the 'barbarians' from the camps of the legions at Chester and York. These practical objectives could have been met in other ways, without the vast expense of the wall's construction. But there was an ideological dimension, too. Hadrian's Wall marked a new phase in the Roman conception of empire, as a fortress of civilization rather than an entity capable of endless expansion and inclusion.

Although their approaches to Rome's frontiers were strikingly different, both Trajan and Hadrian prioritized the core influencing factors on strategic planning that had been in place since the time of Augustus, and which ranged from matters of security to finance and manpower.

Under Trajan, the annexation of Dacia was, from a Roman viewpoint, the logical consequence of problems Decebelus had caused in the Danubian lands. Trajan's decision to create a province protruding north of the Danube (albeit with some goldmines) was typical of Roman understanding of political geography. Areas along frontiers that acknowledged Roman superiority could remain independent – and the groups bordering Dacia (the Quadi, Sarmatians and Marcomanni) had done that. Dacia might have remained somewhat independent if Decebelus had not refused to play along with Trajan at the end of their first war. The annexation of Arabia stemmed from a somewhat different issue: the recognition that a power vacuum, caused by the failure of the Nabataean regime, would be bad for Rome. Trajan's decision to pull out of Parthia reflected a realization that Rome did not have the resources to govern the area – although, before finalizing the Roman withdrawal, Trajan had insisted on some diplomatic theatre through which Parthamaspates acknowledged that he held the throne with the emperor's permission. The theatrics were repeated shortly thereafter, when Hadrian recognized Osroes and, in 129 CE, the next Parthian 'king of kings', Vologaeses III.

Hadrian's decision to fortify the frontier in Germany and build the wall in Britain recognized existing boundaries and the limits of Roman power. Both he and Trajan were aware that the size of their army was limited by the economic resources available to them. The 31 legions in service when Trajan died numbered around 180,000 men, supported by a roughly equivalent number of auxiliary units, meaning that the army amounted to nearly 360,000 men. The disposition of this army around the frontiers reflected perceptions of regional threats, with three legions in Britain, six in the Rhineland, ten in the Balkans, seven in the eastern provinces, three in Egypt, and one each in Spain and North Africa. As military leaders, both emperors nurtured a close relationship with their men, wishing to present themselves as ideal generals, personally overseeing the training of troops, and leading long marches on foot. A long series of surviving speeches by Hadrian, delivered in 128 CE, reveal a great knowledge of military affairs and reflect the way in which he wanted to be regarded by his men:

> *Fortifications which others construct over a number of days, you have finished in one; you built a wall which requires considerable work and is normally built for permanent winter quarters in not much more time than is usually spent constructing a turf wall. For a wall of this type, the turf is cut in equal measures so it is easily carried and moved around and assembled easily, for it is naturally soft and flat; but you worked with heavy, large and uneven stones which no one is able to carry, lift or fit together, without the stones latching on to each other through their uneven surfaces. You dug a ditch straight through hard, rough*

gravel, and, levelling it, made it smooth. When your work was approved you entered the camp rapidly and took up your weapons and food, and followed the cavalry when they were sent out ....

Hadrian, praising troops performing exercises at Lambaesis, an ancient site near the village of Tazoult in Algeria (inscription, 128 CE)

When not present themselves, emperors could make large-scale strategic decisions from Rome because they had professional staff with extensive experience of provincial administration. The imperial fiscal system also worked to collect data that could guide an emperor's decision-making with a high level of precision. One of the more impressive pieces of imperial data collection appears in a commentary on inheritance law by the third-century jurist Aemilius Macer, using an existing formula for the computation of annuity payments. The estimates are based on a reasonably accurate reckoning of life expectancy and suggest that census data was used regularly to estimate imperial income. Variations in the silver content of imperial coinage likewise reflect clear attention to the availability of resources.

Tacitus reflects the importance of finance to imperial planning when he observes, in a book he wrote about Germany, that the area did not have the resources to support Roman administration. It is likely that the Roman economy could not support the size of the army Hadrian had inherited, so he acted accordingly. He allowed the remnants of the battered Ninth Legion from Britain to be absorbed into the Rhine garrison; and, a decade later, he did not replace a legion that vanished during rebellion in Judaea.

Throughout these years, the provincial garrisons began to be integrated into provincial society. Civilian settlements grew up around major military bases, and some – such as Trier and Cologne in Germany, Carnuntum in Austria, and York in England – were on their way to becoming major cities in their own right. In Britain, a treasure trove of evidence in the shape of the Vindolanda Writing Tablets has revealed different aspects of life just south of where Hadrian's Wall was constructed, while other documents, from Vindolanda and elsewhere, give insight into Roman military attitudes.

THE VINDOLANDA WRITING TABLETS

The fortress at Vindolanda in Northumberland, south of Hadrian's Wall, originally housed an auxiliary cohort from Belgium: the First Cohort of Tungrians. In 95 CE they were replaced by the Ninth Cohort of Batavians, a double-strength unit from the area of what is now the Dutch–Belgian border, at which time the fortress was expanded to accommodate the larger garrison. Ten years later the Tungrians returned, remaining until after the completion of Hadrian's Wall. Around 130 CE they departed Vindolanda and history records them next a few miles away, as the garrison at Housesteads. Vindolanda was then abandoned until the early third century, when a new base was constructed during the imperial reign of Septimius Severus. It remained in use until the time of Diocletian, into the early fourth century.

It is from the first period of occupation that this remarkable series of texts illustrating life at the base survives. The Vindolanda Writing Tablets, as they are known, were written in Latin on bark or wax-covered wooden tablets. They were subsequently discarded in layers of bracken and straw flooring in the buildings or in the street, in deposits that look like rubbish dumps and which contain a wide variety of other organic remains and artefacts. It seems that the damp, oxygen-free environment accounts for their preservation.

There are more than 800 writing tablets in total, consisting of letters and documents, both personal and administrative. They have been found in all the phases of occupation before Hadrian's reign, and the majority come from the years of Batavian occupation, as indicated by a reference to Governor Neratius Marcellus (in office in 103 CE) on a document whose handwriting links it with others connected to Flavius Cerialis, the Batavians' commander. Two commanders of the Tungrians also feature: from the earlier period, four letters connected with Julius Verecundus, and from the later period, some correspondence relating to Priscinus.

Many of the documents are very brief, and many words and phrases within them are missing or illegible, requiring a certain amount of informed speculation to establish their meaning. Nevertheless, they are evocative of relationships among and between officers (at different locations), enlisted men, contractors and even slaves. There is even a birthday invitation from the wife of the commander of a nearby fort to Sulpicia Lepidina, wife of the Batavian commander, casting a light on the social relations between women. (All translations given here are courtesy of the online Roman Inscriptions of Britain project.)

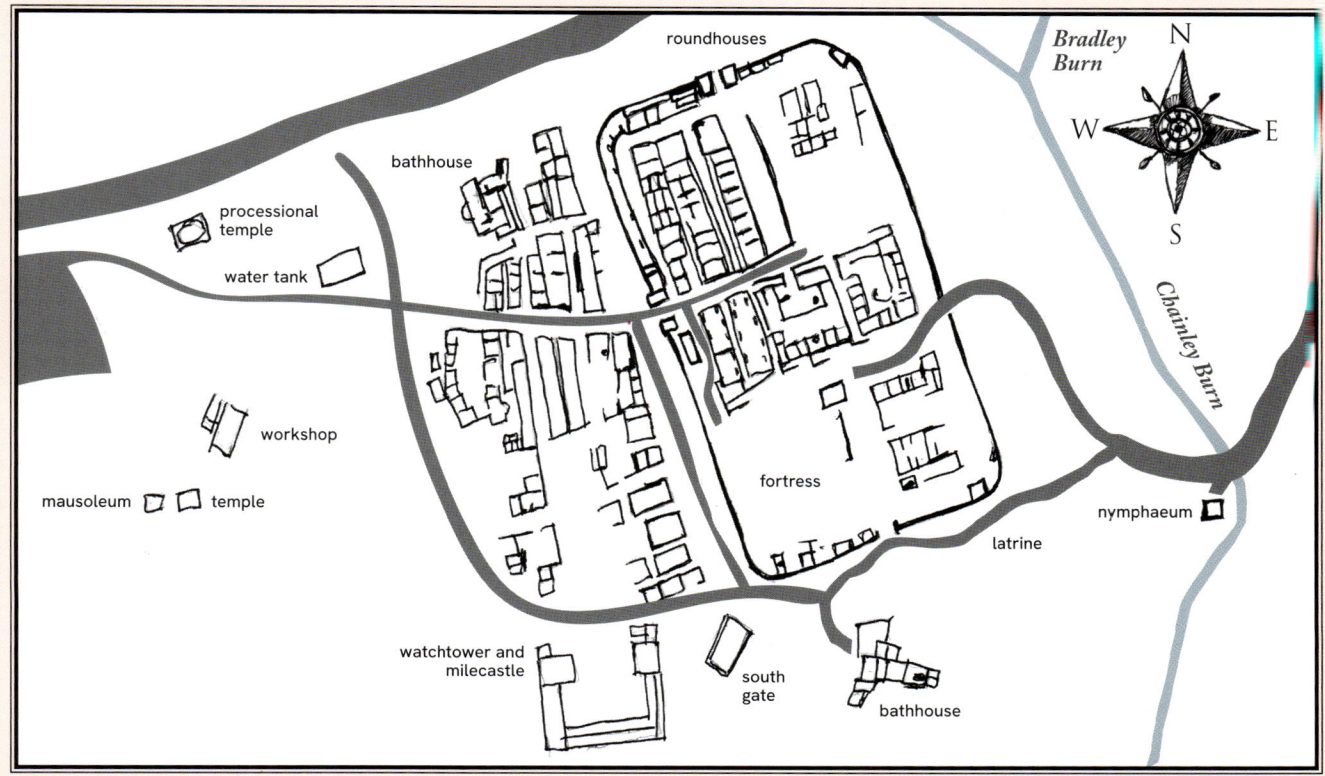

Front: Claudia Severa to her Lepidina greetings. On 11 September, sister, for the day of the celebration of my birthday, I give you a warm invitation to make sure that you come to us, to make the day more enjoyable for me by your arrival, if you are present [?]. Give my greetings to your Cerialis. My Aelius and my little son send him [?] their greetings. I shall expect you, sister. Farewell, sister, my dearest soul, as I hope to prosper, and hail.
Back: To Sulpicia Lepidina, wife of Cerialis, from Severa.
Tab. Vind. 291

The diversity of documents also includes an appeal from a civilian to a senior officer, begging him to prevent further ill-treatment at the hands of one of his subordinates; and a letter between two slaves preparing to celebrate the Saturnalia, the festival where normal master–slave relationships were inverted:

> *... he beat [?] me all the more ... goods ... or pour them down the drain [?]. As befits an honest man [?] I implore your majesty not to allow me, an innocent man, to have been beaten with rods and, my lord, inasmuch as [?] I was unable to complain to the prefect because he was detained by ill-health I have complained in vain [?] to the beneficiaries and the rest [?] of the centurions of his [?] unit. Accordingly [?] I implore your mercifulness not to allow me, a man from overseas and an innocent one, about whose good faith you may inquire, to have been bloodied by rods as if I had committed some crime.*
Tab. Vind. 344

Front: Severus to his Candidus, greetings. Regarding the ... [?] for the Saturnalia, I ask you, brother, to see to them at a price of 4 or six asses and radishes to the value of not less than ½ denarius. Farewell, brother.
Back: To Candidus, slave of Genialis the prefect, from Severus, slave of ... [?]
Tab. Vind. 301

From Vindolanda, too, we obtain a glimpse of the Roman military's dismissive view of its indigenous opponents:

> *... the Britons are unprotected by armour [?]. There are very many cavalry. The cavalry do not use swords nor do the wretched Britons mount in order to throw javelins.*
Tab Vind. 164

EXPANSIONISTS AND CONSOLIDATORS

REVOLT IN JUDAEA

In most of the Roman Empire, relations between the imperial government and its subjects were relatively stable in these years, helped by the increasing integration of provincial elites into the imperial administration. However, there was a notable exception: Judaea. The situation there was worsened by Hadrian's vision of imperial culture, with the result that a brutal revolt erupted in the area in 132–36 CE.

Wherever he went, Hadrian undertook high-profile projects, such as the completion of a vast temple to Zeus, begun by Athenian tyrants in the sixth century BCE (and unfinished in his lifetime), and the enormous villa he constructed near what is now Tivoli. He decided to bring Judaea more closely into the fold by constructing a Roman colony – named Aelia Capitolina, in his own honour – on the site of Jerusalem, which had been abandoned since Titus's destruction of the city. He ordered a temple to Jupiter to be erected on the site of the former Jewish Temple, and for good measure, he banned the practice of circumcision.

Jewish leaders, not unreasonably, saw Hadrian's actions as an attack on their faith. A violent revolt broke out in the Judaean countryside under the leadership of Simeon Ben Kosiba, whom the rabbi Akhiva, a leading scholar of the time, renamed 'bar Kokhba', meaning 'Son of the Star', thus holding him to be the messiah who would drive the Romans out. After initial successes, which enabled bar Kokhba's forces to gain control of the countryside, in 134 CE Hadrian deployed massive forces – six full legions – against him. Bar Kokhba was killed the next year, and the Romans went on to inflict massive destruction throughout Judaea, which was renamed Syria-Palestine and attached to the province of Syria.

> *Simeon, son of Kosiba, the ruler over Israel, to Jonathan and Masabala, peace! That you should inspect and take the wheat which Hanan bar Yishma'el has brought, and send me, after inspection, one hundred. And you should give them with assurance for they have been found to be stolen. And if you do not do this, then retribution will be exacted from you. And send me the man immediately with assurance. And every Tekoan man who is with you, the houses in which they dwell will be burned down, and from you I will exact retribution. [As for] Joshua, son of the Palmyrene, you shall seize him and send him to me with assurance. Do not hesitate to seize the sword which is upon him. You shall send him.*

Letter written by bar Kokhba

While the revolt in Judaea was the only major conflict in Hadrian's reign, the circumstances surrounding it reflect the troublesome aspects of Hadrian's character. He was extremely arrogant and thought himself the cleverest man he knew. The relationship breakdown between himself and Sabina was one sign of how difficult he was to deal with, and his character might have been a reason why Trajan had been reluctant to adopt him. The vast court Hadrian constructed at his Tivoli villa can be construed as a sign of his personal grandiosity; another is his handling of the affair he initiated with a young

Figure IX

This aerial view shows Herodion, the fortified desert palace originally built by Herod the Great. Located about 12 kilometres (just over 7 miles) south of Jerusalem, it served as an important base for the supporters of bar Kokhba in his war against the Romans.

man named Antinous in the 120s. When Antinous died under mysterious circumstances while accompanying Hadrian to Egypt in 130 CE, Hadrian ordered his deification and reorganized the Greek festival cycle so that an athletic celebration of Antinous would occupy a central place in it.

As Hadrian aged, the question of succession became one that he had to face. In 130 CE he adopted as his heir Lucius Ceionius Commodus, who was in his late twenties at the time. But Ceionius died suddenly in January 138 CE, at the same time as Hadrian himself was very ill. A month later Hadrian selected an aging senator, Titus Aurelius Antoninus, to be his new heir, as long as Antoninus adopted Ceionius's son Lucius, then aged eight, as well as Antoninus's nephew Marcus Annius Verus.

When Hadrian died, on the 10th of July, 138 CE, Antoninus duly became emperor. One of his first acts was to insist on Hadrian's deification, despite the hesitation of the senate, many of whose members objected to Hadrian's recent murders of some prominent men. As a result of his devotion to his predecessor, Antoninus would be known as 'Antoninus Pius'.

Figure X (overleaf)

An 'accidental' emperor, Antoninus was adopted by Hadrian at the end of the older man's life, when his original heir apparent had died. Antoninus was known as 'Pius' after he ensured the senate voted divine honours for Hadrian, whom many senators disliked.

EXPANSIONISTS AND CONSOLIDATORS

FROM MY FATHER I LEARNED MILDNESS AND UNSHAKEN RESOLUTION IN DECISIONS MADE AFTER THOROUGH EXAMINATION, NO DELIGHT IN EXTERNAL HONOURS, LOVE OF WORK, WILLINGNESS TO HEAR FROM ANYONE WHO HAD SOMETHING TO SAY FOR THE PUBLIC GOOD, A DESIRE TO AWARD EVERY PERSON ACCORDING TO THEIR WORTH WITH NO PARTIALITY, THE EXPERIENCE TO KNOW WHEN TO PRESS AND WHEN TO RELAX ...

MARCUS AURELIUS
ON HIS FATHER, ANTONINUS PIUS, *MEDITATIONS*
1.16.1–4

prompting the incursions. But economic disruption seems to have been at the heart of the problem. Stability along the frontier was usually secured by the economic self-interest of Rome's immediate neighbours, whose economies were dependent on cross-border trade as well as some Roman subsidies. When peace negotiations ultimately took place, the resetting of trade agreements was a major feature of the resulting treaties. As for the problematic state of the Roman garrison, this may be inferred from the success of the early invaders, who became more aggressive in 167 CE, while the plague prevented the co-emperors, who had planned to campaign together, from leaving Italy. They did, though, reach Carnuntum in 168 CE, inflicting a defeat on the invaders. It was at this point that an incident took place which underscored the damage the health crisis was doing to the imperial economy. The soldiers asked Marcus for a special payment to reward them for their victory; he refused, saying that the extra money should instead be wrung from their parents and other relatives.

At the end of the campaigning season in 168 CE, the emperors returned to Italy. Lucius Verus died there in January or February the next year, leaving Marcus Aurelius as sole emperor. In 170 CE the situation on the northern frontier took a decided turn for the worse when a Roman expedition north of the Danube was defeated. According to one account, Marcus tossed two lions into the Danube – following predictions from a Black Sea holy man named Alexander, who claimed to be a spokesman for a prophetic snake. They swam the river but were sacrificed by the enemy, who went on to kill 20,000 of the Roman forces. Those numbers are probably an exaggeration on the part of the source, who was deeply hostile to Alexander. The raiders then reached northern Italy before they were turned back.

Marcus was more successful in 171 CE, when he managed to reset the frontier on the Danube and base himself at Carnuntum. In response, he praised divine intervention. The great column he erected in Rome to commemorate his victories depicts two miracles. In the first, a lightning bolt (brought on by Marcus's prayers, according to the surviving literary account) shatters a siege machine that is attacking the emperor's fortress; in the second, which was disseminated widely as propaganda, a gigantic divinity intervenes to pour down a storm on the heads of a barbarian army. The most contemporary of the accounts attribute this divine manifestation also to Marcus's prayers, reporting that the army was suffering from exhaustion when Marcus invoked the god.

Figure XI

Marcus Aurelius's reign is today best remembered for his powerful memoirs, the *Meditations*, which indicate that he was a deeply thoughtful man.

NEW EMPERORS, NEW WARS

Antoninus appears to have travelled little and to have looked to maintain peace on the frontiers. The one genuinely aggressive action of his reign may well have come about through the initiative in 142 CE of Britain's governor, who advanced well north of Hadrian's Wall to erect a new wall, from the Firth of Forth to the Firth of Clyde. It would become known as the Antonine Wall. More serious for the empire, though, was Antoninus's inaction when a new regime emerged in Parthia in 147 CE, under Vologaeses IV.

A feature of the settlements with Parthia under Trajan and Hadrian had been that the kingdom of Mesene would remain a notionally independent Roman puppet state. A substantial portion of the trade from India passed up the Euphrates from the riverside port at Charax, where the merchants of Palmyra, some of whom held administrative positions in Mesene, oversaw its onward journey across the Syrian desert into Roman territory. In 151 CE Vologaeses IV invaded Mesene, expelling Mithridates (Meredetes), who had ruled with Rome's blessing since the end of Trajan's war.

Rome failed to respond to Parthia's presumption, potentially sowing seeds for the greater Parthian assertiveness that was to follow in due course. For now, the long years of imperial peace still held. But they came to an end in the spring of 161 CE, with the death of Antoninus.

When Antoninus died, the senate wished to proclaim one of his two designated heirs, Marcus, sole emperor. Marcus resisted, honouring Hadrian's intention that Ceionius's son Lucius become emperor too – and perhaps revealing his own affection for his adoptive brother. The result was that Lucius Verus was proclaimed co-emperor. It was a smart move, given that war was now brewing in the east (even if the threat was underappreciated at this point), as well as trouble in Britain and along the Rhine. Marcus had no experience of war, and neither did Lucius, so both rulers would depend on the advice of their generals for the conduct of any hostilities. What could not be allowed to happen, though, was for some subordinate to gain all the credit for a major campaign. An imperial figurehead would have to be present to take credit for a victory, and the existence of a co-emperor meant that there would be someone to play that role while his colleague managed matters in Rome.

In the east, the situation created conditions whereby Vologaeses IV could initiate his effort to reassert Parthian control over areas that had become Roman client territory without facing overwhelming opposition. Although Rome's frontline eastern army had been strengthened in the wake of the Jewish revolt (and consisted of three legions in Syria, two in Cappadocia, two in Palestine and one in Arabia), it was still primarily a defensive force, substantially smaller than the army Trajan had deployed in his campaigns. There was a further problem for Rome, in that neither the governor of Cappadocia (who would be responsible for any threat to Armenia) nor the governor of Syria was an experienced soldier. For now, the men who would ultimately play a major role were in other parts of the empire.

The eastern war that began was to be unlike conflicts under Nero and Trajan in that it involved several full-scale battles. Vologaeses himself appears to have designed an attack that looked very much like Trajan's plan in reverse, beginning in Armenia, where he expelled the Roman-appointed King Sohaemus (who, although a member of the Parthian Arsacid dynasty, had lived in the Roman Empire for some time, even rising to the consulship). In place of Sohaemus, Vologaeses placed a relative named Pacorus on the Armenian throne.

Rome's interests fared badly to begin with. Severianus, Roman governor of the province of Commagene, northeast of Osrhoene, mishandled the local garrison, which was destroyed at Elegeia, in Armenia. Atidius Cornelianus, who governed Syria when the war broke out, was routed in a full-scale action. However, Parthia failed to capture Antioch in the wake of the victory, possibly reflecting its failure to develop effective siege tactics; the absence of that capacity was noted by Roman authors. In response to the emergency, Lucius Verus was sent to take titular command of the operation, competent generals were gathered to command in the field, and units were brought in from the Balkans to strengthen the eastern garrisons. The reinforcements arrived toward the end of 162 CE. The next year, the army – now commanded by Statius Priscus, fresh from governing Britain – moved into Armenia and captured Pacorus. Priscus led the army down the Euphrates, replacing the king whom Vologaeses had installed in Osrhoene, and destroying the large army the Parthians had deployed along the river, in a battle near Dura.

The year 164 CE appears to have been taken up with preparations for a full-scale Roman invasion of Parthia. The only major event seems to have been the reinstallation of Sohaemus on the Armenian throne. But there was also a changing of the guard in the Roman general staff. Statius Priscus probably died; in any case, he was replaced by two generals: Martius Verus, who was responsible for managing Sohaemus's repatriation; and a younger man, Avidius Cassius. In 165 CE Martius Verus operated in northern Mesopotamia, while Cassius followed in Trajan's path by advancing down the Euphrates and onwards to capture Ctesiphon. A year later Cassius led an invasion of northern Parthia, at which point a serious outbreak of plague (which cannot be identified with any pathogen now extant) forced the Romans to call a halt to further operations, leaving Vologaeses – presumably the target of the campaign – on the Parthian throne.

In the wake of the Roman victories, which included the installation of a Roman client as King of Armenia, and some other territorial adjustments, such as enhanced Roman control over Osrhoene, the eastern provinces were now combined under Cassius Severus's overall command. His title was *corrector totius orientis*, 'governor of the entire east', a move that looks like an effort on the part of Marcus Aurelius, as plague spread across the empire, to enhance the efficiency of the command structure just as a long series of wars on the Danube got underway.

DANUBIAN DISTURBANCES

The first enemy raid across the Danube occurred in 166 CE. Since the plague began to spread in 165, it is quite possible that the devastation it caused – some 10 per cent of the empire's population perished over the next few years – as well as the weakening of the Danubian garrisons, contributed to prompting the incursions. But economic disruption seems to have been at the heart of the problem. Stability along the frontier was usually secured by the economic self-interest of Rome's immediate neighbours, whose economies were dependent on cross-border trade as well as some Roman subsidies. When peace negotiations ultimately took place, the resetting of trade agreements was a major feature of the resulting treaties. As for the problematic state of the Roman garrison, this may be inferred from the success of the early invaders, who became more aggressive in 167 CE, while the plague prevented the co-emperors, who had planned to campaign together, from leaving Italy. They did, though, reach Carnuntum in 168 CE, inflicting a defeat on the invaders. It was at this point that an incident took place which underscored the damage the health crisis was doing to the imperial economy. The soldiers asked Marcus for a special payment to reward them for their victory; he refused, saying that the extra money should instead be wrung from their parents and other relatives.

At the end of the campaigning season in 168 CE, the emperors returned to Italy. Lucius Verus died there in January or February the next year, leaving Marcus Aurelius as sole emperor. In 170 CE the situation on the northern frontier took a decided turn for the worse when a Roman expedition north of the Danube was defeated. According to one account, Marcus tossed two lions into the Danube – following predictions from a Black Sea holy man named Alexander, who claimed to be a spokesman for a prophetic snake. They swam the river but were sacrificed by the enemy, who went on to kill 20,000 of the Roman forces. Those numbers are probably an exaggeration on the part of the source, who was deeply hostile to Alexander. The raiders then reached northern Italy before they were turned back.

Marcus was more successful in 171 CE, when he managed to reset the frontier on the Danube and base himself at Carnuntum. In response, he praised divine intervention. The great column he erected in Rome to commemorate his victories depicts two miracles. In the first, a lightning bolt (brought on by Marcus's prayers, according to the surviving literary account) shatters a siege machine that is attacking the emperor's fortress; in the second, which was disseminated widely as propaganda, a gigantic divinity intervenes to pour down a storm on the heads of a barbarian army. The most contemporary of the accounts attribute this divine manifestation also to Marcus's prayers, reporting that the army was suffering from exhaustion when Marcus invoked the god.

Figure XI

Marcus Aurelius's reign is today best remembered for his powerful memoirs, the *Meditations*, which indicate that he was a deeply thoughtful man.

THE COLUMN OF MARCUS AURELIUS

The Column of Marcus Aurelius, which is 30 metres (97 feet) tall, is located today in the Piazza Colonna, at the heart of Rome, in what was at the time the northern corner of the Campus Martius (Field of Mars). The column illustrates Marcus's campaigns against the Danubian tribes (beginning in 171 CE) in a spiral of 21 turns, and it was probably commissioned at the time of his triumph, in 176 CE, and completed by 193 CE. The image of Victoria, goddess of victory, in the middle of the column appears to divide the campaigns against the Marcomanni from the later campaigns against the Quadi and Sarmatians.

The column's depiction of the army reveals some subtle and significant differences from the treatment on Trajan's Column (see page 121). While, in the earlier column, Romans are seen destroying Dacian towns, they do not slaughter Dacian civilians – who are, after all, on their way to becoming Roman citizens. The fate of prisoners and civilians is very different in Marcus's column, where mass decapitations of prisoners accompany scenes of destruction and battle. Marcus had no intention of expanding the empire north of the Danube. To him, the peoples north of the Danube were enemies, not future subjects.

Two significant features of the campaigns were the development of a new general staff and the promotion of Marcus's son Commodus. The chief figures among the general staff were Claudius Pompeianus, who impressed Marcus so greatly that he arranged for him to marry his daughter Lucilla (the widow of Lucius Verus), and Helvius Pertinax, whose career Pompeianus had promoted very heavily. Pertinax was an extraordinary figure. He was the son of a freed slave who had made a lot of money in the wool trade, and who arranged an appointment for his son in the army through the intervention of an aristocratic patron during the Parthian campaign. As for Commodus, he joined the campaign in 172 CE, aged just 11. He was plainly being prepared for the throne.

The campaigns of 172–75 CE moved east along the Danube, from the territory of the Marcomanni to that of the Sarmatians and the Quadi, until, in the spring of 175, Marcus fell seriously ill. It was thought he might die. In July, believing Marcus's death had already occurred, Avidius Cassius had himself declared emperor from Egypt, where he was suppressing a rebellion in the Nile Delta. Nasty gossip would later suggest that Marcus's wife, Faustina, had a better appreciation of Commodus's qualities than did her husband, and urged Cassius to take the step. Although Cassius was murdered by his guards within two months of his acclamation, the shock of the events brought the Danubian campaign to a halt, so that Marcus could visit the eastern provinces, where he had never shown himself in person.

Figure XII

Commissioned to house the remains of a Roman general who died in the course of Marcus Aurelius's wars along the Danube in the 170s CE, the elaborate Portonaccio sarcophagus (now in the National Roman Museum, Palazzo Massimo alle Terme, Rome) depicts Roman victories over their enemies, which ended shortly after Marcus's death in 180 CE. The cover of the coffin depicts the general's life story.

At the same time, having declared victory, Marcus began to receive requests to rescind special taxes on members of the upper classes, which had been imposed to fund the war effort. One of the most significant of these was a surcharge on the gladiators purchased by people holding priesthoods connected with the imperial cult, so that they could provide the contests required of their offices. The total income from this tax was 20–23 million sesterces, amounting to 3–4 per cent of the roughly 670 million sesterces required to pay the army each year. The bulk of that sum – which constituted 80 per cent of the imperial budget – had come from taxes on land and individuals, collected by provincial communities and paid to provincial officials, as well as taxes on trade, extracted when goods moved from one province to another. The decline in population as a result of the plague meant a decline in the tax base, necessitating such creative surcharges as this gladiator tax.

Marcus's eastern journey lasted for less than 18 months. Returning to Rome, he celebrated a triumph in December 176 CE and elevated Commodus to the rank of co-emperor. He had been ill again earlier that year, and, as the notes he kept of his private thoughts (the *Meditations*) attest, he had a strong sense of his own mortality: 'There are many who do not know your name, and many who will rapidly forget it, as many as praise you now will soon criticize you so neither a memorial or fame or anything else is worth consideration' (*Meditations*, 9.30).

Tax breaks and triumphs notwithstanding, Marcus Aurelius's proclamation of peace on Earth was premature. Fighting broke out again along the Danube in the summer of 178 CE, so towards the end of the year Marcus again departed from Rome, with Commodus in tow. The next year's campaigning season brought major victories over the Quadi and the Marcomanni, as Roman units ranged throughout their territory. Cassius Dio, the major source for these operations, wrote that Marcus now intended to create two new provinces in their territory. This claim, however, which would imply a switch from the ideology illustrated on Marcus's column then being erected, is contradicted by the treaties Dio himself quoted, all of which looked to re-establish the frontier line and control economic activity in the frontier zone.

The opening of a new campaign season, in March 180 CE, was approaching when Marcus fell ill once more. This time he did not recover. On the 17th of March, Marcus Aurelius died. Commodus, already emperor, made peace with the Quadi and Marcomanni and returned to Rome to celebrate a triumph. In the decade to come he would prove that the doubts expressed about his capacities were thoroughly deserved.

Despite the many crises of his reign, Marcus Aurelius was remembered as a fundamentally decent human being who devoted himself to the welfare of his subjects. Cassius Dio concluded his account of the emperor by writing that his work of history would now pass from an age of gold to one of rust and iron.

CHRONOLOGY 97–180 CE

97 CE
Nerva's adoption of Trajan as heir.

98 CE
Death of Nerva (28th of January); Trajan becomes emperor.

100 CE
Trajan's return to Rome.

101 CE
Outbreak of the First Dacian War: ends 102 CE.

105 CE
Outbreak of Second Dacian War.

106 CE
End of Second Dacian War, producing the Roman province of Dacia; annexation of the Nabataean kingdom as the province of Arabia.

113 CE
Trajan's arrival in Syria.

114 CE
Trajan's occupation of Armenia.

115 CE
Trajan's occupation of Osrhoene and Adiabene; great earthquake in Antioch, and the beginning of the Jewish revolt.

116 CE
Trajan's capture of Ctesiphon, and the declaration of Mesene as a client state.

117 CE
Abandonment of Roman provinces taken in 115–16 CE; Jewish revolt suppressed; death of Trajan (August) and succession of Hadrian.

118 CE
Peace of Rhandia with Parthia; Hadrian's return to Rome.

121 CE
Hadrian's visit to the Rhine frontier.

122 CE
Hadrian's visit to Britain, and orders given for construction of the northern frontier wall.

123 CE
Hadrian's travels in North Africa and Syria.

124 CE
Hadrian's travels to Anatolia (and meeting with Antinous), followed by travels to Greece.

126 CE
Hadrian's return to Rome.

130 CE
Hadrian in Egypt; death of Antinous.

132 CE
Outbreak of the bar Kokhba revolt in Judaea: suppressed in 136 CE.

138 CE
Death of Hadrian (10th of July); succession of Antoninus.

140   **150**   **160**   **170**   **180**   → CE

142 CE
Beginning of construction of the Antonine Wall in Britain.

151 CE
Parthia's occupation of Mesene.

161 CE
Death of Antoninus (7th of March); succession of co-emperors Marcus Aurelius and Lucius Verus; Parthian invasion of Cappadocia and Syria.

162 CE
Lucius Verus's command of Roman armies in the east.

163 CE
Roman capture of Artaxata (in Armenia); Parthian occupation of Osrhoene; Roman defeat of Parthians at Sura, on the River Euphrates.

165 CE
Roman occupation of Osrhoene; Roman capture of Ctesiphon, under Avidius Severus; outbreak of plague, spreading across the Roman Empire.

166 CE
End of Roman operations in Parthia.

167 CE
Outbreak of Balkan war around the Danube, after enemy invasion of Pannonia.

168 CE
Command at Carnuntum taken by Marcus Aurelius and Lucius Verus.

169 CE
Death of Lucius Verus (January or February), leaving Marcus Aurelius sole emperor.

170 CE
Defeat of the Roman offensive across the Danube; raids into Italy by the Quadi and Marcomanni peoples.

171 CE
Danubian invaders driven from the Roman Empire.

172 CE
Roman invasion of the territory of the Marcomanni.

175 CE
Defeat of the Sarmatians; revolt of the would-be emperor, Avidius Cassius (April), followed by his murder (July).

177 CE
Marcus Aurelius's son Commodus made co-emperor (1st of January).

178 CE
Renewal of campaigns in Germany.

180 CE
Death of Marcus Aurelius (17th of March).

EXPANSIONISTS AND CONSOLIDATORS

CHAPTER 4

IMPERIAL CHURN, IMPERIAL FAILURE: FROM COMMODUS TO CARUS

Hollywood's Emperor Commodus, as portrayed by Joaquin Phoenix in the film *Gladiator* (2000), was a deeply insecure, homicidal narcissist with an unhealthy interest in his sister. The Emperor Commodus who emerges from the historical record was even more problematic. Brutal and oblivious to the administrative needs of an empire, he had a sense of his own grandiosity that only increased as the years passed, to the point where he projected himself as the earthly embodiment of Hercules.

Tension at the imperial court, already hinted at by Marcus Aurelius in his *Meditations*, exploded as the war on the Danube came to a formal end. Commodus relied heavily on the advice of his *cubicularius* (butler or chamberlain), Saoterus, who even accompanied the emperor in the triumphal chariot when returning to Rome, the two of them kissing as they passed through the streets. At the same time, Commodus showed senior members of the senate less respect than they thought they deserved, and he distrusted men who had held important positions under his father. Unsurprisingly, relations between the court and senatorial aristocracy degenerated. With such an emperor as Commodus, who now stayed in Rome, the palace staff assumed a much larger role in the day-to-day management of the empire, and the greatest influence attached to Saoterus, who controlled access to the emperor in his private moments and had to manage personalities neither compliant nor weak. For women in the palace, the path to power lay rather more directly, via the emperor's bedroom. Commodus kept numerous concubines, who also played a role in determining whom he would hear.

Those who felt that they had been forced out from their proper places in the councils of the emperor gathered around Commodus's sister Lucilla. The actual Lucilla, as opposed to the film version, was considerably older than her brother – she was 19 when he was born – and retained significant privileges, being Lucius Verus's widow. She was an obvious focal point for the discontented, and towards the end of 182 CE a conspiracy took shape that included several senior senators and possibly the Praetorian prefect. A sense of imperial ceremonial dictated the timing for the assassination attempt against Commodus, but an exaggerated sense of theatre was its undoing. As the emperor entered the imperial box in the Colosseum, his would-be assassin cried out, 'Behold! The senate sends you this,' before drawing his concealed dagger. He would have done better to act first and speak second, for he was killed before he could strike a blow. Other conspirators were executed when they were identified, while Lucilla was exiled to Capri, only to be murdered later that year.

The botched assassination attempt gave a new Praetorian prefect with ambition, Perennis, an opening to eliminate his rivals, including his fellow prefect and Saoterus. The executions that followed, of so many senior officials, sent shockwaves through the senatorial aristocracy, while Perennis established himself as the sole power behind the throne – or so he thought.

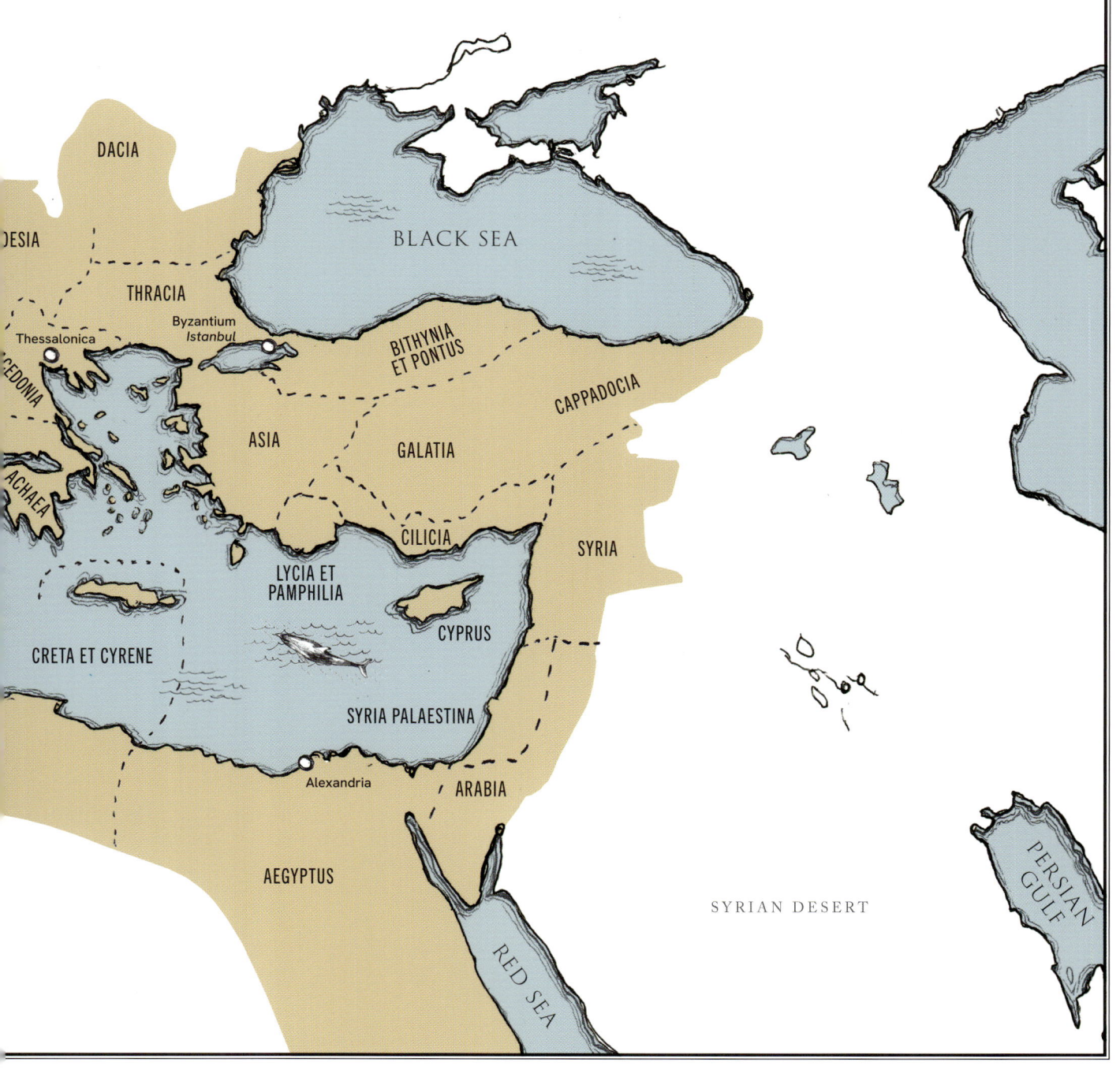

As it turned out, he did not last long in this position, for he failed to pay sufficient deference to Saoterus's successor as *cubicularius*, Cleander, who deftly manipulated the relationship between Commodus and his army. In 184/5 CE, as a result of a military mutiny in Britain, 1,500 men were able to lay their complaints before the emperor in person. But Cleander got to the soldiers before they spoke to Commodus, convincing them that it would be in their interests to identify Perennis as an aspiring usurper. Commodus, swallowing this version of events, turned his prefect over to the men to be killed.

Two years later, Cleander himself was thwarted when his administrative excesses led to a reaction organized by Papirius Dionysius, the prefect of Rome's grain supply, and a remarkable woman named Marcia, whose career recalls that of Vespasian's long-term mistress, Antonia Caenis. The daughter of a freedman from Anagnina, outside Rome, Marcia first appears in the historical record as a senator's concubine. By the time she moved in with Commodus, she had built up a substantial staff of her own, with her own *cubicularius*, Eclectus, who was the servant of one of her previous lovers, and who would become *cubicularius* to Commodus himself. In order to get rid of Cleander, Dionysius fomented a food riot at the Circus Maximus, and, when troops sent by Cleander failed to quell it, Marcia told Commodus that his *cubicularius* was failing in his responsibility to protect the emperor.

The emperor's reaction was uncompromising. He ordered Cleander's death. Much of the butler's erstwhile power now passed to Marcia and Eclectus, although they had to contend with Commodus's increasing eccentricity. In 192 CE he declared that he was Hercules on Earth, and renamed Rome Colonia Commodiana, 'Commodusville'. His interest in public performance became ever stronger, and he spent ever more time training with both gladiators and beast hunters. At the year's end he appeared in the Colosseum to re-enact the twelve labours of Hercules, slaughtering beasts in the morning and fighting as a gladiator in the afternoon.

Figure I (opposite)

The Zliten mosaic from North Africa shows all aspects of arena spectacles. To the left and right of the gladiators in the centre of the detail shown here are matches that have ended or are ending. A gladiator on the left has laid down his shield to surrender, while the fighter on the right has been wounded.

Figure II (overleaf)

Commodus became increasingly detached from reality as his reign extended. Eventually he began to present himself as the new Hercules, as seen here, and renamed Rome after himself.

THE LIVES AND DEATHS OF GLADIATORS

The connections between the emperor and Rome's culture of gladiatorial combat reached a certain peak with Commodus, whose attraction to gladiatorial ostentation was one manifestation of his increasing desire for public acclaim. For the most part, gladiators were slaves, either the property of the games' sponsor or rented for the occasion. But around 40 per cent of gladiators comprised free men and – from the time of Augustus onwards – free women, who were paid to appear by the sponsor.

Gladiators learned their skills in a special training area, or *ludus*, where some might also live, although others lived with their families away from the *ludus*. Some even had neighbourhood fan clubs, which they met in bars. Given the very high cost of training and maintaining gladiators, whether as slaves or as free contestants commanding high fees, the sponsors of games had a vested interest in preventing serious injury, so the bloody death tolls beloved of Hollywood were, in reality, rare. The most famous doctor of the second century CE, Galen, got his start as the doctor to the troupe owned by priests of the imperial cult in Pergamon; he boasted that no gladiator died while he was on the job. Indeed, it was typical for a duel to end when one of the contestants was injured – as shown on the Zliten mosaic and other works of art – at which point, (s)he would ask the referee to stop the fight. Fights to the death were not unknown, but they required special permission from the imperial authorities. The overall death rate in combat seems to have been around 5 per cent and was most often the result, as Galen's comments suggest, of accidental injuries. The referee shown physically restraining a victorious gladiator on the Zliten mosaic is trying to prevent just that sort of injury.

Death, though, was usually the fate of the wild animals hunted in the ring by *venatores* (hunters) for entertainment, as shown in the mosaic. *Bestiarii* – beast handlers – managed not only the animals but also, as an additional role, the unfortunate criminals condemned to die by public exposure to them.

HE APPEARED AND FOUGHT IN THE ARMOUR OF THOSE WHO ARE CALLED SECUTORS: HE HELD THE SHIELD IN HIS RIGHT HAND AND THE WOODEN SWORD IN HIS LEFT, AND HE THOUGHT IT WAS A GREAT THING HE WAS LEFT-HANDED. HIS ADVERSARY WOULD BE SOME ATHLETE OR A GLADIATOR ARMED WITH A CLUB ... WHEN HE HAD KILLED AN OSTRICH AND CUT OFF ITS HEAD, HE CAME TO WHERE WE [SENATORS] WERE SITTING, HOLDING THE HEAD IN HIS LEFT HAND AND WAVING THE BLOODY SWORD IN HIS RIGHT; AND ... SHOOK HIS HEAD WITH A GRIN, INDICATING THAT HE WOULD DO THE SAME THING TO US.

CASSIUS DIO, *ROMAN HISTORY* 73.19.2–3; 21.1–2

Erratic as he now was in public, Commodus became even more bizarre in the palace. Enough was enough. Quintus Aemilius Laetus, the recently appointed Praetorian prefect, joined in with a plan devised by Marcia and Eclectus to dispatch the emperor. On New Year's Eve 192 CE they administered to him a large dose of poison in some beef. When it appeared that Commodus might survive, they sent in a professional athlete, living in the palace, to strangle him.

The conspirators now needed to move quickly, so on New Year's Day 193 CE they presented to the Praetorian Guard and the senate a new imperial candidate: Helvius Pertinax. Serving as the city prefect – a senior senatorial position – Pertinax was also well connected with senior senatorial generals. Service and access to power in the imperial hierarchy were now more important than status at birth, and so it was that at this point the daughter of a freed slave played a major role in the appointment of the son of a freed slave as emperor. The Praetorian Guard proclaimed Pertinax emperor in return for the promise of a substantial bonus, and his acclamation received a very positive response in the senate.

Pertinax promised a return to Marcus Aurelius's style of government. His long-standing connections with other military figures also made him acceptable to the commanders of the major provincial armies, while the fact that he did not immediately anoint his son as his successor appeared to herald a return to the use of adoption to select the best possible candidate. It seemed an auspicious start, but troubles lurked. His restoration of old-style administrative norms did not sit well with Laetus, who, as someone who had engineered Pertinax's sudden rise to power, now expected greater influence for himself; and Pertinax's insistence that the Praetorian Guard return to regular drills irked the men who had been content to serve as Commodus's cheerleaders. To make matters worse, Pertinax was slow to pay the promised bonus. He finally raised the money by selling off Commodus's property from the palace, but it was not enough to save him. On the 28th of March he met with a group of Guardsmen who advanced on the palace to present their complaints. He thought his presence would overawe them. It did not, and he did not escape alive.

As Praetorian prefect, Laetus might have been behind the protest to which Pertinax fell victim, and he now expected the Guard to support his ambition to be the new emperor. But he did not act fast enough. The current city prefect, whom Pertinax had sent to bring order to the Praetorian camp, campaigned for the office as soon as he learned of Pertinax's assassination. He was offering a giant bribe if the Guard supported his claim. Meanwhile, a wealthy senator, Didius Julianus, together with a number of supporters pulled off a series of theatrical stunts, promising even greater rewards if the troops admitted him to the camp. He won the day, as the Guard proclaimed him emperor. The senate had no choice but to follow suit the next morning.

Emperor Julianus might have been rich, and he had enjoyed a reasonable administrative career, but the circumstances of his accession shocked senior staff across the empire, for simply having vast wealth had never, in itself, been regarded as qualifying a candidate to be emperor. Now, to pay off his debt, Julianus quickly began cutting the silver content of imperial coinage. Within

Figure III

These troops, wearing ceremonial dress, are probably Praetorians. Their attire reflects their importance to the imperial regime.

weeks, three provincial governors decided that his regime was untenable and that they would make better emperors. Clodius Albinus (in Britain), Pescennius Niger (in Syria) and Septimius Severus (in Upper Pannonia) were all proclaimed emperor by their respective legions. In Rome, Emperor Julianus responded by executing both Laetus and Eclectus, to try and secure the loyalty of those Guardsmen who still missed Commodus.

THE RISE OF SEVERUS

Septimius Severus, who came from the city of Leptis Magna in North Africa, had had a long career in government, including a term as governor of Syria. While in Syria, he met his wife, Julia Domna, a member of an important family from Emesa (Homs). Being the closest provincial governor to Rome now, he recognized that his competitor Clodius Albinus could not move readily on the capital until he acquired support from the legions in Germany, but that he would at that point become a dangerous adversary. To neutralize the threat, Severus negotiated a deal whereby Clodius would become his heir apparent, or *caesar* – despite the fact that Severus had two sons of his own. The arrangement was concluded as Severus marched on Rome. The beleaguered Julianus attempted to mount a resistance, including the recruitment of elephants from the imperial zoo, but to no avail. In the face of Severus's superior forces, the Praetorian Guard betrayed Julianus, who committed suicide. Severus adopted himself into the family of Julianus's predecessor, Pertinax, replaced the existing Guard with soldiers from his own army and set out east to take on the army that the remaining imperial contender, Pescennius Niger, was even then leading into the Balkans.

After Severus arrived in the Balkans, the troops at his disposal delivered a series of blows to Niger's army. Crossing into Turkey, Severus then pursued Niger's forces into the southwestern corner of Anatolia. A dramatic dispatch to the senate in Rome described fierce fighting as Severus's army broke through Niger's defences in the southern Taurus mountains. The final confrontation came on the plain of Issus, where Alexander the Great had once administered a crushing defeat to the army of the Persian king Darius III. Now, Severus's men destroyed Niger's legions and Pescennius Niger himself committed suicide.

Severus, whose family had begun to become prominent during the later Flavian dynasty, appears to have had a strong sense of imperial history. As he achieved imperial power, he looked to create a public image that echoed admired emperors from the past. The fighting through the Taurus mountains, in which the weather had played a significant role, was articulated in miraculous terms, echoing a claim that Severus's prayers had brought a lightning strike that ended raids threatened across the Danube. Moreover, Severus wished to present himself as a conqueror of Rome's enemies rather than of Rome's armies. With Niger defeated, Severus claimed that the eastern border states of Osrhoene and Adiabene had sent aid to his rival. And so, in the later part of 194 CE he reduced Osrhoene to the status of province and established a Roman garrison at Nisibis (present-day Nusaybin,

Figure IV

Born at Leptis (or Lepcis) Magna in what is now Libya, Septimius Severus was descended from ancestors who were of Phoenician descent. He spoke Latin with a pronounced North African accent.

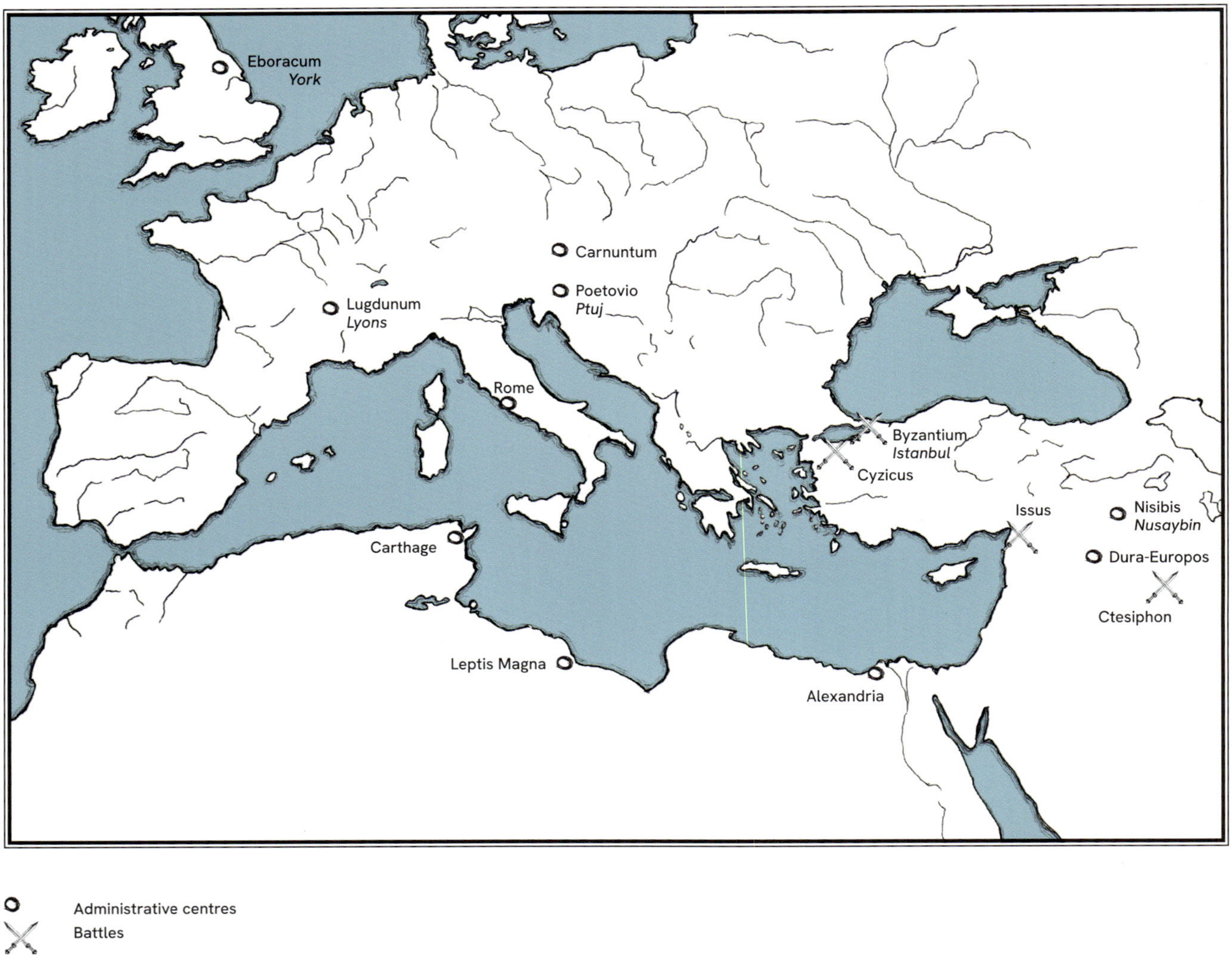

CIVIL WAR 193 CE

- ⊙ Administrative centres
- ✕ Battles

THE GREATER PART OF THE PLAIN WAS SEEN TO BE COVERED WITH THE CORPSES OF MEN AND HORSES; SOME OF THEM WERE MUTILATED BY MANY WOUNDS, AS IF CHOPPED IN PIECES, OTHERS, THOUGH UNWOUNDED, WERE PILED UP IN HEAPS.

CASSIUS DIO

Turkey), overlooking the Tigris. In Cassius Dio's words, Severus claimed to have established a bulwark for Syria before heading back to Rome. The main events of the campaign were to be depicted on one side of the triumphal arch Severus had erected in the Roman Forum.

With victory over Niger, it appeared that, through negotiation and war, Severus had seen off both his imperial challengers. Yet it was clear even before he returned west that war with Albinus was on the horizon, for, while at Antioch, Severus altered the succession. He had already renamed his elder son Marcus Aurelius Antoninus – following Severus's own self-adoption into the line of Marcus Aurelius – although history knows him better as Caracalla, a reference to the hooded garment he favoured. Now, Severus made his son *caesar*, which was effectively a declaration of war, since it invalidated the deal made with Albinus. In February 197 CE, after a quick but brutal winter campaign, Severus crushed Albinus's army in a bloody battle at Lugdunum (Lyons):

> *Severus was victorious; but Roman power suffered severe damage, since countless men had perished on both sides. Many of the victors deplored the loss, for the greater part of the plain was seen to be covered with the corpses of men and horses; some of them were mutilated by many wounds, as if chopped in pieces, others, though unwounded, were piled up in heaps, weapons were scattered everywhere and much blood flowed, even pouring into the rivers. Albinus fled to a house standing next to the Rhone, and when he saw the place surrounded, he killed himself. I am not repeating what Severus reported, but what actually took place.*

Cassius Dio, *Roman History*, 76.7.1–3

A purge of Albinus's followers in Rome followed. His supremacy won, Severus embarked on two major reforms of the military: to double military pay; and to allow soldiers to enter into legal marriages while still in service. Although the first of these would ultimately place the imperial budget under enormous stress, the second simply recognized the situation in Roman military camps throughout the empire.

WOMEN AND THE ROMAN ARMY

Senior Roman officers – as we saw from the correspondence of Cornelia Lepidina at Vindolanda (see pages 134–35) – appear to have been accompanied by their wives regularly when on service. But officers were not the only soldiers to enjoy female company when in camp. Archaeological remains, including women's shoes and jewellery, discovered in a wide range of European countries show that although soldiers were forbidden (until the reign of Severus) from marrying while in service, women were regularly present in military barracks and played a significant role in the domestic life of those establishments. In addition, documents recording the retirement of troops from auxiliary units provide explicitly that they could now legally marry the women with whom they were already in relationships at the time they were granted citizenship. Any children they then had would also be made citizens.

Figure V

Discoveries of women's clothing – such as this sandal, which is one of hundreds found at the fort of Vindolanda, just south of Hadrian's Wall – have revealed the way in which women were integrated into the daily life of the legions.

In 198 CE Severus took off again for the eastern provinces, where the Parthian king of kings, Vologaeses V, was trying to expel the Romans from northern Mesopotamia. The major events of the campaign are summarized on Septimius Severus's Arch in the reliefs facing the Capitoline Hill, and they included the capture of Seleucia, a major Parthian city in central Mesopotamia, as well as of Ctesiphon. After re-entering Roman territory via Hatra in northern Mesopotamia – still an independent buffer kingdom between the Parthian and Roman empires – Severus did not immediately go to Rome. Rather, he engaged in a grand tour of the eastern provinces. He visited Egypt, where he paid homage to the memory of Julius Caesar's ally-turned-rival Gnaeus Pompey, 'Pompey the Great'. Allegedly, one reason for this was Severus's worry that Pompey's assassin, also named Septimius, might have been an ancestor; another was that by virtue of his own self-adoption into the Aurelian line, Severus had made himself a distant relative of Pompey. In Egypt, he also visited the tomb of Alexander the Great.

While Severus was in the east, Plautianus, another tangential relative, was expanding his own power enormously, taking over much of the day-to-day management of government. And after Severus's return to Rome, Plautianus, who was also Praetorian prefect, married off his daughter to the

Figure VI

The arch that commemorates Severus's eastern campaigns is at the base of the Capitoline Hill, at the northwestern end of the Roman Forum, and was dedicated in 203 CE, after Severus's return to Rome. Its four main panels depict critical moments in the two Parthian wars. The first panel, on the southwestern side, shows the Parthian attack on Nisibis, the official cause of the war. The second shows the suppression of the revolt of Edessa, while the third (shown here), which is on the northeastern side, evokes the capture of Seleucia. The final panel depicts the capture of Ctesiphon.

IMPERATOR CAESAR MARCUS AURELIUS AUGUSTUS PIUS [CARACALLA] SAYS: ... WE GIVE THANKS TO THE IMMORTAL GODS THAT THEY PRESERVED ME FROM THE CONSPIRACY WHICH SUDDENLY AROSE. FOR THIS REASON, THINKING THAT, GENEROUSLY AND DUTIFULLY, I SHOULD MAKE A SUITABLE RETURN FOR THEIR BENEFICENCE, IF I WERE NOW TO BRING ALL MEN, AND AS MANY AS ARE NOW JOINING MY PEOPLE ... TO THE CELEBRATION OF THE GODS. I GIVE ROMAN CITIZENSHIP TO ALL UNDER MY RULE THROUGHOUT THE EMPIRE, WHILE MAINTAINING THE RIGHTS OF THEIR COMMUNITIES, WITH THE EXCEPTION OF THOSE IN COMMUNITIES RECENTLY SURRENDERED.

CONSTITUTIO ANTONINIANA,
PRESERVED IN PAPYRUS *P. GIESS.* 40, COL. 1

Figure VII (previous page)

Severus's elder son, Caracalla, was emperor from 211 CE until his assassination near Harran, southern Turkey, in 217 CE.

imperial heir, Caracalla. Being father-in-law to the emperor's son did not, however, prove enough to save Plautianus when, in 204 CE, he fell victim to an elaborate conspiracy and was executed. Nevertheless, his role in government demonstrated that even with a competent man like Severus at the helm, the demands on the office of emperor were now too complicated for any one person to manage them efficiently. The reign of Severus would see the rise in importance of Roman jurists – the most prominent being Ulpian – who codified administrative practice and created handbooks describing the way the empire ought to be run.

Complicating day-to-day administration was the occasional crisis along the frontiers. In 208 CE the boundary of northern Britain was breached. In response, Severus took off for the island with Caracalla and his younger son, Geta, both of whom were now identified as future co-emperors. He remained in the province, based at York, until his death in February 211. Allegedly, Severus's last words to his sons were: 'Get along, make the soldiers rich and don't give a damn for anyone else.'

REGIME CHANGES

Caracalla did not listen to his father. He despised his younger brother and, as their relationship collapsed on their return to Rome in 211 CE, murdered Geta in the arms of their mother on the 25th of December. Early in 212 CE Caracalla even celebrated the event, describing it as salvation from a conspiracy through the providence of the gods – and issuing an edict granting Roman citizenship to all free inhabitants of the empire. A contemporary alleged that this action was not so much the culmination of a centuries-long project, through which the empire's inhabitants were united, as an effort to raise money, because Roman citizens were subject to inheritance taxes that could not be collected from non-citizens. The edict was thus inextricable from the ongoing shortage of money that had plagued the imperial regime since Severus's massive military pay increase. Whatever the reasons for Caracalla's edict, it did nothing for his relationship with the people of Rome, who witnessed mass executions of Geta's alleged supporters in the wake of the assassination.

Three edicts by Caracalla survive in a badly damaged papyrus at the Justus-Liebig University of Giessen in Hesse, Germany. The first of these edicts (see page 167) is a portion of the *Constitutio Antoniniana*, in which 9 lines out of 29 can be read, containing Caracalla's grant of citizenship to free citizens, issued after his claim to have escaped his brother's conspiracy.

In 213 CE Caracalla left Rome for the German frontier, where it appears two recently formed coalitions of Germanic peoples – the Franks in western Germany and the Alamanni further east – were bringing new pressure on the Roman defences. The development of these groups, which anticipated the development of a new coalition north of the Danube, was an important result of the empire's political and economic impact on its neighbours; they found that developing deeper associations among themselves put them in a stronger position to negotiate with their imperial neighbour.

Figure VIII

This painting from about 200 CE shows Septimius Severus with his wife, Julia Domna, and sons Caracalla and Geta. The image of Geta, Severus's younger son, was rubbed out after his assassination by Caracalla in 211 CE.

Moving east in 214 CE, Caracalla began to indulge the fantasy that he might achieve greatness in the manner of Alexander through conquering Parthia, just as the Macedonian king had done 500 years before. On the march, Caracalla created a unit of pike-armed soldiers whose tactics mimicked those of the ancient Macedonian army; no one seems to have pointed out to him that Macedonian soldiers armed in this way had been no match for the legions of the Roman Republic. He also began making demands that the Parthian king should subordinate himself to Roman authority. In 215 CE, while one of his generals engaged in preliminary operations against Parthia, Caracalla visited Alexandria in Egypt, where, in response to a hostile public reception, he ordered his troops to slaughter the crowd. A year later, he launched an ineffectual invasion of what is now northern Iraq, in the region where Alexander had won his decisive victory over King Darius III. There was no battle, but Caracalla's forces did desecrate the tombs of Parthian kings near the present-day city of Mosul.

While the enraged Parthians gathered their forces, Caracalla withdrew to Edessa, and in the spring of 217 CE he decided to visit the ancient temple of the moon outside the city of Carrhae. Unknown to Caracalla, officials in Rome had been writing to him, warning him of prophecies that his Praetorian prefect, Macrinus, would murder him. Unfortunately for Caracalla, Macrinus was the man who dealt with the emperor's mail. He now decided

Figure IX

The women of the Severan dynasty played a very public role in the administration of the empire. From top: Julia Domna, Julia Maesa, Julia Mamaea and Julia Soaemias Bassiana (daughter of Julia Maesa).

he had to act. Macrinus paid a man whom Caracalla had recently insulted to kill the emperor en route to Carrhae. The assassin found his opportunity when Caracalla dismounted to relieve himself by the side of the road.

In the absence of an obvious imperial candidate from the army, Macrinus was now offered the throne. He was born in what is now Algeria, the son of people whom Cassius Dio describes as humble. An accomplished lawyer, he was promoted up the ranks by Plautianus (among others) to become the first man of non-senatorial background to gain the imperial throne. But if he was to stabilize his new regime, Macrinus needed to get to Rome, which was proving impossible while the Parthian war was still going on. After an indecisive battle near Nisibis, he made peace with Parthia but then decided that he needed to remain with the Syrian army for the winter. It was a fatal mistake, allowing the relatives of Severus to strike back. Although Severus's widow, Julia Domna, died in 217 CE, she had a sister, Julia Maesa, who now plotted against Macrinus and enjoyed considerable support from other members of the palace bureaucracy, whom Macrinus had cashiered.

The oldest of Julia Maesa's grandsons was 14 years old. He served as a priest of the chief divinity at Emesa, where a piece of meteorite was worshipped as a manifestation of the sun god, its name Hellenized as 'Elagabalus'. He also bore something of a physical resemblance to Caracalla. On the night of the 16th of May 218 CE Julia had one of her freedman bring her grandson into the camp of the Third Legion, near Emesa, where he was proclaimed emperor, taking the name 'Marcus Aurelius Antoninus'. Macrinus failed to act decisively, or even to rally the full force available to him before encountering the rebel force near Antioch. He was defeated and fled. While the young Antoninus now asserted his control over Rome's eastern provinces, Macrinus was killed as he tried to make his way west to rally support.

In 219 CE Antoninus arrived in Rome with the meteorite in tow. He installed it in front of the statue of Jupiter on the Capitoline Hill, where he would lead dances around the divinity, with the result that – in common parlance among those who despised him – the emperor came to be called by the name of his god. Although Julia Maesa managed to assemble a reasonable administration, including the jurist Ulpian, Antoninus's personal eccentricity quickly became stale, and the palace staff he brought from Emesa did not mesh well with the Roman establishment.

In the end, it was a family rift that sealed Antoninus's fate. He and his mother fell out with his aunt Julia Mamaea, who felt her own son Alexianus was under threat. The situation worsened in early 222 CE. When, on the evening of the 11th of March, the emperor and his mother attempted to smooth things over with Mamaea in the Praetorian camp, they walked into a trap. Both were assassinated, with their closest supporters. Alexianus, just 13 years old, took the throne with the name 'Marcus Aurelius Severus Alexander'. With another young teenager in office, Julia Mamaea effectively became head of state, assembling an experienced council of senior senators to manage the empire, while promoting Ulpian to the position of Praetorian prefect. As for the Elagabalus meteorite, it was sent back to Emesa.

While Julia Mamaea managed Rome, the political situation in Persia took a significant turn. The Arsacid royal house was notably unstable, suffering bouts

Figure X

Alexander Severus succeeded to the throne when he was 13 years old, with his mother, Julia Mamaea, managing the empire's administration.

Figure XI

As Ardashir (left) receives the ring of kingship from the Zoroastrian god Ahura Mazda, his horse tramples the body of Artabanus (the last Parthian king), while that of Ahura Mazda tramples the devil.

of internal rivalry and civil wars, but in 224 CE its king, Artabanus, faced a challenge from a new quarter. In the previous few decades the Sasanian dynasty had taken control of the region of Fars. They appear to have been descended from a Turkic family from farther east, claiming ancestry from a figure named 'Sasan'. In 224 CE the head of the Sasanian clan, Ardashir, declared war on Artabanus. During a decisive battle fought between the two sides in northern Iran, Ardashir killed Artabanus in a duel (or so he claimed), while his eldest son, Sapor, killed Artabanus's vizier. The noble families that had long supported the Arsacids now declared themselves loyal subjects of the Sasanians.

In order to secure his position, Ardashir felt he needed to eliminate surviving members of the Arsacid clan, some of whom had taken refuge in Roman territory, and others with their most powerful kinsman, Chosroes, King of Armenia. However, Ardashir's initial campaigns were not successful; he failed in Armenia, and when he attacked Hatra, which remained loyal to the Arsacid cause, he was repulsed. Nevertheless, reports of Sasanian aggression – and, quite likely, self-interested assertions by Arsacid refugees that Ardashir's regime would collapse if the Romans showed up – led the young Emperor Alexander to announce a war with Persia. From 230 CE he assembled an army along the Roman Empire's eastern frontier.

Alexander's Persian campaign was a failure. Quite possibly because he was being given self-interested but misleading intelligence, he abandoned what was by now the standard Roman advance through northern Mesopotamia into northern Iraq, in favour of dividing his army into three parts. One section went into Armenia and another remained in northern Mesopotamia, while the emperor led a third force down the Euphrates. In so doing, Alexander sacrificed the numerical superiority that Roman armies had enjoyed on battlefields since the time of Trajan, with the result that he achieved no successes but suffered some serious losses. The regime's reputation would never recover, despite the fact that Ardashir offered a peace treaty that left Roman clients and territory intact.

As Rome's Persian operation wound down, news arrived that the empire's northern neighbours had taken advantage of the eastward troop movements to raid across the border. This development further damaged Alexander's relationship with his troops. They were losing faith in the regime's capacity to provide adequate leadership, and they seemed unimpressed by Alexander's visible dependence on his mother, who accompanied him everywhere:

> *The news of these events caused distress to Alexander and distressed the Illyrian soldiers he had with him, who seemed to have suffered a double misfortune; they had suffered hardships fighting the Persians and now learned that their families had been massacred by the Germans. They were angry and held Alexander responsible, having been betrayed on the eastern expedition by his cowardice and negligence as well as by his hesitancy and sloth with respect to matters in the north.*

Herodian, *History*, 6.7.3

Matters came to a head three years later, on the Rhine, when Alexander proposed to invade German territory. The troops mutinied, instead choosing a mid-level officer, Gaius Julius Maximinus, as their leader; he promptly ordered the execution of Alexander and his mother. Given that he had a large army, and that in Rome there were no preparations to deal with such a situation, the senate acquiesced.

THE CRISIS OF THE THIRD CENTURY

Maximinus was the most junior official to claim the imperial throne. Unlike Macrinus, he had no connection with the senior equestrian bureaucracy before he became emperor. Although wild stories later circulated among the many who hated him that he was a shepherd whom Severus had recruited into the army, the likelihood is that he was from a middle-level Balkan family of the equestrian class. The fact that his family name was 'Julius' suggests that his ancestors had achieved citizenship under Augustus or Tiberius. Despite his portrayal in all surviving accounts as a homicidally inclined savage, Maximinus must have been a man of considerable charisma to carry the senior staff of the Rhine army along with him after the murder of Alexander.

As emperor, Maximinus plainly intended to base his power on that army, whose loyalty he would ensure by providing excellent leadership. Archaeological discoveries at Harzhorn in Lower Saxony reveal a battle in 235 CE between some of his troops and local groups who had tried to cut lines of communication between the Romans and their bases to the south. The findings confirm that there was reality in the reports sent by Maximinus to Rome (accompanied by paintings of himself in action) regarding his achievements in Germany. At the same time, he ordered the execution of a number of senators on suspicion of conspiracy, while reducing money to support basic activities in the capital, such as the public grain supply.

Following his German campaigns, Maximinus moved to Pannonia, where he prepared further operations north of the border. At no point, though, did he attempt to visit Rome, an omission that thoroughly alienated the senate and members of the palace bureaucracy, who had never set eyes on their emperor. This alienation was also felt in the old homeland of Severus's family in the province of Africa, which in 238 CE was governed by Gordian, a senior senator of Anatolian roots. That year, a group of young men in Carthage murdered the province's financial administrator for his oppressive conduct and proclaimed Gordian emperor. He wrote to the senate announcing his willingness to accept the position, at which point the senate concurred – and appointed a large senatorial commission to organize Italy's defence against the anticipated military reaction from Maximinus. The committee soon had its work cut out, when both Gordian and his son were killed in battle during conflict with the neighbouring province's governor.

Having lost its imperial candidate, the senate instead proclaimed two senior members of its commission, Pupienus and Balbinus, co-emperors. But when a crowd rioted, backing the 13-year-old son of Gordian's daughter as a legitimate claimant, the senate also agreed to make the teenager *caesar* – heir apparent to Pupienus and Balbinus. He, too, was named Gordian, and is referred to as Gordian III. With the line of succession clarified, it was time to get back to the business of avoiding what promised to be Maximinus's extremely vindictive arrival.

The defence of northern Italy was placed in the hands of an experienced officer, who fortified the city of Aquileia, which sat astride Maximinus's route south. Maximinus, who plainly did not expect any serious resistance, arrived at Aquileia in late March at the head of several legions, and soon found that the region's defenders had stripped the area of the supplies he needed for his troops. As Aquileia resisted, the situation in Maximinus's camp worsened, until in early May Maximinus was murdered in a mutiny. His son, whom he had proclaimed co-emperor, died with him. Pupienus and Balbinus did not have a chance to savour their victory for long, falling prey to the self-interest of the Praetorian Guard, which had remained loyal to Maximinus and now feared they would be replaced. To forestall that eventuality, they murdered the two co-emperors – but agreed to support the young Gordian III as their new ruler.

Another teenaged emperor meant de facto rule by another committee, which, this time, consisted of a number of those who had led the opposition to Maximinus, led by the man who soon became one of two Praetorian prefects, Timesitheus. He cemented his relationship with the new regime by, in 241 CE, marrying off his daughter to Gordian III. That year, too, he led a Roman army east – with Gordian as titular commander – in response to a new challenge

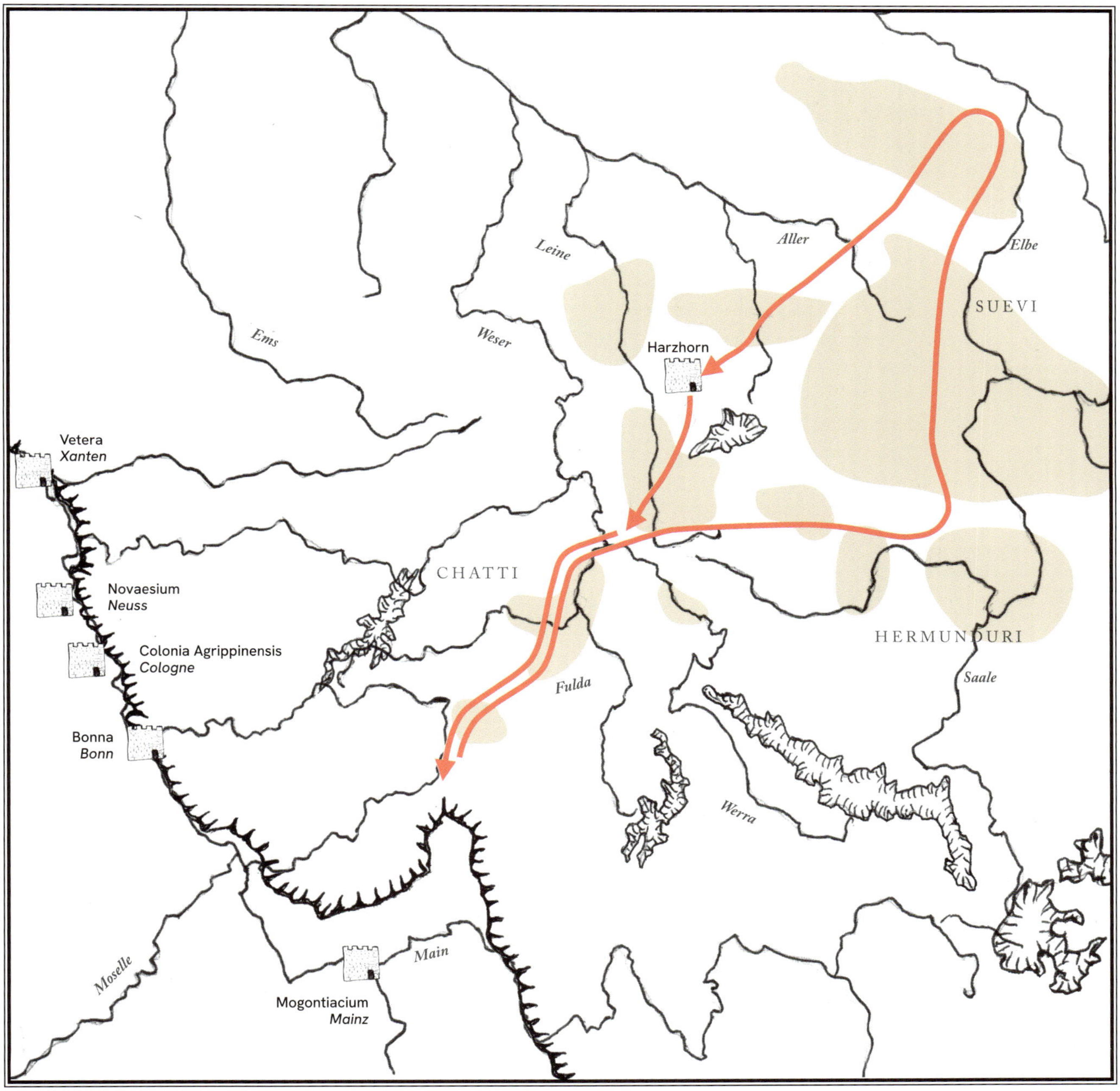

BATTLE OF HARZHORN

→ Possible route of Roman march
⏣ Border of the Roman Empire
▒ Areas occupied by Germanic tribes
🏰 Legionary camp

IMPERIAL CHURN, IMPERIAL FAILURE

from the Sasanian dynasty. Ardashir had taken advantage of Maximinus's concentration on western issues to seize the province of Mesopotamia. He then retired as ruler in favour of his son Sapor, who would emerge as Rome's most formidable foe since the days of Hannibal the Carthaginian some 450 years earlier.

Timesitheus must have been a good soldier, for in 243 CE he managed to defeat Sapor and restore Roman control of Mesopotamia. From there, though, things went downhill. Timesitheus died, and in the early spring of 244 CE the Roman army headed down the Euphrates, where it suffered a heavy defeat before withdrawing to Zaitha, a town slightly north of the city of Dura-Europos (now in ruins). With Rome anticipating an easy victory – a repeat of Alexander the Great's conquest – several philosophers accompanied the expedition, including Plotinus, father of the Neoplatonic school of philosophy. According to his biographer, Plotinus escaped a camp mutiny that brought about the assassination of Gordian III. With Gordian dead, power passed shortly thereafter to Philip, a Praetorian prefect absent from the mutiny. He negotiated a treaty with Sapor that evidently involved the payment of a large subsidy to the Persians and an agreement to abandon the Arsacid regime in Armenia.

Philip returned to Rome, leaving his brother Priscus as deputy emperor in the east, while appointing another relative to a similar position in the Balkans. The aim of these appointments seems to have been to ensure greater control of provincial forces and better extraction of revenue; the regime was short of cash after the expensive failure in Persia, and furthermore, there was the prospect of a wildly expensive party at Rome in 248 CE. That year marked the 1,000th anniversary of Rome's foundation. It is a sign of the ongoing fiscal crisis that the silver content of the Roman *denarius* continued to decline throughout these years, being mixed with increasing amounts of bronze. The nominal value of the coinage remained the same, with 25 *denarii* being equivalent to 1 gold coin, the *aureus*. This prevented significant inflation, although people expressed a preference for 'old' coins, rather than the new ones, in their transactions.

Philip's policies appear to have alienated provincial populations. An essential aspect of imperial relations with communities throughout the empire was that they were self-governing entities that interacted with the imperial authorities only at well-defined times, such as major games or the annual visit by an imperial governor. Locals collected the taxes that would be passed on to the imperial authorities, and they had their own police forces. As was the case with Boudicca's revolt in Britain, centuries before, an intervention by imperial authorities that upset existing relationships was deeply problematic. Nor did it help, now, that the image of Roman military might projected by the imperial government was called into question by the defeat in Persia. As tension rose, a revolt against Philip's regime broke out in Syria, followed, in 249 CE, by a rebellion in the Balkans. The relative whom Philip had placed in charge of the Balkans seems to have died or been removed, so the emperor sent an experienced commander named Decius to suppress the revolt. No sooner did Decius arrive than he joined the rebellion and led his army to Italy, where he encountered

GOTHIC INVASIONS OF 250–51 CE

- Carpi advance
- Cniva advance
- Roman territory
- ☆ Attacked site
- ○ Provincial capital or administrative centre
- ● Other centre
- ⚔ Battle site

Philip near Verona. Philip died in the battle, while Decius took the spoils as Rome's latest emperor.

Decius's plan appears to have been to 'make Rome great again'. To do that, he decided he must reinforce the empire's relationship with the gods. He issued an edict ordering all citizens to make a sacrifice in front of a local board of overseers, and to obtain a certificate stating that they had done so. Within months of gaining the throne, in the spring of 250 CE, Decius had to take the field against a swarm of invaders from north of the Danube, including – possibly for the first time – the peoples described as 'Goths'.

Decius was successful in checking the raids into Pannonia, but then things started to go very badly in the western Balkans, in the provinces of Thrace and Moesia. First, the city of Philippopolis (now Plovdiv) was sacked. Then, after leading three legions in pursuit of the raiders, Decius's army was annihilated at Abritus, a spot near the present-day village of Drynovets in Bulgaria. Not only did Decius himself die in the fighting, but also, on this one afternoon, nearly 10 per cent of the Roman army was destroyed, a catastrophe on a similar scale to that of Varus centuries earlier. The contemporaneous historian Publius Dexippus, who wrote a history of the wars with the Goths (from Decius until the reign of Aurelian 20 years later), plainly thought Decius a fool, one critical failure being his inability to realize that defence of the empire required the coordination of regional militias with imperial troops, and another being his underestimation of the danger posed by the Goths:

Figure XII

The god Elagabalus is depicted in the chariot on the reverse of this coin issued by the third-century usurper Uranius Antoninus.

> *When the advance of Ostrogotha's force was announced to him, he thought that it was an opportune time to encourage his troops, and, when they had gathered, Decius spoke in this way. 'I could wish, men, that the army and the whole empire was doing well and not humiliated by the enemy. Since, however, the events of human life bring misfortune (for such is the fate of mortals), it is the duty of prudent men to accept what happens, and not to lose their spirits, not being distressed by mishap on the battlefield or the capture of the Thracians, in case any of you are disheartened by these things, for each of those misfortunes offers arguments against your discouragement: the former was brought about by the treachery of the scouts, rather than by a fault of ours, and they took the Thracian town by trickery rather than strength, their attacks having failed ....'*

Words attributed to Decius in Dexippus, *Scythica*

Another perceived failing was Decius's lack of understanding that negotiation, rather than fighting, could be an effective way of ending a war. His successor as emperor was the man who had been serving as his chief lieutenant during the Balkan campaign, Trebonianus Gallus. But he proved no better in office than Decius, as events would show within a year.

In 252 CE Sapor struck the province of Syria. Guided by a Syrian rebel named Mariades, he advanced up the Euphrates, crushed Syria's garrison in battle, and sacked Antioch (the Syrian capital) and many other places throughout the region, before returning home with many captives, whom he set to work in the heart of his kingdom. The only effective resistance after the

Roman army's disastrous encounter with Sapor was offered by the leader of the city of Emesa, who claimed to be operating under the divine protection of Elagabalus. In the wake of Sapor's offensive, Emperor Gallus was overthrown by a general named Aemilianus in the summer of 253 CE; he, in turn, fell victim to his own men when confronted by Gallus's ally Valerian, who arrived in Italy from Gaul at the head of a larger army than Aemilianus had mustered.

Valerian proved to be a truly awful general, but he did have some administrative sense. Ever since Septimius Severus, emperors were expected to lead their armies into battle, a circumstance that left an administrative vacuum throughout much of the empire. Realizing this, Valerian appointed his adult son Gallienus co-emperor while he first restored imperial authority in Syria and then tried to manage incursions from north of the Danube. Like Decius, he seems to have been concerned with maintaining the goodwill of the gods, and to this end he instituted the first empire-wide persecution of the Christian Church.

Figure XIII

In his edict ordering the persecution of Christians, Valerian expressed special concern about Christians in imperial service. The reason may be deduced from the fact that two of the earliest-known Christian meeting houses are associated with Roman military bases, both dating from the 230s CE. One is at Dura-Europos in Syria; the other, at Megiddo in Israel, has this mosaic with an inscription stating that it was donated by a Roman centurion named Gaianus.

IMPERIAL CHURN, IMPERIAL FAILURE

In 260 CE Sapor struck again, attacking across northern Mesopotamia. Valerian led whatever he had for an army against him, reaching the city of Edessa. What happened next is the subject of varied accounts. In Sapor's version, he captured Valerian with his own hand:

> *In the third campaign, when we advanced upon Carrhae and Edessa and were besieging Carrhae and Edessa, Valerian Caesar marched against us. He had with him a force of 70,000 from Germany, Raetia, Noricum, Dacia, Pannonia, Moesia, Istria, Spain, Africa [?], Thrace, Bithynia, Asia, Campania, Isauria, Lycaonia, Galatia, Lycia, Cilicia, Cappadocia, Phrygia, Syria, Phoenicia, Judaea, Arabia, Mauritania, Germania, Lydia, Osrhoene and Mesopotamia. And in the region of Carrhae and Edessa we had a great battle with Valerian Caesar. We took Valerian Caesar our prisoner with our own hand, and the others, chiefs of that army, the Praetorian prefect, senators: we made all prisoners and deported them to Persis.*

Inscription of Sapor from Naqsh-e Rostam, Iran

Figure XIV

Philip the Arab kneels before Sapor after Sapor's victory in 244 CE, while Sapor grasps the hand of Valerian, symbolizing his capture of the emperor in 260 CE.

In one Roman version, Valerian was taken captive in a treacherous negotiation. In what appears to have been Dexippus's version, Valerian surrendered himself and his army to Sapor after a defeat in the area of Carrhae – and that is probably what actually happened. The victors took Valerian and a substantial number of his soldiers back to central Persia, where they were charged with working on construction projects at Sapor's behest. Valerian died in captivity. His co-emperor son made no effort to get him back; the disgrace was too great.

With a significant section of the Roman army out of the way, Sapor again ravaged the eastern provinces. But the fact that he did not try to annex territory outside northern Mesopotamia is quite possibly a reflection of the limited resources at his disposal. In the end, his westernmost operations were terminated when the surviving Roman forces in the region united with an army emerging from Palmyra under the leadership of Septimius Odaenathus, whose actions illustrated Dexippus's point about the importance of coordinating regional forces with those of the regular army. Joining with Odaenathus, Valerian's generals drove the Persian forces from Syria – and promptly decided they should become emperors. Odaenathus, however, remained loyal to Gallienus, and, when his former colleagues took off for the west, he defeated their remaining comrades. Gallienus now placed him in titular charge of the eastern provinces.

A contemporary composed an oracle as propaganda to support Odaenathus's regime, in which he appears as the lion from the sun to preserve his people. The text known as the *Thirteenth Sibylline Oracle* is the most extensive surviving narrative of the mid-third century CE. Like Dexippus, the editor of the verses that make up the text regards the alliance between imperial and local government as crucial for success. He describes the rise of Odaenathus and his overcoming of the Roman usurpers Macrianus and Ballista, as well as the Persians:

> *After him another will come[,] a well-horned hungry stag [Macrianus] in the mountains desiring to feed his stomach with venom-spitting beasts [Persians]; then will come the sub-sent, dreadful, fearful lion, breathing much fire. With great and reckless courage he will destroy the well-horned stag and the great venom-spitting fearsome beast discharging many shafts and the bow-footed goat [Ballista]; fame will attend him; perfect, unblemished and awesome, he will rule the Romans and the Persians will be feeble ....*

THE STEEP ROAD TO RECOVERY

In the surviving Latin sources, Emperor Gallienus receives a very bad press. As early as the beginning of the fourth century CE, writers were alleging that with his rule, the Roman Empire had reached its lowest point. Later writers stressed his personal debauchery as the reason for the near collapse of the imperial system. A rather more reasonable view is that his actions in the face of extraordinary challenges laid the foundation for the empire's recovery.

Shortly after Valerian's catastrophe in the east, the troops serving Postumus, governor of Germania Inferior, proclaimed him emperor. Postumus rapidly gained control of the rest of Roman Germany, along with the Gallic provinces and Britain. As for Gallienus, with only the Danubian army at his disposal, and facing usurpers both in the Balkans and from the eastern provinces, there was little he could do in response. It is to his credit that he managed to see off the threats, overcoming the Balkan issues and, learning from his father's disaster, arriving at the creative solution for the eastern provinces, involving Odaenathus. Over the next few years of his reign, he built up an exceptionally competent military organization, based on the Balkan army, and removed senators from positions of command. This was essentially a formalization of existing trends whereby extensive command experience was increasingly required of senior officers, who might then become senators, but who did not enter the system as such. Gallienus also created an independent cavalry corps, which served as a central reserve, outside legionary commands. This unit heralded important changes in the years to come – although quite soon it spelled trouble.

In 268 CE Gallienus faced two exceptional challenges. One was a revolt in Italy at Mediolanum (Milan), led by Aureolus, the commander of his cavalry corps; the other was a massive invasion of the Balkans, over land and sea, by the peoples north of the border. One of the most dramatic moments of this invasion occurred when a fleet manned by Goths sacked Athens. It was the historian Dexippus who rallied local defenders and inflicted a notable defeat upon the invaders when they tried to launch raids inland from the city.

Gallienus decided that he must first deal with the revolt in Italy, but he was killed outside Milan; whether this was as a result of a conspiracy or of simple bad luck is unclear. His successor, chosen by the army's general staff, was an experienced militaryman, Marcus Aurelius Claudius. He suppressed the Italian revolt before turning his attention to the Balkans. It was in an area outside what is now the Serbian city of Niš that he inflicted a crushing defeat on his adversaries. This was the first really big victory by a Roman army in decades, but, as 269 turned to 270 CE, Emperor Claudius II was pursuing the Goths into the mountains when he died as a result of an epidemic that had been sweeping the empire for some years. After a brief effort on the part of his brother to claim the throne, the general staff selected another experienced general to be their leader: Aurelian.

Aurelian completed the Gothic war, but by now the empire was yet again engaged in civil conflict among competing power blocs. He turned his attention eastwards, where, in 267 CE, Odaenathus had been murdered, his power passing (in theory) to his son Vaballathus. In reality, it was Odaenathus's

Figure XV

A remarkably resilient emperor, Gallienus preserved the imperial regime after his father's capture in 260 CE and forged the Balkan army that would reunify the empire after his own assassination in 268 CE.

GOTHIC INVASIONS OF 267–68 CE

Gothic advance

Roman territory

Attacked site

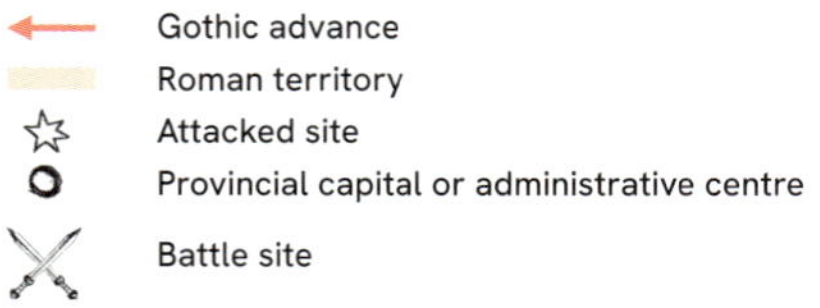

○ Provincial capital or administrative centre

⚔ Battle site

widow, Zenobia, who wielded influence. She had claimed that her husband's control over the eastern provinces was inheritable, but Claudius had demurred, dispatching an expedition eastwards to reassert imperial control. That expedition was a failure, allowing Zenobia to send armies to occupy other provinces, most notably Egypt, while suggesting now that her son share power with Aurelian.

In 272 CE Aurelian arrived in Syria at the head of an experienced army, winning a decisive victory outside Emesa. He seems to have felt that Elagabalus (now known simply as Invincible Sun) had assisted him, and he would order an enormous temple in the god's honour to be erected in Rome. Palmyra surrendered shortly after the battle at Emesa on what appears to have been generous terms. Zenobia survived. She was removed from power but sent to Rome, where she, or possibly a child of hers, married into the Roman aristocracy; in the next century, there were senators who claimed descent from her.

Although Zenobia and her family were gone, other members of the Palmyrene hierarchy were not happy with the reduction in their power. In 273 CE they rebelled, but this time Aurelian was less merciful. He sacked Palmyra before heading west to bring the Gallic Empire, now ruled by a man named Tetricus, to an end, the decisive battle taking place outside Châlons. In truth, that result was predetermined after Aurelian offered Tetricus a pardon, including a generous pension, if he would deploy his army in such a way as to facilitate Aurelian's victory.

Aurelian might have been an exceptional general, but he was a dreadful economist. The empire's silver coinage had been so debased through the years of crisis that it was essentially now another bronze coinage, whatever its notional value. Aurelian decided to issue new 'silver' coinage that raised the silver content to 5 per cent. The new coins had the effect of rendering illegitimate all coinage issued by various regimes on the old standard, destroying faith in the validity of the imperial coinage system. The result was hyperinflation, which continued for more than a decade.

The emperor was more concerned to nullify the shame still felt as a result of Valerian's surrender than to solve the economic crisis. And it was not a bad time to attack the Persians. Sapor was no more – he had died in 272 CE – and a weak regime surrounded his son, dominated by an extremist Zoroastrian priest named Kartir, who injected what would prove to be a strong religious element into Sasanian rule from this point onwards. But before Aurelian could reach the Persian frontier, and even before his army could exit the Balkans, he met the well-worn fate of emperors past. A highly placed cabal of officers assassinated him.

Aurelian's killers fled, while the staff remaining with the army seem to have been deeply divided, unable to agree on a candidate to succeed him. Aurelian's widow, Ulpia Severina, might have played a role in negotiating the settlement through which an elderly official, Marcus Aurelius Tacitus (no relation to the historian), became emperor and led the army in pursuit of the assassins, who had fled east. The crisis deepened when the Tacitus-appointed governor of Syria was assassinated on account of his oppressive administration, and the Syrian nobility and garrison (neither of which had been fully

reconciled to the post-Palmyrene regime) invited Aurelian's assassins to take over the province. Tacitus's attempt to negotiate with this group resulted in his murder.

In the ensuing contention to become emperor, Tacitus's brother was eliminated, allowing the general Marcus Aurelius Probus to emerge victorious. Over the next few years, Probus regained control of Syria, executed Aurelian's assassins, and headed west to deal with several rebellions – with some success – until his Praetorian prefect, Carus, declared himself emperor and, in 282 CE, arranged for Probus's demise. Carus's vision of his imperial goals once again involved avenging Valerian by attacking Persia, whose monarch was dealing with revolts in the eastern portion of his kingdom. The Roman army advanced as far as Ctesiphon before pulling back. Carus did not have another chance, for in 283 CE he was murdered, although it was said that his tent was struck by lightning – deeply unlikely in Turkey during the late summer.

The leaders of Rome's eastern army now faced a conundrum. At some point they would have to deal with Carus's sons and heirs, now technically co-emperors: Carinus, who had remained in Italy; and his younger brother, Numerian, who was with the army in the east. So, the army leaders needed an imperial candidate of their own. But who would take the job? As events of recent years had shown, life expectancy in the position was poor. They temporized. Even after murdering Numerian (in 284 CE), they carted his body along with the army, putting out a story that he was confined to his litter by an eye injury, until they reached Nicomedia in western Turkey. At that point, the odour of the decomposing body was so bad that they had to admit to his death.

A meeting of the senior staff seems to have produced no willing imperial candidate. Instead, a mid-level Praetorian officer was put forward for the job. Gaius Aurelius Valerius Diocles was an experienced soldier, but he had no experience of high command. Despite that, he accepted the imperial role – and changed his name to Diocletian. Within a decade, he would transform the Roman Empire.

Figure XVI

Marcus Aurelius Probus was the third of the Balkan generals who restored unified government of the Roman Empire.

CHRONOLOGY 180–284 CE

180 CE
Commodus sole emperor.

182 CE
Failure of conspiracy against Commodus.

185 CE
Fall of the Praetorian prefect, Perennis.

190 CE
Fall of Commodus's *cubicularius*, Cleander.

192 CE
Rome renamed 'Colonia Commodiana'; assassination of Commodus (31st of December).

193 CE
Pertinax proclaimed emperor; assassination of Pertinax (28th of March); accession of Didius Julianus (29th of March); Septimius Severus proclaimed emperor at Carnuntum (9th of April); Didius Julianus killed (1st of June).

194 CE
Defeat of Pescennius Niger (May); annexation of Mesopotamia.

197 CE
Defeat of Clodius Albinus at Lyons.

198 CE
Defeat of Parthia.

199 CE
Severus's visit to Egypt.

205 CE
Execution of the Praetorian prefect, Plautianus.

207 CE
Severus's departure for Britain.

211 CE
Death of Severus (4th of February), and accession of sons Caracalla and Geta; murder of Geta (25th of December).

212 CE
Constitutio Antoniniana, granting Roman citizenship to the empire's free inhabitants.

213 CE
Caracalla's campaign in Germany.

216 CE
Beginning of Caracalla's Parthian war.

217 CE
Assassination of Caracalla (8th of April). Accession of Macrinus. Peace with Parthia.

218 CE
Revolt of Elagabalus begins (May), and Macrinus defeated (8th of June).

219 CE
Emperor Elagabalus's arrival in Rome.

222 CE
Assassination of Emperor Elagabalus. Accession of Alexander Severus.

224 CE
Murder of the jurist Ulpian.

225 CE
Ardashir's succession as King of Persia.

230 — 240 — 250 — 260 — 270 → CE

232 CE
Alexander Severus's invasion of Persia.

235 CE
Alexander Severus's murder (March). Succession of Maximinus.

235–36 CE
Ardashir's occupation of Roman Mesopotamia.

238 CE
Gordian revolt in North Africa (March), but Gordian and his son killed. Pupienus and Balbinus proclaimed co-emperors, and Gordian's grandson (Gordian III) made heir apparent. Maximian killed (May). Pupienus and Balbinus killed (August). Accession of Gordian III.

240 CE
Sapor's succession in Persia.

241 CE
Beginning of Gordian III's Persian war.

243 CE
Persians driven from Roman Mesopotamia.

244 CE
Sapor's defeat of Gordian III at Misiche, Mesopotamia, and his assassination at Zaitha. Accession of Philip 'the Arab'.

248 CE
Celebration of the 1,000th anniversary of Rome's founding.

249 CE
Decius's revolt, the killing of Philip, and Decius's succession. Edict on sacrifice issued.

250 CE
Gothic invasion of the Balkans.

251 CE
Battle of Abritus (June). Death of Decius. Accession of Gallus.

252 CE
Sapor's sack of Antioch.

253 CE
Gallus overthrown by Aemilianus. Aemilianus overthrown by Valerian, naming his son Gallienus co-emperor.

258 CE
Valerian's persecution edict against Christians.

260 CE
Sapor's capture of Valerian. Sapor's defeat by Roman and provincial forces. Revolt of Postumus in Gaul.

262 CE
Odaenathus recognized as chief administrator of eastern provinces. Repeal of Valerian's persecution edict.

267 CE
Assassination of Odaenathus.

268 CE
Gothic raids into the Balkans and sack of Athens. Revolt of Aureolus. Death of Gallienus. Accession of Claudius II.

269 CE
Claudius II defeats the Goths at Naissus.

270 CE
Breakdown in relations between Rome and Palmyra. Death of Claudius. Accession of Aurelian. Death of Sapor.

271 CE
Beginning of new defensive wall for Rome.

272 CE
Aurelian captures Palmyra.

273 CE
Revolt of Palmyra, and Aurelian's sack of the city.

274 CE
Aurelian's conquest of the Gallic Empire. Reform of the Roman currency.

275 CE
Assassination of Aurelian. Accession of Emperor Tacitus.

276 CE
Assassination of Tacitus. Accession of Probus.

282 CE
Assassination of Probus. Accession of Carus.

283 CE
Carus's campaign against Parthia, and his assassination.

284 CE
Accession of Diocletian (20th of November).

CHAPTER 5

EMPIRE RESHAPED AND REFORMED: FROM DIOCLETIAN TO JULIAN

On the 20th of November, 284 CE, Gaius Aurelius Valerius Diocles mounted a platform outside Nicomedia (present-day İzmit, in Turkey), where the assembled army acclaimed him Emperor of Rome. Shortly afterward, he changed his name to the one that would be remembered: Diocletian.

The new emperor, about forty years old at the time, was born near Split, in what is now Croatia. He began his ascent through the ranks under Gallienus, most likely seeing action under Claudius II and Aurelian, as well as Probus and Carus. The result was that he had solid first-hand experience of the eastern and Balkan regions, but little knowledge of Italy, Africa or the western Roman Empire – facts that would condition his policy choices over the years. Diocletian appears to have deeply considered several aspects of imperial rule and military organization: the failures of previous commanders; the impossibility of a single person ruling such a vast empire; the perception that while emperors required victories to retain the throne, they did not need to be present in battle; and the awareness that stationing legions in one area for many years made it very difficult to move large numbers of men to campaigns at a distance. He was also attentive to the possibility that alliances – between provincial commanders and local communities – could provide the foundations for breakaway regimes.

However, before he could act upon such thoughts, Diocletian needed to solidify his own claim to the throne and deal with the former Emperor Carus's imperial heir, Carinus. Luckily for Diocletian, it appears that Carinus did not command affection among several senior associates, including the governor of Dalmatia, Flavius Constantius. Given that Diocletian later rewarded these men, it is likely that they betrayed Carinus, whose army lost to Diocletian's in

Figure I

The elaborate Baths of Diocletian in Rome were lavishly decorated with painted stone reliefs that survive in remarkable detail. This one shows Mithras, originally a Persian divinity, who was very popular in the Roman Empire from the first to the third century. A key aspect of his cult is the legend that he created the universe by slaying the primordial bull.

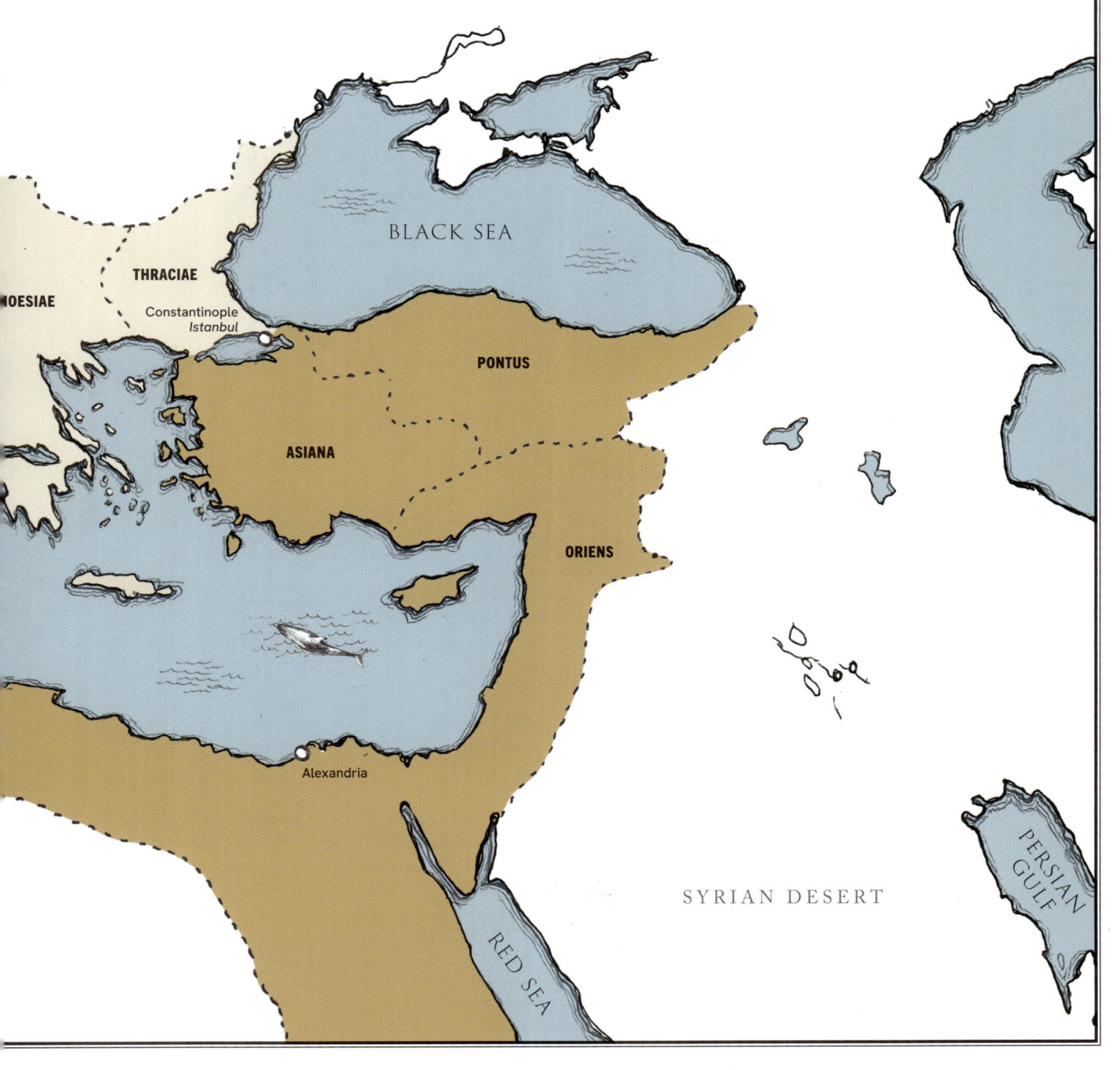

July 285 CE at the River Margus in Moesia (now in Serbia). Carinus escaped, only to be murdered a few days later.

Diocletian advanced into northern Italy but probably went no further than Milan, which would soon be developed as an imperial capital while Rome ceased to be a centre of government. Milan presented advantages in that it was closer to the frontier and did not have a large population requiring control by a substantial garrison – which, as past events demonstrated, could be capable of acting on its own to select a new ruler. The central theme for the next several years of Diocletian's reign would be imperial security. He took a major step in that direction at Milan when he elevated his friend Maximian to deputize for the emperor as his *caesar*, dispatching him to Gaul, while Diocletian himself returned to the east.

In the western empire, as had been the case after the failure of the Palmyrene regime in the 270s, the local elites were not readily reconciled to the rule of a distant emperor. The imperial hold over Gaul had not been securely established after the arranged surrender, in 274 CE, of Tetricus to Aurelian. Evidence from coinage confirms that two men, Bonosus and Proculus, had asserted their imperial credentials against Emperor Probus – before he had them killed – and now a man named Amandus was issuing coins as emperor. Sources describe him as a jumped-up thug, whose power was supported by rural brigands. Whatever the truth about Amandus, his imperial pretensions were ended by Maximian near Paris in autumn 285 CE. Maximian proceeded to the Rhine, where he defeated a raid by the Franks.

At this point, Diocletian made a remarkable decision. He sent word from Nicomedia that Maximian would henceforth be not merely a deputy but

Figure II (left)

This image of emperors Diocletian and Maximian from the former's palace at Nicomedia in western Turkey, retaining traces of the original paint, stresses the unity of the two rulers. That unity was a crucial aspect of the ideology of collegial rulership set out by Diocletian.

Figure III (opposite)

This representation of Emperor Maximian, who was depicted as Hercules acting for Diocletian – who was representing Jupiter on Earth – stresses his military bearing.

joint *augustus* – co-emperor. Under Diocletian's new theory of government, the two *augusti* were not exactly equal; Diocletian's own role would be like Jupiter's, and he would label himself 'Jovius', whose task it was to direct the world, while Maximian would be his version of Hercules, known as 'Herculius', charged with eliminating the forces of evil from the Earth. The image of their association is preserved in sculptures from Diocletian's palace at Nicomedia, showing the two large men in their purple cloaks, clasping each other.

The purple cloaks reveal another aspect of Diocletian's programme: a substantial increase in court ceremonial and an elevation of imperial status, whereby the cloaks were reserved, for the first time, for the emperor alone. Emperors might hug each other, but no ordinary mortal could expect such treatment, and those who approached the emperor were now expected to bow before him. Nothing could be further from the image of collegiality promoted by Trajan or Marcus Aurelius, but a century of imperial assassination informed Diocletian's new, more distanced style of contact with his subjects.

> *He [Diocletian] was a great man, but he had the following habits: he was the first to really want a mass of silk, purple and gems for his gilded robe and his sandals. Although these were excessive and a sign of a vain and arrogant disposition, they were minor compared to other things. He was the first emperor after Caligula and Domitian to wish to be called 'Lord' as well as allowing himself to be worshipped and addressed as a god ... However, these faults in Valerius were obscured by other good qualities; because he wished to be called 'Lord' he acted like a parent.*

Sextus Aurelius Victor, *The Caesars*, 39

Whatever Diocletian hoped to achieve by his change in style, it did not prevent new revolts. Shortly after Maximian took office as *augustus*, the commander of the Roman fleet in the English Channel, Carausius, declared himself emperor. Allegedly, he was about to be charged with absconding with plunder taken from pirates in the North Sea. He proved a wily adversary. Maximian attempted an invasion of Britain, to which Carausius had withdrawn after losing his mainland European bases, but the situation became so difficult that Diocletian himself had to come west.

The co-emperors met at Milan and perhaps agreed on a future reorganization. An *augustus* needed deniability if things went wrong. There followed further promotions. In the spring of 292 CE, presumably as a result of prior consultation with Diocletian, Maximian promoted Flavius Constantius to deputize as his *caesar*. Having played his part in smoothing Diocletian's path to the throne, Constantius – an able soldier – was becoming increasingly prominent in the western imperial court, and by now he was also Maximian's Praetorian prefect and son-in-law. A few months later, Diocletian bestowed the same office on a man named Galerius, who would then marry Valeria, Diocletian's daughter and only child. This rule by two *augusti* and two *caesars* is generally known as the Tetrarchy.

Over the next few years, Constantius overcame first Carausius, then another imperial challenger, Allectus, in Britain, while Galerius would prove

Figure IV

Constantius served as Maximian's Praetorian prefect in the western provinces before his marriage to Maximian's daughter Theodora and his promotion to serve as Maximian's deputy, or *caesar*. The terms of his marriage required him to divorce his first wife, Helena, the mother of his son Constantine.

his own merit in the east, against the Persians. Persistent civil strife among Sapor's descendants had enabled Diocletian to make a treaty with Persia that restored an Arsacid, Tiridates, to Armenia's throne in 287 CE. However, six years later Sapor's ambitious son Narses emerged as Persia's king, looking to recapture land taken by Rome in northern Mesopotamia and Armenia. In 296 CE Narses crushed the forces of Galerius – who may have been underprepared – outside Carrhae, in the wake of which a revolt broke out against Roman rule in Egypt.

The resulting crisis was Diocletian's most serious test to date. He led an army from the Balkans into Syria (where he had a rather testy encounter with Galerius) before heading to Egypt. Narses, who overestimated his success the previous year, launched an invasion of Armenia, where Galerius – showing considerable initiative and spying out the Persian camp on his own – defeated him in two battles and captured the king's camp, complete with harem. Narses's wife was sent to live outside Antioch until peace could be negotiated, while Galerius's victory was shortly to be memorialized in a triumphal arch.

Figure V (below)

The porphyry image of the four emperors shows Diocletian grasping his deputy, Galerius, while Maximian grasps Constantius.

Figure VI (opposite)

The Arch of Galerius in Thessalonica celebrates the crucial victory of the eastern emperors and the treaty that was imposed on Persia in 299 CE.

THE ARCH OF GALERIUS

The triumphal arch commemorating Galerius's victory over Narses was erected outside what was once his palace at Thessalonica (in Moesia, now northern Greece), probably between 299 and 305 CE. In its original form, the structure consisted of eight piers arranged in two parallel rows of four, creating three arched openings, of which the central arch was the largest. The four central piers were decorated with marble slabs depicting Galerius's victory and the ideology of the Tetrarchy. The arch was subsequently linked, on the northeastern side, to a portico that extended outwards from the massive rotunda that Galerius ordered to be built, possibly intending it to be his mausoleum. His palace lay to the southwest.

The surviving sculptures on the south side of the central arch stress the unity of the Tetrarchs, while the panels on the north side, which focus on the campaign against Narses, appear to echo Sasanian art by inventing a scene depicting Galerius's personal victory in a duel with Narses.

EMPIRE RESHAPED AND REFORMED

Present on the staff of Galerius was Constantine, the teenage son of his fellow *caesar*, Constantius. He was the offspring from Constantius's first marriage and had no obvious hope of high office, so his assignment to Nicomedia might have been a convenience for his father, who was starting a new family with his second wife, Theodora. Constantine's education, in Diocletian's capital, had included instruction from a Christian named Lactantius, although the tutor does not appear to have dared to share his faith with an imperial princeling who, at this stage, was being brought up to be a soldier. More prominent would have been, for example, the chance for Constantine to watch Galerius in action.

During the 290s CE Diocletian began transforming the empire's military structure, expanding the cavalry corps that Gallienus had created to include substantial bodies of infantry, who would serve under the direct command of one of the Tetrarchs. These *comitatenses* were distinguished from the men of the old legions, now much reduced in strength, which were called the *riparenses* (border forces). The job of the latter was to operate locally, defending

Figure VII

One of the earliest surviving pieces of Christian art, this painting from the Catacombs of Domatilla in Rome shows Jesus dining with his Apostles.

IN THOSE MATTERS WHERE SAVAGE AVARICE BURNS, PLACING NO LIMIT TO ITSELF, WITHOUT REGARD FOR THE HUMAN RACE, IT HASTENS TO INCREASE AND AUGMENT ITSELF NOT BY YEARS OR MONTHS OR DAYS, BUT ALMOST BY HOURS AND MOMENTS.

EDICT OF DIOCLETIAN, SETTING MAXIMUM PRICES ACROSS THE EMPIRE

Figure VIII

Maximinus was appointed Galerius's *caesar* when the latter (Maximinus's father-in-law) succeeded Diocletian as *augustus* in 306 CE. The representation of Hercules on the reverse of this coin stresses Galerius's continuation of Diocletian ideology concerning the relationship between senior and junior members of the imperial college.

a frontier against attack until – if needed – a Tetrarch showed up with the more elite *comitatenses*. Diocletian's reform effectively recognized the reality that legions of the old army, stationed for generations in the same place, were unwilling to be shipped across the empire, and were all too prone to support a regional usurper if their terms of service were threatened with change. To be transferred was now the most serious collective punishment that could be inflicted on a unit whose conduct an emperor found unsatisfactory.

Economic reform was on the agenda, too. In the mid-290s Diocletian reformed the coinage wrecked by Aurelian, although without great effect. But in the wake of victory over Persia, Diocletian attempted something more radical: he issued an edict fixing prices for goods and services across the empire, underpinned by an appeal to justice and morality:

> *The memory of the wars we have fought successfully rightly gives thanks to the Fortune of our State, together with the immortal gods, for the tranquil state of the world placed in the embrace of the most profound peace, and for the goods of peace on account of that which was striven for with great sweat; decent public opinion as well as Roman majesty and dignity demand that it be stabilized faithfully and ordained decently so that we who, by the favour of the gods, have stifled the seething ravages of barbarian nations in previous years by the slaughter of those nations, will surround the peace founded for eternity with the proper foundations of Justice … If some thought of restraint were curbing its means, or if our shared fortunes could calmly endure this raging as it rips them apart, day after day in the worst way with conditions as they are, perhaps a place would be left for pretending it all away and keeping quiet, since the shared endurance of our spirits would moderate the detestable enormity and the pitiable state of affairs.*

It did not work out as planned, for the result was to create shortages everywhere. Other reforms included an edict banning the Egyptian practice of closer kin marriage than was typical elsewhere, on the grounds that it was amoral and 'unRoman'. In addition, Diocletian took aim against the dualistic religious thought of Manichaeism, on the grounds that it had spread from its Persian roots to become a corrupting influence in the Roman Empire. He turned on the Christians, too, whose faith had been legal ever since Gallienus's edict in 262 CE. Diocletian's first anti-Christian edict was directed against those serving in the Roman army; another, in 303 CE, ordered the incineration of Christian scripture, the destruction of churches, the removal of Christians' legal rights and the reversion of Christian freedmen to slavery. Those who protested were executed.

For all its severity, the edict against the Christians did little to eradicate the faith, although it did foment bitter divisions within Christian communities. It was, however, implemented only briefly, for a year after issuing it, Diocletian rescinded his edict. By now, the *augustus* had other matters on his mind, for he was contemplating an unprecedented act for a Roman emperor: abdication. He travelled to Rome, where he met with Maximian, explaining that they would both be stepping down on the 1st of May, 305 CE, so that the two *caesars*, Constantius and Galerius, could assume the positions of *augusti*. Diocletian rigged the succession in such a way that Constantius, technically inheriting Diocletian's role as senior *augustus*, would have as his new *caesar* not a man from the western bureaucracy, but rather a friend of Galerius named Severus. Neither Maximian nor Constantius was happy about these arrangements, but such was the power of Diocletian's personality that they did not oppose his decision. As *augustus* in the east, Galerius now promoted his nephew Maximinus Daia to be his *caesar* and heir.

> *There is a high place about three miles from the city [Nicomedia], on the top of which Galerius had received the purple. A pillar, with a statue of Jupiter, had been erected there. The procession went to that spot. An assembly of the soldiers was summoned. Diocletian, with tears, spoke to the soldiers. He said that he was unwell, that he wished rest after his labours, that he would hand the empire over to stronger men and appoint new Caesars ... Diocletian put the purple cloak he had taken off on this man [Maximinus Daia] and became Diocles once again. He descended from the tribunal, and the former emperor, transported through Nicomedia in a cart, was dismissed into his own country.*

Lactantius, *On the Deaths of the Persecutors*, 19

NEW REGIMES AND THE RISE OF CONSTANTINE 'THE GREAT'

Constantius and Maximian had plainly been close associates, at times diverging from decrees emanating from the empire's east. For example, the edict on Christian persecution had not been enforced in the Roman provinces covering France and southern Germany, where Constantius held court. There is not even any evidence that Diocletian or Galerius met with Constantius in the decade after he became *caesar*. The consequence was that, despite Diocletian's ambition to eliminate local power structures, this is exactly what had evolved in the western provinces under Constantius. The men who held senior positions under him sensed that their jobs were threatened should Severus come to power in the west, and there was plainly strain between Severus and Maximian's agents, too. The uncertainty was aggravated by Constantius's poor health, and the fact that his several children with Theodora were too young to be potential successors. It was time for Constantine to come home.

Constantine was, by now, a minor official in Galerius's eastern court. Stories would later be spread that Galerius had tried to find ways for him to have a fatal accident, but it appears that Constantine was living quite peacefully with his new wife, Minervina, and son Crispus. Galerius complied with Constantius's request to send Constantine to him, and he duly arrived, with his family, in the summer of 305 CE – despite having had to flee through the night to avoid Galerius's assassins, if the stories are to be believed.

Soon, both Constantius and Constantine – now on his staff – were in Britain, dealing with a large-scale attack from across the Scottish border. The operation was a success, and it gave the senior staff a chance to observe Constantine in action, so that when Constantius died on the 25th of July,

Figure IX

Crispus was Constantine's first son, by his first wife, Minervina. This coin dates from 323 CE, when Crispus started to play a major role in his father's military operations.

306 CE, at York, they proclaimed Constantine *caesar*, rebuffing Diocletian's plans for Severus. He wrote to Galerius explaining his new position and ordered troops to the Alpine passes, to prevent Severus from entering what would be the core territory of his regime. Galerius had no choice but to accept the situation, for Severus's administration had been destabilized by an edict Galerius had issued, eliminating the tax exemption that Italy's inhabitants had enjoyed for centuries. Resentment was sufficiently widespread that Maximian's son Maxentius had himself proclaimed 'Leader of the Youth' at Rome (28th of October), in effect claiming his own form of regional imperial rule. When Severus tried to suppress Maxentius's revolt, his father emerged from retirement, and Severus's troops – who plainly retained considerable affection for their old general – deserted to Maximian. Severus surrendered and was confined in a villa on the Appian Way in Rome.

This was a dangerous situation that Galerius could not ignore. In the face of expected action from him, Maxentius and Maximian moved rapidly to shore up support from Constantine, who was campaigning against the Franks; accusing their leaders of acting in bad faith, he had two of their kings thrown to the lions in the amphitheatre at Trier. Maximian now offered his young daughter Fausta – not even a teenager – in marriage to Constantine, who divorced Minervina and duly complied. With this alliance cemented, Maximian returned to Italy, ahead of Galerius's invasion, in September. Maxentius and Maximian allowed Galerius to advance as far as Rome without offering serious resistance, but there he ran out of steam, for he lacked the wherewithal to storm the heavily fortified city. Deprived of an opportunity to fight in open battle, Galerius withdrew to the Balkans. His withdrawal was a death sentence for Severus, who was executed shortly afterwards.

It was in the wake of Galerius's failed invasion of Italy that Diocletian emerged from retirement to help broker a new deal, whereby Galerius would recognize Constantine's legitimacy as *caesar*, while appointing an experienced general named Licinius as the new *augustus* for the western empire. In practice, Licinius did nothing to enforce his claims to Maxentius's territory in Italy and Africa or Constantine's lands. But the arrangement did not calm the power play among the leading actors, for that same year (308 CE) Maximian tried to replace his son as head of their regime; he failed and fled to Gaul, where Constantine offered him refuge. Two years later, while Constantine was again on campaign on the Rhine, Maximian, who was at Arles, spread the rumour that Constantine was dead and had himself proclaimed *augustus* in his place. An unhappy Constantine moved rapidly south, shutting up Maximian in Marseilles.

What happened when the city opened its gates to Constantine remains unclear. In one version, he forgave Maximian and readmitted him to the palace, where he later committed suicide after he was discovered trying to murder Constantine. More likely, Maximian killed himself in the aftermath of his revolt, as the author of a panegyric in honor of Constantine suggested:

Be thankful, Constantine, for your character and habits, because Constantius Pius gave birth to you this way, and the decrees of the stars formed you so that you cannot be cruel. Nor do I think that man, when he was about to emerge into the light of day and receive a choice of the life he would lead, encountered a fate that had to be avoided, which brought injustice to many men, and finally a voluntary death to himself. For, not to speak of other matters, did not the inevitability of fate cause this to happen, that he gave you this in return for your piety, when you had received him, driven from Rome, fleeing from Italy, repudiated by Illyricum, in your provinces, armies and the very palace.

From the Panegyric in honour of Constantine, 6.14.5–6

Maximian's death, unfortunately, undermined the prevailing justification for Constantine's claim to power – that he was continuing his father's relationship with Maximian. It is presumably why the author of the panegyric suddenly 'revealed' a hitherto unknown fact about Constantine's family: that he was the descendent of Claudius II.

Galerius did not long survive Maximian, but his death in 311 CE set up a fresh round of civil warfare. Maximinus Daia – Galerius's son-in-law and supposedly his heir – was jealous of Licinius, who had been promoted over his head. With war beckoning, Maxentius would be a useful ally to Daia, since his army could threaten Licinius's western frontier and prevent the full concentration of Licinius's forces in the east. Licinius could see what was coming, and he reached out to Constantine, offering to recognize his claim to be *augustus* in the west if he would eliminate Maxentius. Constantine agreed.

DEFEAT OF MAXENTIUS AND THE BATTLE OF THE MILVIAN BRIDGE

The campaign that Constantine would fight in Italy during the summer and autumn of 312 CE would be one of the truly masterful military operations of the age. When he led his army across the Alps, the main forces of Maxentius were already in northern Italy, concentrated around Milan. Needing to move quickly, Constantine chose a transalpine route near Mount Cenis. The first garrisoned city he encountered was Segusio (Segusium). According to reports that formed the official tradition of the campaign, the place refused to surrender but fell to an immediate assault when Constantine's men scaled the walls and set fire to the gates.

Turin, a major city, would be next. Maxentius could neither abandon it, because of the potentially serious impact on morale, nor reinforce it, because his major formations were still around Milan. Yet the destruction of Segusio had sent a message to the citizens of Turin that, in the event of a siege, their fates would be tied to that of the garrison. Constantine was fully aware of the stress he was causing, as is evidenced by a contemporary comparison of his actions to Julius Caesar's in a decisive campaign of 48 BCE. Had Constantine been studying Caesar? Certainly, Constantine's understanding that war was a political as well as a military process reflected that of Caesar. So too did the attention Constantine paid to understanding his enemies' constraints and to grasping the details that were necessary for a successful operation.

Maxentius's general decided to defend Turin, even though he was outnumbered. The battle itself seems to have been a dramatic affair, turning upon Constantine's ability to deal with his enemy's superior heavy cavalry. When these were defeated, with Constantine allegedly fighting in the front ranks, the people of Turin closed the gates on their former defenders and were consequently spared the fate of Segusio.

The battle for Turin marked the turning point in the campaign. Maxentius's surviving forces pulled back toward Verona, leaving open the road to Milan, which surrendered without a fight. Winning control of an imperial capital was an important symbolic victory, which caused other cities to switch sides. After a few days in Milan, Constantine set out in pursuit of Maxentius's surviving forces. The final battle of the northern campaign was fought outside Verona. The army fighting for Maxentius fled, much of it subsequently going over to Constantine. One account has Constantine imitating Galerius in the Persian war by going on a scouting mission beforehand. Both stories may be fabrications, but they emphasize a stress on the role of the emperor in all phases of a military operation.

Constantine's victories in the Po Valley made it impossible for Maxentius to rely on the defences of Rome, and, with a substantial portion of his original military establishment now destroyed, it is unlikely that he mustered a force much greater than that of Constantine – if at all greater. Treason may well have been in the air, too, for many of Maxentius's associates would rapidly find places in the highest echelons of Constantine's regime, suggesting that negotiations were opened as he moved south. There are also suggestions of unrest among the urban population. All these factors created circumstances very different from Galerius's invasion, when Maximian and Maxentius had been able to wait him out. And then, the gods stepped in. Maxentius even ordered a consultation of the ancient collection of Sibylline Oracles. The priests in charge of the consultation allegedly found an oracle telling him he was better off fighting Constantine in the open. The text was presumably a forgery designed to encourage Maxentius' men by suggesting that the gods were on their side.

On the 28th of October – the anniversary of his original seizure of power – Maxentius rode to war, although with what confidence might be surmised by the fact that he deposited the symbols of his imperial power, including his sceptre, in wooden boxes under a shrine near the Palatine Hill. He seems to have known there was a good chance that he would not come back.

The battle that took place was known as the Battle of the Milvian Bridge. Constantine allowed Maxentius to draw up his army with the river at his back. Perhaps this was a sign that Maxentius was trying to inspire his troops with thoughts of their imminent demise, should they fail to conquer. In the event, his army did not withstand the first assault.

Constantine's battle at the Milvian Bridge was not simply a celebrated *military* victory, for he ascribed his success to his new-found religion. In the months before the campaign, Constantine had come to the decision that he would, henceforth, worship the Christian God – a decision that marks a moment of revolutionary significance for the intellectual and religious history of Europe.

Figure X (opposite)

Constantine's success in the first part of the Battle of the Milvian Bridge undermined support for Maxentius in Rome. This was one factor in Maxentius's decision to fight, while he was also encouraged by a Sibylline Oracle, which stated that an enemy of Rome would perish on the 28th of October. Consequently, Maxentius led his army across the Tiber with its back to the river, where Constantine's experienced force was able to rout it. Maxentius died in the flight.

Figure XI (overleaf)

The Dove of Peace greets Noah at the end of the Great Flood, symbolizing the rebirth of the world.

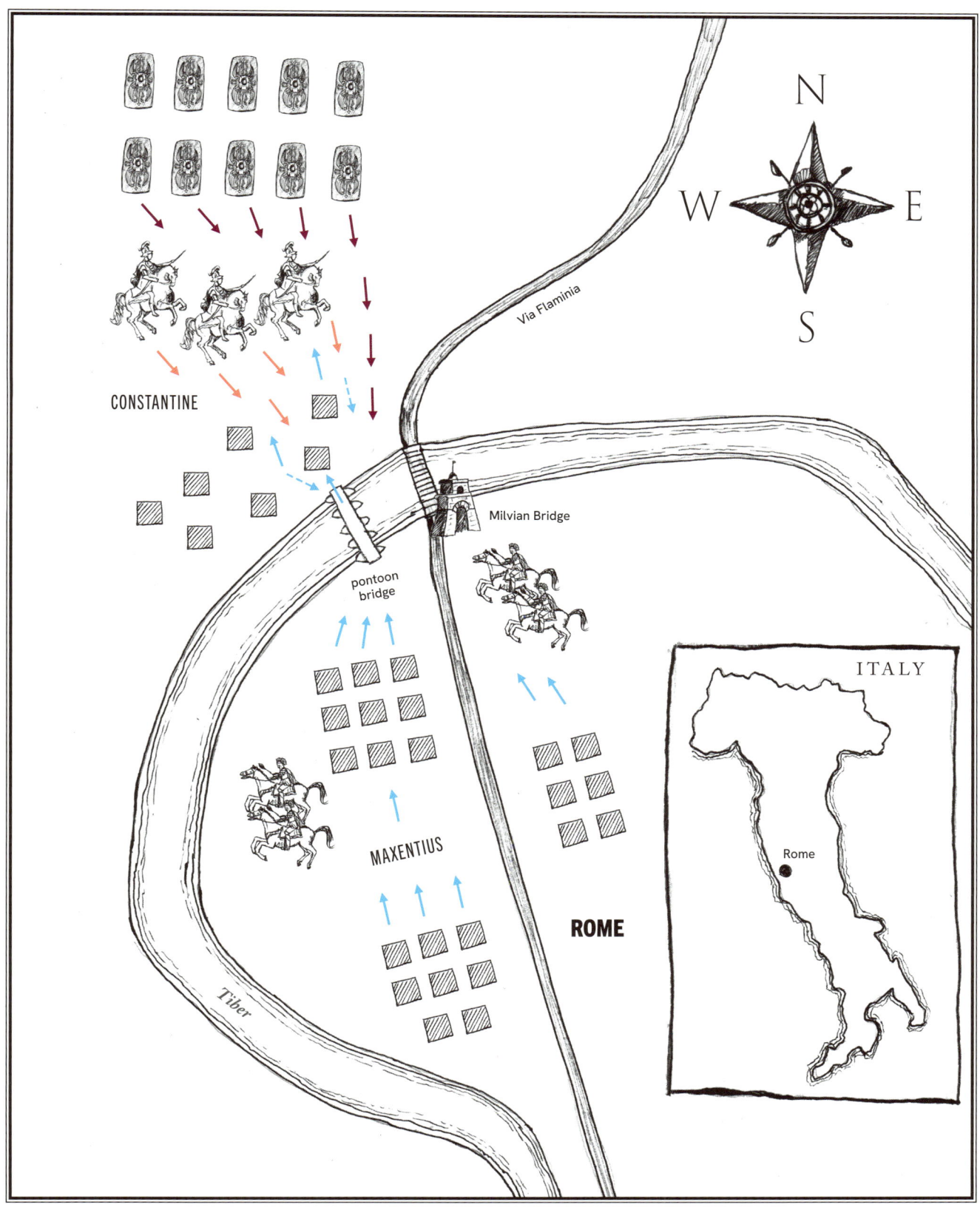

THE CONVERSION OF CONSTANTINE

Figure XII (above)

One of the legends about Constantine's conversion, emerging long after the event, was that he had been struck with leprosy while persecuting the Church. Cured through the intervention of Pope Silvester, he became a Christian and bestowed authority over the Church upon the Bishop of Rome (the so-called Donation of Constantine).

The evidence for the timing of Constantine's conversion to Christianity varies across the sources. It seems to have been the case that while he was explicit about his faith when talking with Christians, he was much less so when conversing with others. The earliest evidence to indicate that Constantine attributed his victory over Maxentius to the special guidance he received from a divinity appears in the panegyric delivered in his honour in 313 CE at Trier. There, the author – who presumably had been told what to say by sources in the palace, and who knew a great deal about the course of the campaign – referred to an unnamed, singular god who overruled negative omens and prompted Constantine to invade Italy. The author adds that Constantine later took advice from a divine, singular power.

Writing a few years later, Lactantius wrote that Constantine had had a dream in which the Christian God advised him to put a Christian symbol on the shields of his troops, for protection. The scene is rather similar to a dream he attributed to Licinius before his decisive victory over Maximinus Daia, and it might not reflect official communication from Constantine's court. The most extreme version of Constantine's conversion is provided by Bishop Eusebius of Caesarea, in his biography of the emperor, completed after Constantine's death. Eusebius asserts that Constantine saw a cross of light in the sky with the inscription 'by this you will conquer,' a sign later confirmed in a dream. Although Eusebius states that Constantine swore to him that this is what happened, it is likely that the tale was made up well after the event.

The most important account of the conversion derives from a letter Constantine wrote in 314 CE to the Council of Arles, which had assembled to adjudicate a dispute between Christian groups in Africa. In it, he wrote:

The eternal and incomprehensible religious piety of our God will not allow the human condition to wander uselessly for long in the shadows, nor does it allow the hateful desires of certain men to prevail for long so that he should not allow them to be saved, opening a path with shining beams of light to turn them to the rule of justice. I have learned this through many examples, and I measure these things through myself. For there were of old things in me that seemed to be lacking in justice, nor did I think that the heavenly power could see those secrets that I bore within my breast. Truly what should have been allotted to these things? Plainly one abundant with all evils. But the all-powerful God who sits in the watch post of heaven gave me what I did not deserve; truly I cannot say, nor can those things be enumerated which heavenly benevolence granted me, its servant.

A reasonable interpretation of this statement, in conjunction with the evidence for public pronouncements made at the time, is that Constantine was happy to advertise the guidance he felt he had received from a single divinity, seen in a vision, but that he did not reveal widely his belief that this divinity was the Christian God. That his vision occurred before he crossed the Alps in 312 CE might be inferred from both the panegyric of 313 CE and the fact that three Gallic bishops accompanied him on the campaign. The senate, when dedicating the arch to celebrate his victory (see page 214), spoke of Constantine being inspired by the Divine Mind (mentioned as a possible guide for Constantine in the panegyric). For the next decade, Constantine would place images of Sol Invictus (Invincible Sun) on his coinage: a choice of a divinity that could be identified not only with a tradition of imperial victory (dating back to Aurelian), but also with the Christian God.

Figure XIII (overleaf)

This bust of Constantine survives from a colossal statue, estimated to have been 10–12 metres (33–39 feet) tall, which was erected near the basilica of Maxentius, a building that Constantine finished. It would have looked down on Constantine's triumphal arch. The square face, aquiline nose, wide-open eyes and distinctive hairstyle with the fringe of hair forming an almond shape on the forehead are characteristic of Constantinian portraiture.

[MAXENTIUS], VAINLY TRYING TO ASCEND THE STEEP OPPOSITE BANK WITH HIS HORSE AND SHINING ARMOUR, WITH ITS WHIRLPOOL SO THAT SUCH A GROTESQUE MONSTER WOULD NOT LEAVE THIS STORY BEHIND OF HIS DEATH, THAT HE HAD FALLEN TO THE SWORD OR SPEAR OF SOME BRAVE MAN. THE RIVER SWEPT THE BODIES AND ARMOUR OF THE ENEMY REVOLVING HEADLONG, BUT IT HELD HIM IN THE PLACE WHERE HE HAD DIED SO THAT THE ROMAN PEOPLE WOULD NOT HESITATE IF THE THOUGHT AROSE THAT HE HAD ESCAPED, OR WANTED PROOF OF HIS DEMISE.

LATIN PANEGYRIC 12.16.5–17.3 (DELIVERED AT TRIER IN 313 CE AND PROBABLY BASED ON AN ACCOUNT CIRCULATED BY CONSTANTINE'S COURT)

THE ARCH OF CONSTANTINE

Figure XIV

Although a Christian, Constantine preserved the traditional symbolism of imperial power: addressing his troops with their traditional eagles, and allowing a sacrifice scene to be placed on his arch.

Once Rome was in his possession, Constantine began to eradicate the memory of Maxentius from the urban space. Today, one of the most stunning reworkings is the great arch that stands in the valley of the Colosseum, dedicated in 315 CE. Its position was significant, for it straddled the by then traditional triumphal route along the Via Sacra and framed the colossal statue of the Sun God, first erected by Nero in his own image but lately redesigned to display the features of Maxentius's deceased son Romulus. In fact, Maxentius had chosen this site for an arch intended to commemorate his own victories.

Constantine's version of the arch linked him with both divinity and earlier imperial traditions. Anyone travelling up the Via Sacra from the south would see the smiling visage of the Colossus re-carved in Constantine's image emerging over the top of the arch and gazing down at the bronze statue of Constantine in a four-horse chariot, which stood atop the arch. Aside from the use of the Colossus, one of the most stunning aspects of the new arch was the reuse of sculpture from earlier periods. The practice itself looked back to a tradition that began under Diocletian, whose own triumphal arch had made use of sculpture from the Julio-Claudian era, and to Maxentius's recycling of earlier material for the tomb of Romulus. But the Arch of Constantine goes beyond those earlier experiments in the complexity of its message, whereby the heads of earlier emperors were re-carved to represent Constantine, Licinius, and – in one case – Constantius.

The sculptural programme consists of elements arranged in three registers. In the top register are ten tableaux, four each on the north and south faces, one each on the east and west, set behind eight statues of defeated barbarians taken from a monument of Trajan's time. At this level, the tableaux all derive from monuments of Marcus Aurelius and depict fundamental types of imperial action. On the south side, the images are of the emperor 'giving' a king to a barbarian people, his speech to his army, as well as the performance of a ritual before military standards, and the display of barbarian prisoners. Depicted on the north side are the emperor's arrival and departure from Rome, a triumphal procession and the distribution of bounty to his people. The east and west sides show victories over barbarians. The central element on each side is the dedicatory inscription of the arch.

The central register also has four images each on the northern and southern sides, this time taken from a monument of Hadrian. On the southern face they show a hunt, with the emperor and his companions standing outside a gate, then sacrificing to the god of the woods, and hunting a bear; and finally, there is a sacrifice to Diana, the goddess associated with hunting. On the north side, the scenes depict a boar hunt, a sacrifice to Apollo, a dead lion and a sacrifice to Hercules.

The third register focuses on the victory of Constantine. The southern face shows the capture of Verona and the victory at the Milvian Bridge, while the northern face reveals scenes of Constantine's arrival in Rome, with the emperor standing on the speaker's platform in the heart of the Forum, and statues of Hadrian and Marcus on either side. Behind the figure of Constantine, the four columns erected in honour of Diocletian and his colleagues in 303 CE are visible, flanking a statue of Jupiter, while off to the left the triumphal arch of Septimius Severus can be seen. The story of the conquest continues on both the east and west faces of the arch with, on the west side, a frieze showing the departure of the army from Milan, beneath the image of the setting moon, and on the east side, the sun rising above the triumphal entry into Rome.

By means of the arch, Constantine propagated his preferred image of imperial power, harking back less to Diocletian than to the era of the Antonine dynasty. The gods depicted – the Sun and Moon, Apollo and Diana, Silvanus – are all divinities who had little place in the regime of Diocletian, but who suggest the extent to which Constantine's regime is as one with the natural world.

The left-hand side of the relief depicting the Battle of the Milvian Bridge shows Constantine on the riverbank, looking over Maxentius, who falls from the bridge into the water. Beside Constantine is the goddess Roma. Although by now a Christian, Constantine was happy to be presented to the public as a highly traditional figure.

CONFLICT WITH LICINIUS

Figure XV

Promoted to the rank of *augustus* in the Balkans by Galerius in 308 CE, Licinius seized the eastern portion of the empire from Maximinus Daia in 313 (at which point he issued a decree legalizing Christianity). He married Constantine's half-sister, but fell out with Constantine in 316/17. He was defeated and killed after a second war with Constantine, which ended in 324.

Constantine did not remain long in Rome, departing for Trier shortly after his victory. On his way, he met with Licinius at Milan. There, they solidified their alliance through Licinius's marriage to Constantine's half-sister Constantia, and it seems they discussed religion, too. In the spring of 313 CE war commenced with Maximinus Daia, who sent an army across the Hellespont.

The (allegedly) outnumbered Licinius met Maximinus Daia at Adrianople, the vital crossroads city that was so often the scene of deadly conflict. As the armies prepared for battle, Licinius publicized a dream in which a divine messenger told him to pray to the Supreme God. On the morning of the 30th of April he wrote out a prayer that he claimed to have received verbatim from an angel – an event scarcely unparalleled in the history of ancient visions – and distributed it to his men. When they had recited it three times, Licinius and Maximinus met briefly to see if they could resolve their differences; and when that failed, they joined battle. Licinius was completely victorious, while Maximinus rapidly fled east, pausing briefly at Nicomedia to gather up his family. He planned to make a final stand at Tarsus, but failed to defend the narrow passes into the Cilician plain from the Anatolian plateau. His end came by way of suicide, as Licinius's army approached.

In life, Maximinus Daia was a brutal persecutor of the Christian faith, and when he was defeated, Licinius issued a powerfully worded statement on religious freedom for Christians. The document is sometimes known, erroneously, as the Edict of Milan. It was issued from Nicomedia on the 13th of June, 313 CE, and, although it was the work of Licinius, it is highly probable that Constantine had encouraged him to take a step that firmly disassociated his regime from that of Diocletian.

By the end of 316 CE the relationship between Constantine and Licinius had soured, in part because their spouses bore children. Fausta's first child, another Constantine, was born in the spring of 316, at about the same time that Constantia gave birth to a son, another Licinius. A direct result was that Constantine transferred the seat of his government from Gaul to Serdica (present-day Sofia, Bulgaria). He would remain there, or at Sirmium, thereafter, with just one brief journey to Italy in 318 CE.

Constantine now sought to exclude his nephew from the succession by naming Bassianus (the husband of his half-sister Anastasia) *caesar*, with authority over Italy. The arrangement did not last long, since Bassianus was charged with treason and executed. Constantine then sent an ambassador to Licinius demanding that he hand over a relative of Bassianus who was in his court. Licinius refused to comply with what seemed like imperial blackmail, instead ordering that statues and images of Constantine be destroyed in a frontier city, an act that constituted a declaration of war. In the next few months Constantine showed both the ability that had brought him victory over Maxentius and a new overconfidence that nearly caused his destruction. The first battle was joined on the 8th of October, 316 CE, at Cibalae, at the western end of Licinius's domain. Constantine was the aggressor in a battle that raged from dawn until evening. Taking personal command of his own right wing, he routed Licinius's left wing, at which point Licinius fled,

CONSTANTINE'S CONFLICT WITH LICINIUS

Figure XVI

This mosaic from Aquileia in northern Italy symbolizes the fight between good and evil. The rooster represents daylight and the turtle was regarded as a nighttime animal.

withdrawing to Thrace and allegedly breaking bridges behind him to slow the pursuit. Licinius managed to rally his forces, appointing an experienced officer named Valens his *caesar*, before more fighting at Adrianople, where again Constantine emerged victorious. It is a tribute to Licinius's abilities that he was able to keep his army together in the wake of a second defeat – and take advantage of Constantine's natural aggression. Anticipating that Constantine would press on after him towards the Hellespont, Licinius placed his army across Constantine's lines of communication at Beroia, in what remains one of the epic acts of deception in Roman military history.

Although the strategic advantage now lay with him, Licinius chose to negotiate, which might have been a sign of the fear that Constantine's string of battlefield successes had instilled in him. So too might be the fact that the final terms were highly advantageous to Constantine. Licinius ceded his European territories (other than Thrace) to Constantine and agreed to execute Valens. New *caesars* were appointed, confirming the principle of biological succession, so that Constantine's sons Crispus and Constantine II received the office, along with Licinius' son, which was a major concession on Constantine's part, even though it ensured that descendants of Constantius would dominate the next generation.

The peace between Constantine and Licinius lasted six years, although it was clear as early as 321 CE that fresh conflict was pending. Two years later

Constantine pursued a band of Gothic raiders into Licinius's lands, implying that Licinius was in some way responsible for an attack on his territory; he also began to assemble a powerful fleet.

Significant naval actions had been noticeably absent from the annals of Roman warfare after the Battle of Actium. The only major operations involving fleets in the ensuing centuries had been Aurelian's reconquest of Egypt and the war waged by Maximian and Constantius against Carausius. In the Mediterranean, the poor quality of Roman naval forces was amply demonstrated during the mid-third century by their failure to contain raiders, be they tribesmen from the Black Sea who ravaged the Aegean coastline in the time of Valerian and Gallienus, or adventurous Franks who looted the western Mediterranean while Probus was emperor. Therefore, a major Mediterranean Roman fleet was something new – and its construction showed that Constantine was planning a campaign to carry his forces into the heart of Licinius's realm. The fleet was to be commanded by his son Crispus.

Constantine's invasion began in the summer of 324 CE. Licinius again mustered his forces at Adrianople, but on the 3rd of July he was utterly defeated. Constantine again led the decisive attack, during the course of which he was wounded in the leg. Licinius fled the field for Byzantium, which Constantine then besieged. The wound is somewhat problematic for Eusebius's *Life of Constantine* (written long after the event), which has Constantine going into battle accompanied by a kind of battle-standard with miraculous powers to protect those around it. According to Eusebius, when one of the 50 specially selected guardsmen carrying the standard let go of it, a javelin skewered him, while the man who took his place was saved from all peril. The standard itself attracted so many javelins that it resembled a giant pincushion.

In truth, Constantine had no need of supernatural support. With Licinius in Byzantium, the campaign shifted to the sea, where the western fleet, handled in a thoroughly professional manner, took control of the Bosporus. Licinius now abandoned his men in Byzantium to take command of fresh forces near Chalcedon. Constantine landed his army without opposition north of Licinius's position, forcing him to fight, probably on the 18th of September, and with thoroughly predictable results. Licinius fled again, this time to Nicomedia, as the troops left in Byzantium surrendered and the campaign entered its final stage. On (or slightly before) the 16th of December, 324 CE, Licinius's wife, Constantia, assisted by Nicomedia's bishop, negotiated the surrender of her husband, who was sent into exile at Thessalonica. He was executed there shortly afterwards, allegedly for conspiring with barbarians, leaving Constantine sole ruler of the Roman Empire.

SCANDAL AND SUCCESSION

The challenge from Licinius defeated, reconstruction began on the city of Byzantium to transform it into the emperor's eponymous eastern capital: Constantinople. Constantine moved into Diocletian's old palace at Nicomedia. Following a tour of the eastern provinces as far as Syria, he settled back in the imperial capital district – and confronted a serious dispute in the Christian community.

Followers of an Alexandrian priest named Arius insisted that Jesus had a human aspect distinct from his divinity, while Arius's rivals held that he was wholly divine. Constantine acted decisively to see if he could end this quarrel, summoning a council of the eastern clergy at Nicaea (in western Turkey) in June 325 CE, and delivering (with the aid of his future biographer, Eusebius) a new statement of faith to which all Christians were expected to adhere. The so-called Nicene Creed – easily the best-known piece of Roman legislation in the world today – was the first official statement of the Christian faith.

Constantine's theological intervention reflects the development of his understanding of Christianity over the previous decade. He had employed his old teacher, Lactantius, to instruct his children, and appears to have become familiar with Lactantius's teachings. He quoted him heavily in a letter to bishops before the Council of Nicaea and in a remarkable letter to Sapor II, the young King of Persia, in which he advised Sapor to convert (and attributed Sapor I's capture of Emperor Valerian as God's vengeance for Valerian's career as a persecutor).

As the letter to Sapor suggests, Constantine's promotion of Christianity was rather more direct when dealing with Rome's neighbours than when dealing with his own subjects; he had observed the failure of Diocletian's persecution and was not going to alienate his subjects by trying to compel adherence to his faith. He very rarely closed temples, but he did make it clear that people seeking favours from him were more likely to be successful if they were Christians – as long as they were acting within traditional avenues of approach. For example, he told the people of Orcistus (in central Turkey) that their desire for civic status, and thus self-government, would succeed in part because they were followers of his 'sacred faith'.

While Constantine was in the east, a crisis of some sort was brewing in the west. Crispus had returned to Trier in the spring of 325 CE as titular head of the western government, but in May 326 CE he was tried for treason and executed at Pola (in present-day Croatia). Wild stories later spread via a pagan historian: that Crispus had rejected sexual advances from his stepmother Fausta, who then accused him of trying to rape her; and that Helena outed Fausta as a liar, so Constantine had steamed Fausta to death in a bathhouse. Other passing references to the episode suggest something less lurid: that Crispus had asserted some inappropriate prerogatives, or that his fate was linked to a more general revamping of the western administration.

What is certain is that Crispus was now dispatched, and Fausta exiled, quite possibly for objecting to Constantine's treatment of the young man with whom she had grown up in the palace at Trier. She died a year later. While Constantine's wife, she had typically accompanied him on campaign,

Figure XVII

Helena, mother of Constantine, is represented here as the embodiment of Ceres, the goddess of plenty, aligning with Constantine's adaptation of traditional imagery. Also a devout Christian, Helena was credited with the rediscovery of the remains of the Cross upon which Jesus was crucified.

so the suggestion that she and Crispus were together in the west while Constantine was away is most unlikely. What does seem true, however, is that Constantine deeply regretted what happened. He would not remarry and would return only once more to the west, to lead a military expedition against the Franks in 327/8 CE. He was otherwise in the Balkans, where he campaigned several times against the peoples north of the Danube or in the region around Constantinople, which was officially dedicated in May 330 CE.

Constantine 'the Great' died on the 22nd of May, 337 CE. He had created a new model of imperial government, according to which there were now four *caesars*: his three sons by Fausta and a nephew named Dalmatius, whose father had held numerous important positions in recent years. In this system, Constantine's eldest son, Constantine II, was based at Trier; the youngest, Constans, was in Italy, while the middle child, Constantius II, was in the eastern provinces. Dalmatius was based in the Balkans. In all cases, they appear to have been accompanied by senior officials, who were charged with the actual government of the empire.

THE SONS OF CONSTANTINE

Constantine's death occurred just as he was preparing for war with Persia, after he declared Dalmatius's brother Hannibalianus King of Armenia. Those succession plans collapsed within months. Constantius II did not want to share power with his cousin Dalmatius, and several up-and-coming officials did not want to wait out the superiors who remained in power and who were loyal to Constantine's vision. In September 337 CE Dalmatius, Hannibalianus and virtually every other member of the family descended from Constantius and Theodora were executed at Constantinople on the trumped-up charge of having conspired to kill Constantine. The slaughter included some of Constantine's most trusted lieutenants. The only ones spared were two young descendants of that line, Gallus and Julian, who were soon sent to be raised on the estate of a bishop in central Anatolia.

Shortly after the murder of their relatives, the three brothers met to decide how to govern. Constantine II appears to have asserted that he should be the senior *augustus*, since he was the oldest. The two younger brothers disagreed and, it seems, were on very bad terms with each other.

The empire's military resources were now divided into three separate commands, consisting of the 'border forces', that is, Diocletian's *riparenses* – now known as the *limitanei* – and three mobile reserve armies, *comitatenses*, each numbering about 40,000 men. As a result of the division of empire, the *comitatenses* in the Balkans had been split between Constans and Constantius II. The total size of the army was probably near 240,000 men, with a roughly 50-50 split between *comitatenses* and *limitanei*. After years of fiscal chaos, this army was the army the Roman state could afford to pay.

The division of forces meant that it was not possible for Constantius II to gain local superiority in numbers over the Persian army. When his brother

Constantine II offered to help, leading an army into Constans's territory, he was assassinated, with the result that Constans took over his portion of the empire in 340 CE. In the meantime, the war with Persia had become a series of sieges, with the Persians focusing their attention on the city of Nisibis, which they attacked for the first time – unsuccessfully – in 337 CE. Their defeat was sufficiently embarrassing for Constantius II to be able to restore Roman control of Armenia the next year, as well as to make a treaty with the Arabs inhabiting the desert regions between the Tigris and the boundaries of Syria.

Sapor II returned to the attack in 343 CE, and this time – the only occasion on which this would happen – Constantius II met him in open battle, near the city of Singara (now Sinjar, Iraq). After some preliminary success, which allowed the Romans to breach the Persian camp, the Persians counterattacked and inflicted a serious defeat, taking advantage of the Roman mistake in breaking formation to loot the camp. The action continued into the evening, and Constantius was forced to flee the field. It was last time he confronted Sapor in person. The victory encouraged Sapor to launch another attack on Nisibis, in 344 CE, although this siege was no more successful than the first.

Ammianus Marcellinus – later a historian, but at this time serving with Constantius II on the eastern front – would criticize Constantius's unwillingness to confront the Persians, which, he believed, nearly cost Ammianus his life; but the Persian record before Nisibis suggests that Constantius II was pursuing a reasonable course. Soon, however, the fate of his brother Constans meant he had other things to worry about.

Constantius II had had a frosty relationship with Constans, aggravated by his tendency to support Christian leaders who were antagonistic to Constantius – a very devout Christian himself – on matters of doctrine. Constans had also made a serious political mistake when he decided to take up residence for several years in the Balkans, ignoring the western provinces. By the time he returned, the western bureaucracy was thoroughly fed up with his regime and supported a man named Magnentius, who, in January 350 CE, claimed the throne for himself, tracked down Constans (who was away from court on a hunting expedition) and killed him. Whatever his misgivings about his brother, Constantius II could not ignore this murder.

Over the course of the following summer, Constantius united his Balkan forces with those who had served Constans and augmented them with defectors from Magnentius's regime, who had initially backed the imperial pretensions of their own general, Vetranio. Constantius then defeated Magnentius at an extremely bloody battle at Mursa, near Cibalae, where Constantine had once vanquished Licinius (these places were on a major road). Magnentius retreated to Gaul, where Constantius caught up with him in 352 CE, and where, after a second defeat, Magnentius committed suicide.

The revolt forced on Constantius II a number of decisions. One was to leave it to Nisibis to deal with another attack by Sapor, which failed, but not without witnessing dramatic tactics to try and breach the walls. Sapor II redirected water from the River Mygdonius (JaghJagh) around the city walls, before deploying ships equipped with siege engines:

Figure XVIII (overleaf)

Sapor became king of Persia at his birth in 309 CE and ruled for 70 years. An able warrior, he regained the territory Persia had lost to Rome under Diocletian.

[WHEN] SAPOR REACHED 16 YEARS OF AGE AND WAS ABLE TO BEAR WEAPONS ... HE SUMMONED TOGETHER THE COMMANDERS [AND] MENTIONED HOW BOUNTIFUL GOD HAD BEEN TO HIM AND TO THEM THROUGH HIS FOREFATHERS, WHAT THESE LAST HAD ACCOMPLISHED THROUGH THEIR GOOD CONDUCT ... HOW ALL THESE ACHIEVEMENTS OF THEIRS HAD, HOWEVER, FALLEN INTO CONFUSION ... HE THEN TOLD THEM THAT HE WAS GOING TO START ON THE WORK OF RESTORING THE POSITION BY SECURELY DEFENDING THE HEARTLAND.

AL-TABARI, *HISTORY*, 838

The king of the Persians, crossing the Tigris from his zone, surrounded the city with ditches, and then let the Mygdonius flow into them and turned the area around the city into a lake, and completely surrounded the city as if it was an island, and only the ramparts showed above the water. Then he attacked it by bringing up ships with siege engines onboard, and this was not a matter of a few days, but of nearly four months, but the defenders constantly drove the barbarians back by hurling fire darts at the war machines and hauling many of the boats into the walls or destroying them through the force of their weapons hurling large stones at them ... when this had been going on for many days in a row, the dyke holding back the water broke, flooding the area and carrying away a large portion of the wall ....

[When the Persians attempted to take advantage of the failure of the wall, they became stuck in the mud.]

Many of the attackers were killed and all at once turned their horses in flight, though it was only through their gestures that it could be determined that they were seeking to flee, for as they were in the act of turning around their horses fell, carrying their riders with them. Weighed down by their armour, they fell ever deeper into the swamp and the destruction that followed has no parallel in any siege.

Julian, Panegyric on Constantius

(A Syriac bishop, Ephrem, present in the city at the time, provides confirmation that these events took place with the third siege of Nisibis, rather than the earlier sieges.)

The second decision Constantius II made was to appoint a *caesar* as a stand-in for himself in the east. The job went to Gallus, the elder of his two nephews, who was sent to Antioch. It did not go well. Gallus had no experience as an administrator, and his performance in the role was generally terrible, including violence against subordinates who showed him insufficient deference. In the summer of 354 CE Constantius decided to relieve him of his position; as he learned more about what had gone on under Gallus, he had his nephew tried – and executed – at Pola.

Constantius II knew he was going to have to return to the east, but he was very uncertain of the loyalty of the staff remaining from Constans's regime. The situation was complicated by the brutal inquisitions carried out by his own staff and a coup led by a senior general, Silvanus, after he discovered that members of that staff were circulating bogus letters to prove he was a traitor. In 355 CE Constantius dispatched one of the senior officers from the eastern army, Ursicinus, to assassinate Silvanus. The events that followed were reported vividly by Ammianus Marcellinus, who accompanied Ursicinus, and who describes the fear felt by himself and others on what they suspected would be a suicide mission. Instead, a too-trustful Silvanus received them well, assuming that Constantius's other subordinates shared similar experiences to his own. As his reward, in September 355 CE Silvanus was killed while attending church, by Frankish auxiliaries recruited by Ursicinus.

Constantius II now summoned his surviving nephew, Julian, to Milan, where he appointed him *caesar*. In later times, Julian was very clear that he understood his task at this point was simply to represent the imperial household, while the actual business of government would be carried on by Constantius's staff:

Constantius gave me 360 soldiers and sent me to Gaul in the middle of the winter, which was then in a state of great disorder. I was sent not to be the commander of the garrisons there but rather as a subordinate to the generals. Letters had been sent them and explicit orders given that they were to watch me as closely as they did the enemy, for fear I should try to cause a revolt. And when all this had happened as I have described, he allowed me to join the army in mid-summer and to carry his dress and image with me. He had both said and written that he was not giving the Gauls a ruler but one who should convey to them his image.

Julian, *Letter to the Athenians*, 24–25

But Julian, who had become a devotee of some esoteric schools of pagan philosophy – a fact unknown to Constantius – soon developed other plans.

In the summer of 357 CE Constantius ordered a complicated operation against the Alemanni in southern Germany, which involved moving many troops under a senior general west, from the region of what is now Switzerland, to meet up with Julian, who was commanding a smaller army. But the uncompliant Alemanni first defeated the larger Roman force, before encountering Julian's army in the vicinity of Argentoratum (Strasbourg), where the barbarians were crushed. Julian's victory established him as a major figure in his own right.

As for Constantius, after a campaign along the Danube he returned to the eastern frontier, where Roman forces continued to suffer significant setbacks. Most important of these were the losses of Amida, which was captured in 359 CE after a long siege, and of Singara, which was betrayed by its defenders the next year:

We waited there [in what is now northern Iraq] for two whole days, when the sun shone on the third day, we saw the whole expanse of the countryside, stretching as far as what we Greeks call the horizon, filled with innumerable columns of troops and the king going on ahead gleaming in his robes. Next to him [Sapor II] on the left rode Grumbates, king of the Chiniotae [a tribe to the east of the Persian Empire], a man of middle age with withered limbs but famous as a result of his great courage and ennobled by many famous victories; on the right rode the king of the Albanians, equal in rank and age; behind them rode a number of leaders, eminent from their power and authority, after whom came the mass of men of all ranks drawn from the neighbouring peoples and experienced in enduring harsh circumstances from long experience.

Ammianus, spying on an anticipated advance by the diverse allies that made up the Persian army in 359 CE

Figure XIX

Even before the death of Constantius, Julian advertised his paganism widely. The image of the bull on this coin is a symbol of traditional sacrifice.

The fate of Amida ultimately proved to be Constantius II's undoing. He needed to respond to the Persian successes, and to do that he required more men, so he ordered Julian to dispatch a portion of the *comitatenses* from Gaul. But the soldiers were unhappy. Two of the legions that had defended Amida were previously in the Gallic army, before being transferred east, never to return, as a punishment for supporting Magnentius. Julian, whose relationship with many of Constantius's officials was frosty at best, and who was increasingly convinced that his destiny was to restore the worship of Rome's traditional gods, connived to create a scene in Paris whereby the soldiers there proclaimed him emperor. There was nothing Constantius could do about this turn of events. He accepted Julian's statement that he would be *augustus* in Gaul but remain *caesar* in the east. The promise counted for little, for in 360 CE, after further successes along the Rhine – by contrast with further setbacks for Constantius against the Persians – Julian decided to invade the eastern empire. A lightning march along the Danube enabled him to absorb the Balkan *comitatenses*. Constantius II, whose health was failing, began to move west at the end of the eastern campaigning season; but on the 3rd of November, 361 CE, he died at Mopsuestia (in southeastern Turkey).

Julian now began openly to worship the old gods. He did not unleash persecution of the Christian Church *per se*, but the officials he killed were Christians, while those he favoured were not. Even a religious fellow-traveller like Ammianus – generally very favourable to Julian – thought his religious policies were extreme, and that the philosophers with whom Julian surrounded himself were frauds.

Julian was quite clear in his own mind that his policy required the prestige accruing from a major victory over the Persians. With the substantial portion of the western *comitatenses* that he had, he might confidently expect that outcome. The key figure in his plan of campaign was a brother of Sapor II named Hormisdas (Hormizd), who had fled west many years before, and whom Julian thought would be welcomed back by the Persians if he showed up in the company of a Roman army. This view was based on the dubious assumption that the average Persian must dislike Sapor II as much as the Romans did. As the campaign progressed in the summer of 363 CE, it became increasingly clear that Julian was not interested in hearing from anyone who doubted the truth of his view.

The campaign's plan involved dispatching a portion of the army to northern Mesopotamia. The intention was that they would distract Sapor from the main thrust of the operation, in which the bulk of the army would march along the Tigris, then follow Trajan's route across Mesopotamia to Ctesiphon, which – it was hoped – would abandon resistance and acknowledge Hormisdas as king. Strikingly, Julian planned to show up outside the city without even a siege train.

In the event, the Roman advance was slowed because the Persians opened the irrigation canals along the route across Mesopotamia, flooding the area of Julian's march. When he reached Ctesiphon, the city was fully prepared to withstand a siege that Julian was in no position to press, lacking not only a siege train but also supplies. It turned out, too, that the Persians had no interest in Hormisdas, whom they presumably took to be a Roman

A FORTUITOUS WONDER! THERE MET ME NEAR THE CITY THE CORPSE OF THAT ACCURSED ONE WHICH PASSED BY THE WALL; THE BANNER WHICH WAS SENT FROM THE EAST WIND THE MAGIAN TOOK AND FASTENED ON THE TOWER SO THAT A FLAG MIGHT POINT OUT FOR SPECTATORS THAT THE CITY WAS THE SLAVE OF THE LORDS OF THAT BANNER.

EPHREM SYRUS, *HYMN AGAINST JULIAN III*, 1

stooge. Julian had to withdraw, but, with the land behind him flooded, he could not return the way he had come. He intended, instead, to pillage his way up the Euphrates until he could cross back into Roman territory; he had not planned on the Persians ravaging the country ahead of him, nor that Sapor II, when he arrived at the head of his army, would be happy slowing the Roman progress north with raids rather than committing to a full-on battle. It was while rallying his men against one of these attacks that Julian, who appeared in the battleline without his armor, was stabbed by a Saracen serving in Sapor's army.

Julian died on the evening of the 24th of June, 363 CE. The general staff assembled to choose a new emperor, selecting for the job a relatively junior guard officer named Jovian. Senior officials made it clear that they were not interested in a task that would involve negotiating a very difficult truce with the Persians, nor in starving to death with the army. For his part, Sapor II saw that he could gain a great deal through negotiation. He drew up a treaty. By its terms, the Roman army would be unmolested on its return to Roman territory, but Rome would have to surrender any claims to influence in the regions of northern Iraq that had been surrendered by King Narses, and, furthermore, Rome would have to surrender Nisibis.

Fantasy, allied with arrogance and ignorance, had informed Julian's plan of conquest, and so it was that he – the last emperor who would worship the old gods – undid the successes of Diocletian and Galerius. The imperial division between east and west, solidified by Constantine's sons, would not now be undone. Henceforth, the entrenched bureaucracies of the eastern and western empires looked first to their own internal interests, even if that meant they lacked the capacity to dominate their neighbours. And all the empire's frontiers would be vulnerable to those neighbours.

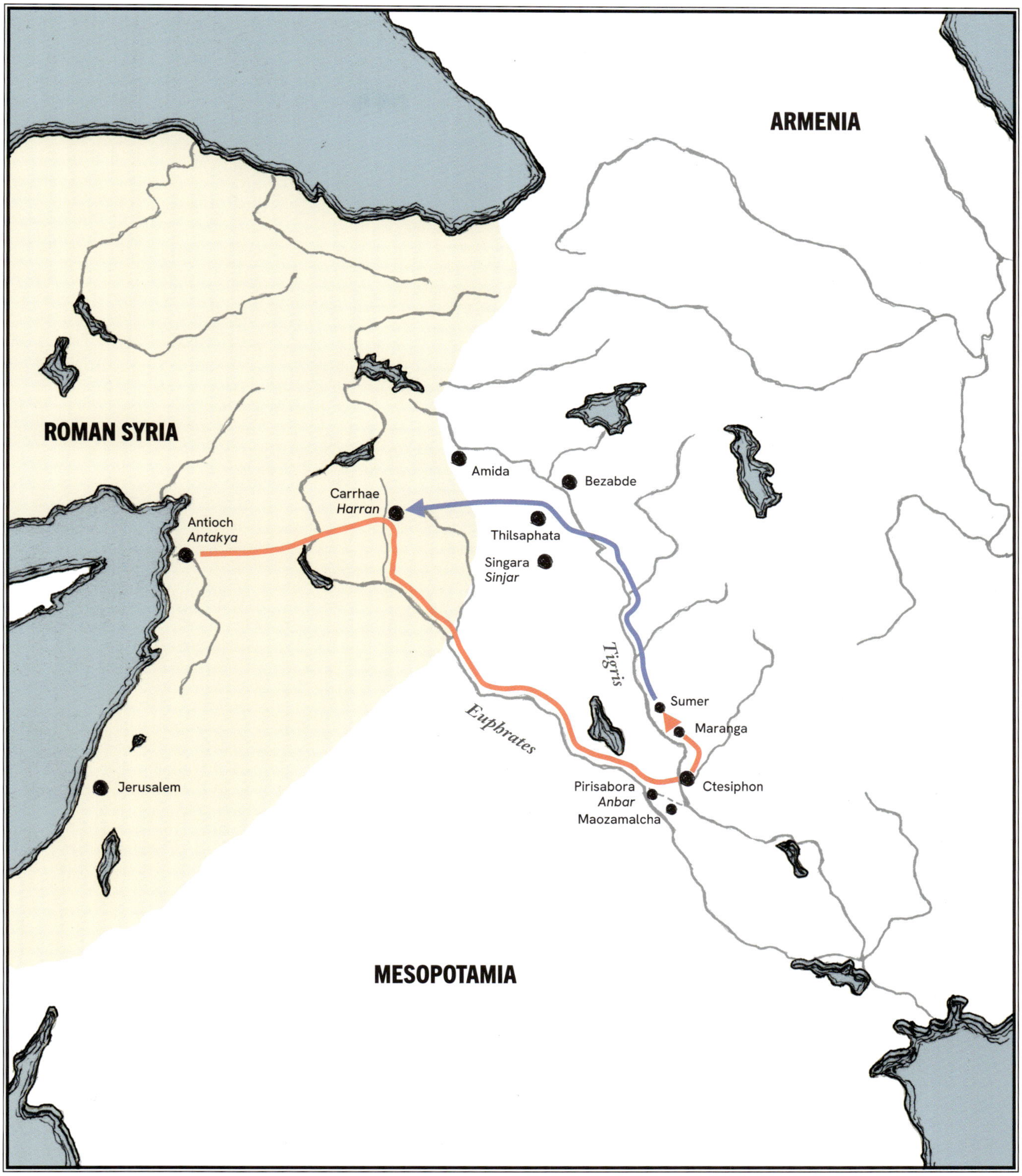

JULIAN'S INVASION OF PERSIA

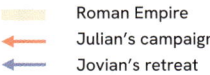

- Roman Empire
- Julian's campaign
- Jovian's retreat

CHRONOLOGY 280–370 CE

284 CE
Diocletian proclaimed *augustus* (20th of November).

285 CE
Defeat of Carinus; Maximian proclaimed *caesar* (21st of July); Maximian's campaigns in Gaul; Diocletian's campaigns in the Balkans.

286 CE
Maximian promoted to *augustus* (1st of April).

286 CE
Revolt of Carausius.

287 CE
Diocletian's treaty with the Persians, making Tiridates King of Armenia.

289 CE
Constantius's marriage to Theodora (daughter of Maximian).

290 CE
Carausius's defeat of Maximinus; Diocletian and Maximian meet in Milan.

293 CE
Constantius promoted to *caesar* (1st of March); Galerius promoted to *caesar* (21st of May); Galerius's marriage with Valeria (daughter of Diocletian); Diocletian reforms coinage.

296 CE
Persian invasion of Syria and defeat of Galerius at Carrhae.

297 CE
Revolt in Egypt, suppressed by Diocletian; Galerius's defeat of Persian King Narses.

299 CE
Peace of Nisibis: Persia cedes control of parts of northern Iraq to Rome.

301 CE
Diocletian's edict on maximum prices.

302 CE
Persecution of Manicheans ordered.

303 CE
Persecution of Christians ordered (23rd of February).

304 CE
Diocletian's meeting with Maximian in Rome, to celebrate twentieth anniversary of his reign.

305 CE
Abdication of Diocletian and Maximian (1st of May); Constantius and Galerius made *augusti*; Severus and Maximinus Daia made *caesars*.

306 CE
Death of Constantius in York (25th of July); Constantine acclaimed as *caesar* and recognized by Galerius; Severus promoted to *augustus*; Maxentius acclaimed as a de facto emperor in Rome (28th of October).

307 CE
Severus's abdication and imprisonment; Constantine's campaigns against the Franks; Constantine's marriage to Fausta (July or August); Galerius's failed invasion of Italy; Severus executed.

308 CE
Maximian's failed attempt to overthrow Maxentius; Licinius appointed (by Galerius) *augustus* for the western empire (11th of November).

310 CE
Constantine's campaigns against the Franks; Maximian's failed attempt to seize power, and his suicide; Constantine's claim of descent from Claudius II.

311 CE
Death of Galerius (April/May).

312 CE
Constantine's invasion of Italy: Battle of the Milvian Bridge (28th of October).

313 CE
Licinius's defeat of Maximinus Daia; Edict of Nicomedia, granting religious freedom to Christians.

316 CE
Constantine's attack on Licinius.

317 CE
Peace between Constantine and Licinius (1st of March): some Balkan provinces ceded to Constantine; Crispus, Constantine II and Licinius II recognized as *caesars*.

324 CE
Licinius deposed by Constantine; beginning of reconstruction of Byzantium to be the eastern imperial capital: Constantinople.

325 CE
Constantine's 'Oration to the Holy' at Easter; Council of Nicaea, and the Nicene Creed issued.

326 CE
Crispus executed; Fausta removed from public life.

232 — ATLAS OF THE ROMAN EMPIRE

330 — 340 — 350 — 360 — 370 — CE

330 CE
Dedication of Constantinople (11–12th of May).

336 CE
Death of Constantine 'the Great' (22nd of May); Constantine II, Constans and Constantius II become *augusti*; war with Persia.

337 CE
Sapor II of Persia repulsed from Nisibis.

338 CE
Roman control in Armenia restored (by Constantius II); Sapor II repulsed again at Nisibis.

339 CE
Constantine II assassinated: Constans takes over his territory.

343 CE
Persian victory at the Battle of Singara.

344 CE
Sapor II repulsed at Nisibis.

350 CE
Constans murdered on the orders of Magnentius, who becomes *augustus* in the west; Sapor II repulsed from Nisibis again.

351 CE
Gallus promoted to *caesar* by Constantius II; defeat of Magnentius at Mursa.

353 CE
Magnentius defeated again by Constantius II, at Mons Seleucus; Magnentius's suicide; reunification of the Roman Empire under Constantius II; Gallus executed.

355 CE
'Conspiracy' of Silvanus; Julian appointed *caesar* in Gaul.

356 CE
Julian's defeat of the Alamanni at Strasbourg.

359 CE
Persian capture of Amida.

360 CE
Julian proclaimed *augustus* in Gaul.

361 CE
Death of Constantius II (3rd of November); worship of traditional gods practised by Julian.

363 CE
Julian killed while invading Persia (26th of June); Jovian becomes emperor; treaty with Persia: the territory taken by Galerius and Nisibis surrendered.

CHAPTER 6

ENEMIES AT THE GATE: FROM JOVIAN TO THE SACK OF ROME

The new, Christian, Emperor Jovian's first task in 363 CE was to salvage the army that was now his, as both he and they retreated through Persia. In the circumstances, he had no choice but to negotiate an unfavourable treaty with his Persian enemies, but it enabled him to bring his surviving troops back to Antioch. Jovian would now have to try to reunite the badly divided society that his predecessor, Julian, had left behind, a task not helped by the bitter aftertaste of the surrender of Nisibis, necessary though it had been. Memories of the glorious defences of Nisibis under Constantius II were now wiped away by the sight of the Persian banner waving over the walls of the city (see page 229).

Jovian managed to negotiate the daunting task in front of him with considerable skill, seeking compromise wherever possible. Imperial compromise was a quality not much in evidence of late. Ammianus's comments on the tomb that Jovian erected for Julian at Tarsus indicate the bitterness the former emperor's pagan supporters felt, and suggest their capacity to create a fantasy image of Julian. At the same time, the Christian community remained deeply divided over doctrine, which played out with different factions vying for possession of the property that Julian had confiscated and which Jovian was now returning.

Jovian was reasonably successful in his effort to calm the controversies he faced, despite the whining of Ammianus and others. Perhaps he was even too successful. His assertion of control over the government, when he declared that his infant son (Varronian) would be consul in 364 CE, suggested that he had forgotten he was meant to act as a figurehead for the great and powerful on his staff. It should not be totally surprising that he was found dead on the 28th of February, 364 CE, in the village of Dadastana, western Anatolia. No investigation of the circumstances was carried out. According to one version, he died from inhaling noxious fumes in his bedroom; in another version, he suffered fatal indigestion. These stories seem as likely to be true as the tale that Carus had been struck by lightning to usher in the age of Diocletian.

The general staff met to choose a new emperor. The probability was that the people who had found Jovian too independent a soul would now seek a more pliable individual. Again, no senior officer would take the job, so another mid-level officer, Valentinian, was selected as *augustus*. To cement his positions, he then arranged for the murder of Varronian and the elevation of his own brother Valens to be his colleague. In their job division, Valentinian would govern the western empire, while Valens managed the east. They shared certain characteristics. Both men were notoriously bad-tempered, and neither had the capacity to manage the bureaucracies they inherited. Their failure would ultimately prove fatal to Rome's imperial project.

The first sign of the brothers' weakness involved Julian's nephew Procopius. He had gone into hiding after receiving news of his uncle's

Figure I

Jovian, a relatively junior guard officer when he was thrust into the role of emperor after Julian's death, restored Christianity as the empire's principal religion and attempted to reconcile the divisions caused by Julian.

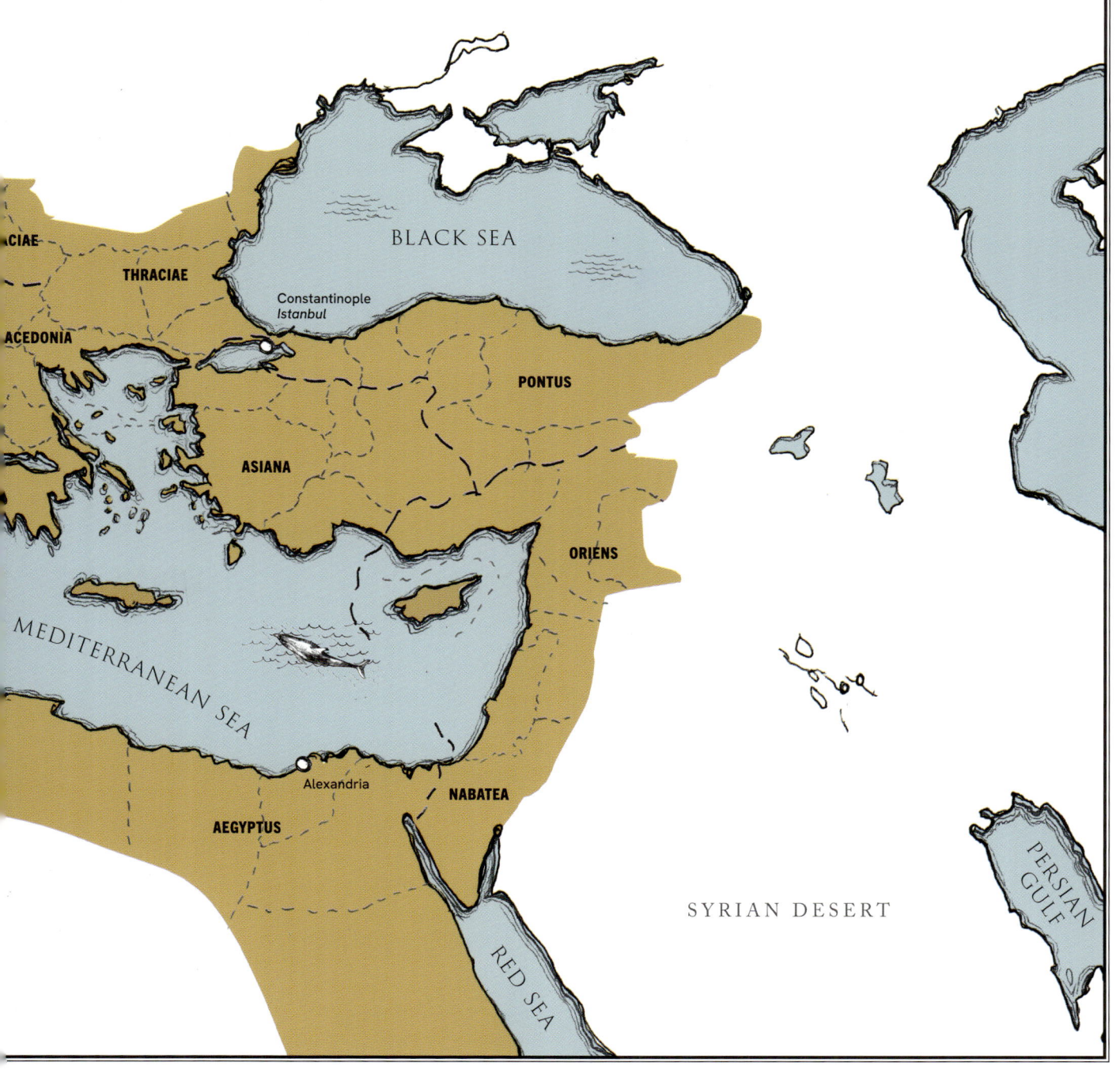

demise, only to emerge in September 365 CE, with the support of senior officials who had tired of Valens' brutality, to lead a revolt in Constantinople. Praetorian regiments there acclaimed him emperor. Procopius was able to win an initial battle with Valens, who was in western Turkey at the time, and gain further support by parading around Constantinople with the late Emperor Constantius's young daughter and widow. Had he moved more rapidly into the eastern provinces, he might have prevailed. However, his failure to act decisively enabled Valens to rally his forces. Now outnumbered, Procopius found himself deserted by many of his supporters, who went directly over to Valens, and two of them now turned Procopius over to Valens, who had the would-be emperor decapitated.

Procopius's revolt revealed a number of essential weaknesses in the administration of Valens in the eastern empire. Prone to cruelty, he possessed limited ability as a general. He was aware, however, that his continued rule depended upon his ability to construct a faction of supporters in the court; in this regard, his situation did not differ from that of Valentinian, whose generals explained to him that his job was in the west, and they would not follow him east if he tried to take on Procopius. The limitations on Valentinian's power were further illustrated a year after Procopius's defeat, when he fell seriously ill. The general staff elected Gratian, Valentinian's eight-year-old son, his co-*augustus* without asking Valentinian if this was what he wanted.

Plainly, Valentinian's general staff were not very interested in dealing with an emperor who would presume to order them around. Soon, the head of the general staff for each emperor's army would be in the form of a new role, *magister militum* (master of the soldiers), a post invented in the early 370s CE to create a new level of command above the *magister peditum* (master of infantry) and *magister equitum* (master of cavalry). The *magister militum* would become the military equivalent of the Praetorian prefect, as the officials who had been in effective control of the civilian administration had been known since the time of Diocletian. In the company of these officials, the emperor was something of an odd man out.

The weakness of both Valentinian and Valens was a factor in their persistent displays of ill-temper, and limited the extent of their military operations. Valens launched some minor operations north of the Danube, where the Gothic tribes along the river were developing new political structures, dividing into two coalitions: the Greuthungi and the Thervingi. As for Valentinian, who remained in the Gallic provinces throughout his reign, he launched raids on the Alamanni and the Franks. Both *augusti* were constantly looking over their shoulders at their senior

Figure II (left)

Valentinian, who became emperor upon the death of Jovian and ruled from 364 until 375 CE, was also a relatively junior guard officer before his selection. Noted for his fierce temper, he formalized the administrative division of the western and eastern empires.

Figure III (opposite)

Valens, the younger brother of Valentinian, had some difficulty asserting control over his senior administrators after his appointment in 364 CE. His insecurity led to several scandals and was a factor in his catastrophic defeat at Adrianople in 378.

Figure IV (opposite)

Gratian, Valentinian's elder son, was proclaimed his father's co-emperor by the senior administrators of the west when his father was ill in 367 CE. He was murdered after his army deserted him for Magnus Maximus in 383.

Figure V (above)

Theodosius I seized the throne of the eastern empire in 379 CE. He was a devout Christian who enforced the Nicene Creed as the definition of Christian orthodoxy and allowed the settlement of Gothic communities within the empire's boundaries.

subordinates, concerned lest one of them should obtain a success that overshadowed their own. One such man was Valentinian's *magister militum*, Theodosius, who won significant victories – in Britain, against invaders from Scotland, then along the Danube. His alleged ambitions were curtailed by his execution, on suspicion of aspiring to the throne, and ironically after he had suppressed a usurper in Africa. The dispatch of Theodosius in 375 CE proved to be Valentinian's final major decision. He died shortly thereafter, having suffered an apoplectic fit while listening to an embassy from the Quadi, a Germanic group based north of the Danube.

THREE EMPERORS – AND A GOTHIC INFLUX

As news of Valentinian's demise spread, a major split in the government of the western empire manifested itself. Gratian, now aged 16, was based in Gaul, but the leadership of the army in the Balkans, as well as the civilian authorities there and in Italy, had no interest in subordinating themselves to the Gallic government. They suspected those officials of having connived in Theodosius's death as well as some bloody interventions in Italy, where prominent members of the senate had been executed for engaging in supposedly magical practices. Under the leadership of the *magister peditum*, Merobaudes, they arranged to elevate Valentinian's four-year-old son, also named Valentinian, to the throne in Italy and the Balkans. From the east, Valens acquiesced in this decision, as did the Gallic aristocracy, for to do otherwise would have been to start a civil war. The Roman Empire now had three *augusti*. In one of the more remarkable statements in his historical

Figure VI

The Gothic communities that entered the empire after 375 CE had been shaped by long contact with the empire. The diverse units they deployed were modelled on the contemporary Roman army, with a combination of cavalry with heavy and light infantry.

writing, Ammianus gives a perspective on how Gratian took the elevation of his younger brother to *augustus* of his own portion of the empire:

> *When this was done, some thought that Gratian would take it badly that another emperor had been put in place without his permission, but this fear was later put aside and peace of mind returned because Gratian was a kindly and intelligent man who cherished his kinsman with great devotion and guided his ways.*

Ammianus Marcellinus, *History*, 30.10.6

As the regime was changing in the west, Valens' domain in the east was experiencing fresh challenges. A few years previously in Antioch, in 372 CE, the emperor had dealt with a bizarre event in which a senior official named Theodorus had told him he was destined to be Valens' successor. Theodorus had learned this because some colleagues, consulting a prophetic device, had discovered that the next emperor would have a name beginning with the Greek letters *theta* (th), *eta* (e), *omicron* (o) and *delta* (d):

> *The device was placed in the middle of a house scented with Arabian spices throughout, covered with a round dish made from a variety of metals. The outer edge of the dish was inscribed with the twenty-four letters of the [Greek] alphabet ... A priest dressed in linen garments ... recited a set prayer to invoke the divine power that presides over prophecy. He then stood above the tripod in accordance with his knowledge of ceremonial acts, and set a ring swinging, suspended from a very thin cotton thread. The ring moved in a series of jumps over the marked-out spaces, coming to rest on certain letters, which made up the verses appropriate to the question, perfect in number and meter just like the verses of the Delphic oracle or the oracle at Didyma. Then, when we asked who would succeed the present emperor, since it had been said that he would be excellent in every way, the ring touched upon two syllables THEO, and when the next letter was added, one of those present shouted that Theodorus was indicated by the decision of undeniable fate.*

Ammianus Marcellinus, *History*, 29.1.30–32

Valens exploded. He demanded the immediate execution of Theodorus and rounded up all those connected with the prophecy, ordering their torture and execution. That Theodorus even imagined he could have the conversation he did with Valens suggests how weak Valens was perceived to be.

Valens treated anyone suspected of having been connected with Theodorus with intense brutality, violating laws that ordinarily protected senior officials from torture and the most brutal death penalties. Ammianus wrote that the ghosts of those killed as a result of the Theodorus affair were still haunting the empire when a great crisis arose along the Danubian frontier in the mid-370s CE. Valens had been in Antioch because he engaged in a desultory conflict with Sapor II over the succession to the throne of Armenia. But while this was going on, aggression from the people known as the Huns upset the political order north of the Danube. While the Thervingi and Greuthungi were agriculturalists, supported in large measure by trade across the frontier with Rome, the Huns appear to have been a more nomadic group, albeit related to other Gothic peoples. Although their aggressive tendencies had hitherto been kept in check by their more settled neighbours, they suddenly achieved a series of bloody victories. These enabled them to raid the territory of the Greuthungi at will and to threaten the territory of the Thervingi, who now sought refuge in Roman lands.

No preparations had been made to receive a large group of people into the empire, but Valens saw the refugees as a potential source of new soldiers whose presence would preserve the empire's tax base, since they would replace the need to draw new recruits from the tax-paying population. In addition, a supply of fresh recruits would become especially useful if the situation in Armenia headed in the direction of all-out war. So it was that the Thervingi, followed by a large band of Greuthungi, were allowed to cross the Danube.

The official in charge of receiving these Goths was a man named Lupicinus, who appears to have been over-promoted from the mid-level commands he had held in the Balkans during the previous decade. His immediate subordinate, Maximus, described by Ammianus as 'that disastrous general', was plainly no better. They had made no preparation to feed the new arrivals, and, when they saw them starving, they began to offer them dogs in exchange for humans, whom they proceeded to enslave as the column moved inland towards an as yet undetermined location. When the Goths reached the city of Marcianopolis (present-day Devnya, Bulgaria), Lupicinus invited their leaders to dinner. As they ate together, the Goths who had been allowed into the city began to loot the marketplace. Lupicinus murdered the bodyguards who had accompanied his dinner guests, but allowed the important Gothic leader Fritigern to leave with his companions, because Fritigern said he could calm things down in the city. It did not turn out quite like that. Rejoining his people, Fritigern began raiding the region – and inflicted a serious defeat on Lupicinus when the Roman official tried to stop him. There were now no substantial Roman forces to resist the Goths.

Fritigern led his people through the Roman provinces, looting as he went but avoiding towns, saying he 'didn't wage war with walls'. In the meantime, Emperor Valens ended his conflict with the Persians over Armenia and began to assemble a fresh army in the Balkans, while appealing to Gratian for assistance. Gratian agreed to send aid, but the numbers were not as great as Valens might have hoped, given that the *magister peditum*, Merobaudes, again began acting rather independently. He convinced many of the troops sent on the expedition to abandon it, on the grounds that too many threats remained in the west. Those who did arrive from Gratian's western empire were led by a man named Richomer, who, like Merobaudes, was descended from Frankish ancestors. He joined with the small detachment arrived from the eastern army, at the end of 377 CE, to engage Fritigern's Goths in battle. They fought all day, but neither side could claim a decisive victory; the Roman troops withdrew, however, and the Goths continued to ravage the Balkans.

Figure VII

The infantry of the later Roman army, when deployed in the field, had largely abandoned the heavier armour of earlier periods to promote greater tactical flexibility.

The story of the Gothic migration to this point reveals significant lack of coordination on the part of the Roman regime, and a comparable degree of incompetence. The situation would worsen in the coming year. It started off well; Gratian opened the year campaigning along the Rhine with considerable success, before beginning a march east to assist his uncle. Unfortunately, Valens, who arrived from Syria in the summer with a substantial force, became anxious that Gratian was obtaining the kind of success that had so far eluded him. He decided not to wait for his nephew's arrival before taking on the Goths. The Goths had now moved east, from raiding the province of Thrace to areas closer to Constantinople. On the 9th of August, 378 CE, Valens encountered them near Adrianople. The result was a disaster for the Romans. Valens died on the battlefield, along with some twenty thousand of his men. It was a momentous event, for the Roman Empire would never recover from the consequences of this defeat.

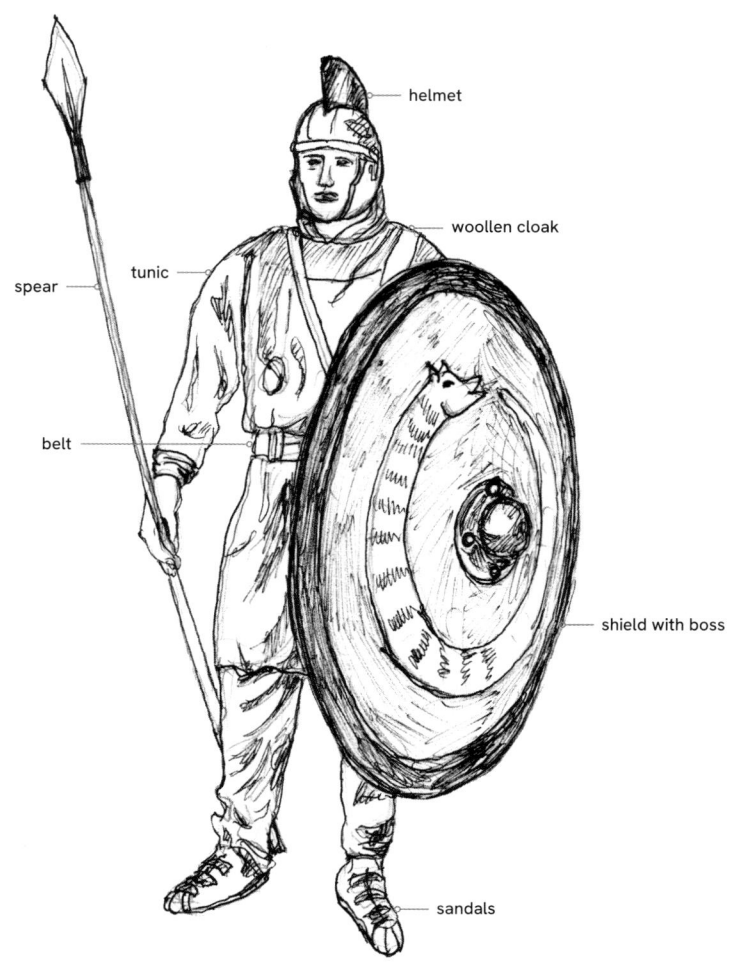

THE BATTLE OF ADRIANOPLE

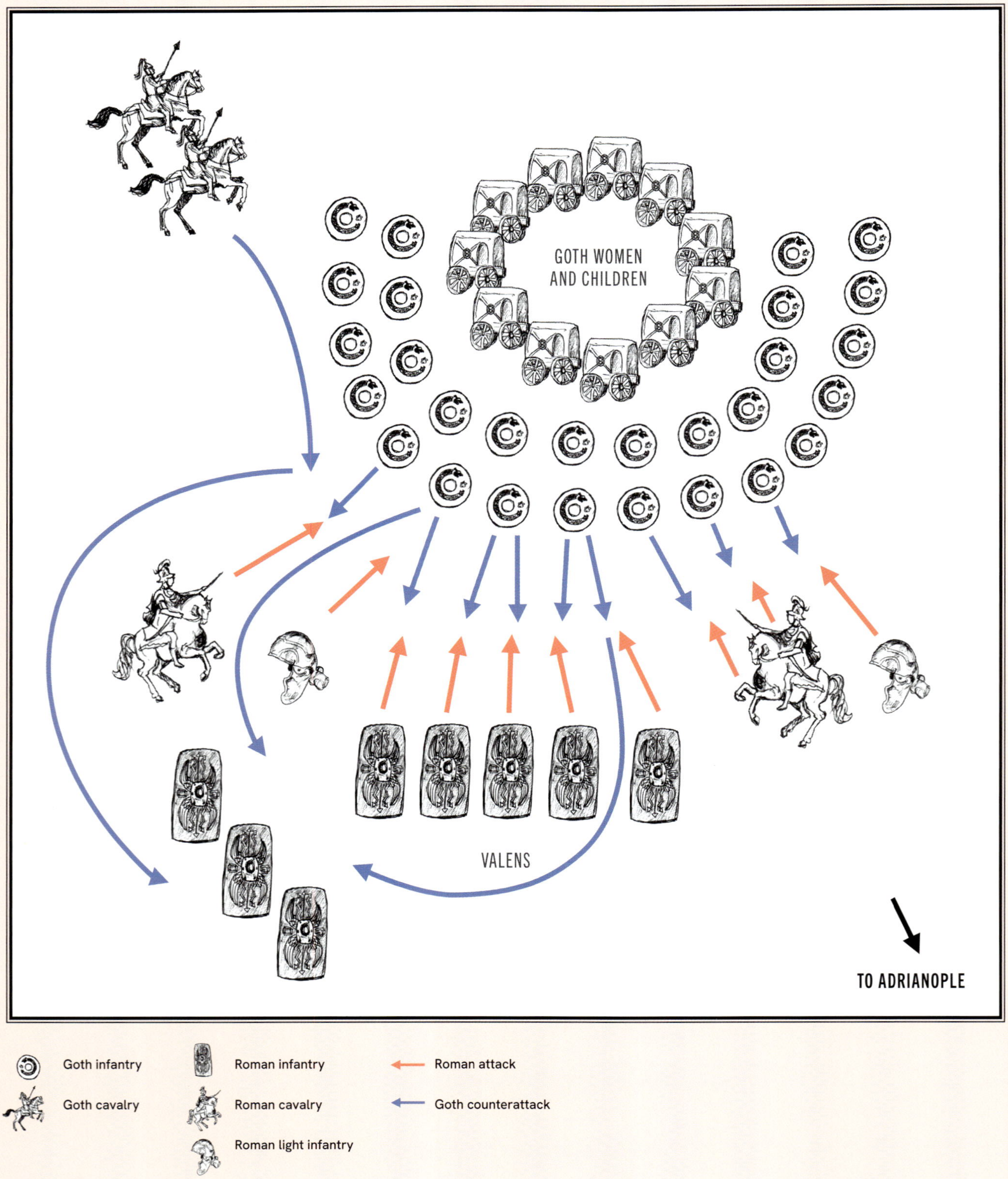

VALENS

TO ADRIANOPLE

 Goth infantry
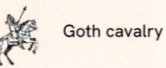 Goth cavalry
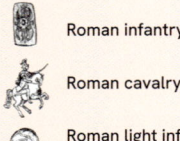 Roman infantry
Roman cavalry
Roman light infantry
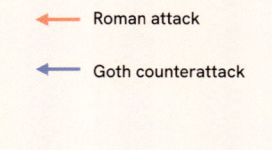 Roman attack
Goth counterattack

The present-day Turkish city of Edirne is on the site of the ancient city of Adrianople. It was there, in mid-August 378 CE, that Emperor Valens erected a camp for his army, sending scouts to observe the movement of the Goths in the region. Although some of his officers urged him to await his nephew Gratian and so obtain a significant numerical superiority over the enemy, who were led by Fritigern, 'the fatal resolve of the emperor and flattery of some courtiers' prevailed (Ammianus Marcellinus, *History*, 31.12.7). Valens decided to attack the Goths on his own. On the morning of the 9th of August the Roman army marched 13 kilometres (8 miles) through the blazing sunshine to find the circled wagons of the Gothic encampment. When they arrived, Fritigern – who was waiting for his cavalry to return from a raid – pretended to negotiate. At the same time, his men set fires in the neighbourhood to worsen the situation of the Roman forces, who had insufficient water, had not eaten in hours and were further worn down by the weight of their armour.

While the sham negotiations continued, a unit on the Roman left wing launched its own attack on the Gothic wagons. This was repulsed, however, when the long-awaited Gothic cavalry returned and fell on the disordered ranks of the Romans as they retreated. The Gothic cavalry then overwhelmed the Roman left wing, allowing the Goths to surround the rest of the Roman army, who were now so crowded that they could not use their weapons effectively. Some died without knowing who had struck them; many others were crushed by the weight of numbers, and yet others were killed accidentally by their own comrades. Only a third of the Roman army at Adrianople escaped. Valens himself vanished in the rout. Rumour had it that he had been wounded and was taken to a hut that was burned by the Goths, who did not realize he was in it. The only consolation for the Roman side was that afterwards Fritigern failed to capture Adrianople, where the Roman survivors had fled. He mounted a brief raid in the direction of Constantinople before returning to ravage the Balkan provinces.

THEODOSIUS AND HIS CHALLENGERS

With his uncle now dead, Gratian could – as the senior surviving *augustus* – have claimed sovereignty over the eastern empire. But could he be sure that the eastern bureaucracy would accept him? The signs were that he would be a hard sell to them. Instead of doing battle with the Goths, he returned to the west and appointed two senior military commanders (*magistri militum*), one for the eastern frontier and one for the diocese (as this group of provinces and other, similar groups had been known since Diocletian's time) of Illyricum. The latter was a rather ill-defined appointment, which probably included authority over the idle armies of his brother Valentinian II, as well as the remnants of Valens' forces in the Balkans. The man Gratian chose to take command of Illyricum was named Theodosius – son of the Theodosius whom Gratian's father had executed a few years before.

Although he had no experience of senior command, the younger Theodosius was a fast learner. After a victory over the Sarmatians – another group from north of the Danube that had moved south after Valens' demise – he prepared to claim the title of *augustus* for himself. In the official version of events, which we have from a speech delivered by an imperial propagandist in the summer of 379 CE, it was Theodosius's inherent virtue – as announced by Gratian – that made him emperor; Gratian and his advisers appear to have felt that anyone who wanted to be eastern Emperor under the circumstances was welcome to the job.

Nevertheless, Theodosius knew that he must tread carefully. He could not really claim the throne, or indeed show himself in Constantinople, until he had solved the problem of the Thervingi and Greuthungi, whose shared experience of victory and pillage was gradually shaping them into a cohesive new community. Having set up court at Thessalonica, and after suffering a defeat of his own at the hands of the Goths, he made a treaty with them. By its terms, they received their own, autonomous territory in the Balkans, which was largely taken from the lands technically controlled by Valentinian II; in return, the Thervingi and Greuthungi offered service, when required, as *foederati* (confederates) with the army of the eastern empire, fighting under their own leaders rather than Romans. Although this treaty seemed to hark back to such deals as the one Gallienus had made with the Palmyrenes, in this new arrangement the Gothic leaders had no official position within the Roman state. They remained independent contractors. It was, in fact, a blueprint for the break-up of the Roman Empire.

Despite the weakness of the arrangement Theodosius had made with the Goths, Gratian could imagine that the course of events had solved the crisis and established a regime that he could present as being a product of his own generosity in the east. But he had spent too much time away from his base in Gaul. In 383 CE he took his court to northern Italy to confront the Alamanni. In strategic terms, this move made sense; in political terms, it was a serious mistake. There seems to have been a general view that Gratian was too readily influenced by those around him, and by withdrawing from the headquarters of the Gallic armies at Trier, he was cutting off his commanders from access to him. Failure to understand the lens through which his subordinates viewed him would soon prove fatal.

Even as Gratian was settling into his new base, Magnus Maximus, the governor of Britain, rebelled and brought his army over to Gaul, where his troops acclaimed him *augustus*. In the spring of 383 CE his army confronted Gratian's forces near Paris, in a stand-off that ended after five days with the bulk of Gratian's men deserting him. Gratian fled as far as Lugdunum (Lyons), where he was killed on the 25th of August. The Greek historian Zosimus reported his downfall:

Figure VIII

Magnus Maximus gained a reputation as an excellent soldier while commanding Roman forces in Britain. Overthrowing Gratian in 383 CE, he shared power with Gratian's brother Valentinian until 387, when he expelled Valentinian from Italy. That act led to a war with Theodosius I, which Magnus lost.

> *While the affairs of Thrace were set in order, those of Gratian were overturned. Having put his trust in the advice of courtiers who usually corrupt the habits of emperors, he took in some fugitives called Alans, whom he not only introduced into his army, but honoured with valuable gifts, and entrusted them with his most important secrets, placing little value in his own troops. This produced a violent hatred against the emperor among his troops, which was gradually inflamed and increased a desire for revolt, especially in those who formed the garrison of Britain since they were especially wilful. Maximus, a Spaniard, who had been a companion of the Emperor Theodosius in Britain, encouraged this mood in them. He was offended that Theodosius should be thought worthy of being made emperor, while he himself obtained no powerful position. He built up the animosity of the soldiers towards the emperor. They were thus easily convinced to revolt and to declare Maximus emperor. Having presented to him the purple robe and the diadem, they sailed across the sea to the mouth of the Rhine. When the German army and all who were in the area approved of the election, Gratian prepared to fight him, with the considerable part of the army which was still with him. When the armies approached each other, there were skirmishes for five days; until Gratian, seeing that his North African cavalry deserted from him and declared Maximus Augustus, and then that the remainder of his troops were gradually taking up his rival's cause, relinquished all hope and fled with three hundred cavalrymen to the Alps.*

Zosimus, *New History*, 4.35.3–4

The next year, both Valentinian II and Theodosius recognized Maximus as their co-*augustus*.

Maximus remained a powerful figure in British folklore into the Middle Ages. In Welsh myth, he was identified as Macsen Wledig, a Roman emperor who fell in love with a Welsh woman he had seen in a dream, and with whom he would continue to live, in Wales; and when the Roman people elected a new emperor in his absence, he returned to the continent and reconquered his empire. That version, which prefigured the career of King Arthur, was picked up in the twelfth century by the Welshman Geoffrey of Monmouth and included in his chronicle of British kings.

The real Magnus Maximus was less successful. He had initially left Valentinian II alone, tacitly recognizing the authority of Theodosius as the person who would maintain the balance between the two groups, and he allowed Theodosius to extend his influence over the Italian regime. As for Theodosius, he found Maximus (a tangential relative who had served under his father) to be an acceptable new co-emperor. This situation ended at the end of 386 CE, when Maximus launched a sudden invasion of Italy. Valentinian II fled to Thessalonica, where his mother, Justina, is said to have convinced Theodosius – who would marry her daughter Galla – to invade the west. In the summer of 388 CE Theodosius moved faster than Maximus expected, defeating his advanced forces in the Balkans, seizing his supply depots and arresting Maximus himself, who had no time to organize an adequate defence, at Aquileia. Having overreached himself, Maximus was executed. Valentinian II, who had returned to Rome by sea while Theodosius's armies advanced on Italy, was restored to his nominal position of *augustus*.

Theodosius now took advantage of his position to strip the western field army of several units for service in the east, and to staff the western government with his own people. His marshals began to exert an iron grip over the region. Prominent among them was his *magister militum*, the Frankish general Arbogast, who ruthlessly mopped up any of Maximus's remaining sympathizers and placed Valentinian under virtual house arrest in Vienne, after Theodosius returned to Constantinople. In 392 CE Valentinian II tried to depose Arbogast by letter; Arbogast tore up the missive and replied that, as an appointee of Theodosius, he did not take orders from Valentinian.

A few days later Valentinian II was found dead. He had allegedly committed suicide, but the historian Orosius, writing in the early fifth century CE, disagreed. He regarded the empire's problems as stemming from the misconduct of pagans, a view expressed in his seven-volume *History against the Pagans* (*Historiae Adversus Paganos*). In Orosius's opinion, the pagan sympathizer Arbogast had arranged for Valentinian to be murdered:

> *Thus, Valentinian the Younger was restored to his throne, with Maximus and his son Victor, whom Maximus had left as emperor in Gaul, dead. Valentinian came to Gaul. Here, while he ruled a tranquil state in peace, he was strangled at Vienne through the treason of his count, Arbogast, and then suspended from a noose so that people might think he had ended his own life.*

Orosius, *History Against the Pagans*, 7.35.10

The fact that Arbogast was a Frank disqualified him from taking the throne himself, given the residual anti-German sentiment in the empire. Instead, he selected a senator named Eugenius to play the role of *augustus*. The move looks as though it was intended to create an alliance between Arbogast and the wealthiest elements of the Italian aristocracy, who appear to have become tired of taking orders from the imperial court at Milan. They also resented Milan's bishop, Ambrose, who seemed to them to have become excessively powerful in recent years. Arbogast is reported to have told Ambrose that if he defeated Theodosius, he would turn Ambrose's church into a stable.

Ambrose, the son of a Praetorian prefect, had first asserted his power in a dispute with Valentinian II about where the emperor's Gothic soldiers could pray. The priest had argued that since they were not orthodox believers, they could not use his church. It was generally asserted at the time that the Goths had been converted by followers of the Alexandrian Arius, with his emphasis on Jesus's humanity; by this time the Goths themselves might have adopted this anti-orthodox identity for themselves, even though there is no reason to think Arius's followers had anything to do with their conversion, which began under Constantine. After a tense stand-off and the miraculous discovery of the relics of two martyrs, Ambrose had got his way. A few years later he had played a leading role in removing the Altar of Victory from the senate house. This was a pure power-play on his part, since the Bishop of Rome was willing to leave the altar in place, and the majority of senators who convened in its presence were Christians. In addition, he had quarrelled with Theodosius on two occasions, once even excommunicating the emperor and forcing him to submit to ecclesiastical authority in order to be readmitted to communion.

In light of Ambrose's history, there is no need to assume that Arbogast's well-advertised hatred of the man stemmed from anti-Christian feeling rather than a weariness of Ambrose's meddling in secular affairs. Their mutual animosity would, however, lend the emerging conflict between Arbogast and Theodosius a religious dimension. Theodosius's propagandists suggested that Arbogast openly placed his faith in the power of the old gods. For his part, Theodosius – as his own willingness to tolerate Ambrose's combative conduct shows – was a devout Christian and an aggressive supporter of the definition of the faith deriving from the Nicene Creed. He went further than Constantine had ever done when, in 392 CE, he issued a law banning all forms of pagan sacrifice.

When the forces of Eugenius (under Arbogast) and Theodosius came to blows in what is now western Slovenia, at the Battle of the Frigidus (6th of September, 394 CE), Theodosius attributed his eventual victory to the intervention of a violent storm, which he proclaimed to be a divine miracle. More prosaically, his victory appears to have stemmed from miscalculations by his opponents and the courage of his own Gothic *foederati*, whom Theodosius had deployed in large numbers – and with serious losses – against Arbogast's defences. Theodosius's willingness to fight to the last Goth is unlikely to have endeared him to the future commander of those forces: Alaric.

THE BATTLE OF THE FRIGIDUS

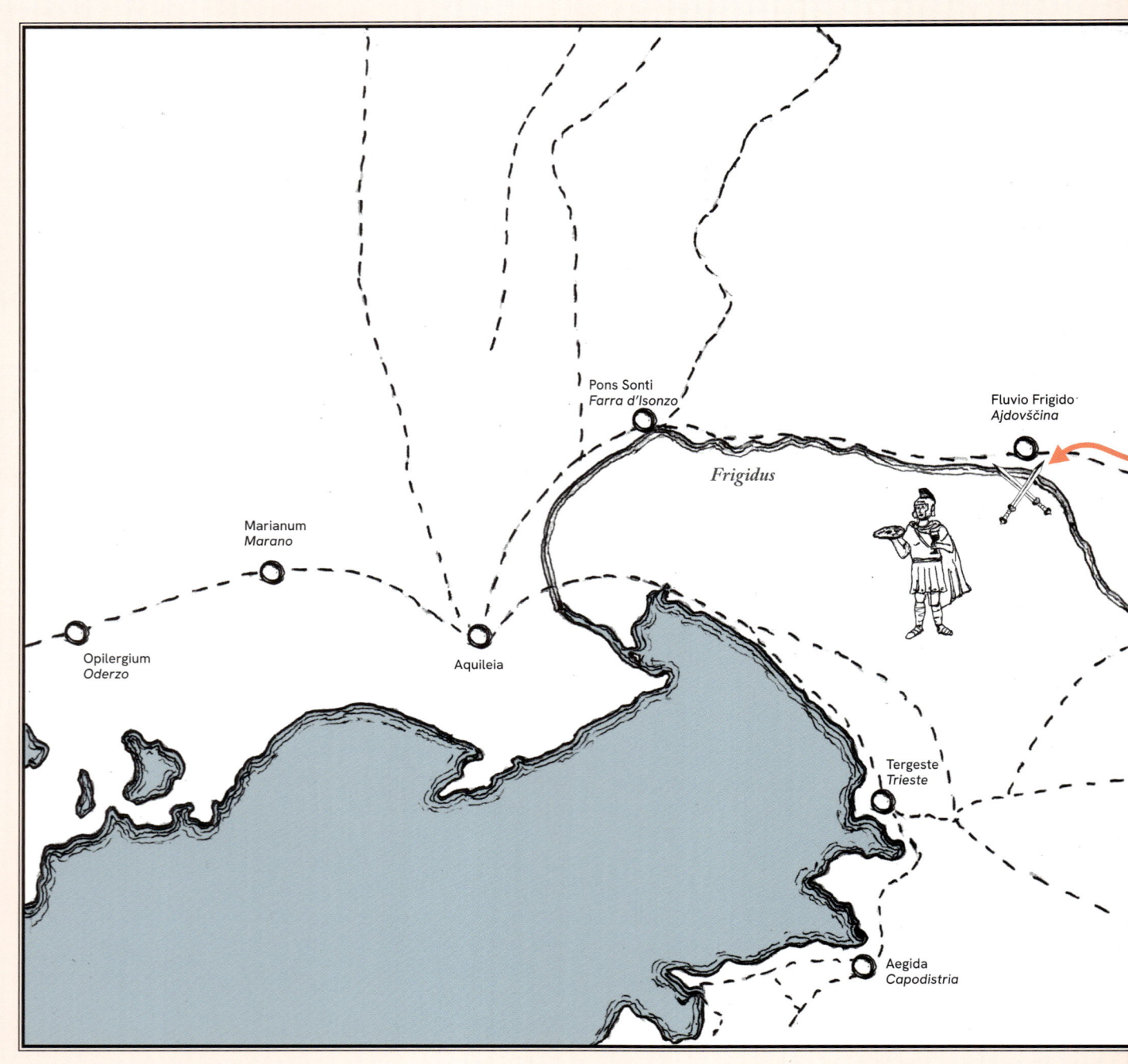

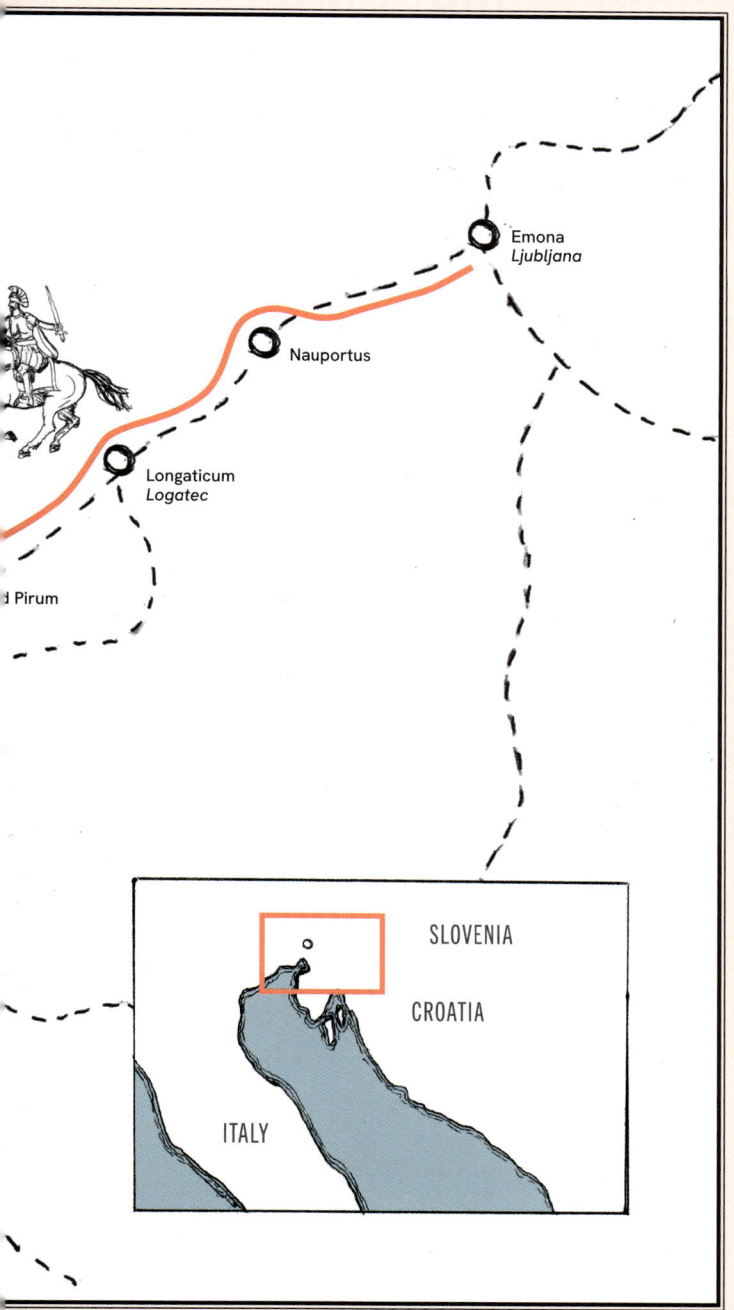

The River Frigidus, where Theodosius defeated Arbogast and Eugenius in 394 CE, is in western Slovenia. Although the precise location of the spot remains controversial, contemporary descriptions of the battle indicate that the terrain through which the river ran was bounded on either side by ridges. According to a description in a history composed by the pagan Zosimus in the sixth century CE, Theodosius used his Gothic allies to launch a series of unsuccessful and costly attacks on Eugenius's forces throughout the first day of the conflict, during which time there was an eclipse of the sun. In the wake of his successful defence, Eugenius fed his men a generous dinner – so generous that they were still weighed down by the banquet the next day, when Theodosius launched a fresh attack that overwhelmed them. Christian sources assert that Eugenius and his colleagues made sacrifices to the ancient gods in order to secure the aid of demons; they also acknowledge that Theodosius deliberately allowed his Gothic allies to be routed because he did not want to seem to triumph through the aid of barbarians. Instead, when he saw the Goths being driven back, he prayed to the Christian God, who sent a powerful wind that blew in his enemies' faces, turning their missiles back against them and breaking their spirit.

It is plain that the Christian versions of the story, which falsely characterize Arbogast and Eugenius as pagans, are heavily influenced by Theodosius's propaganda and his desire to assert the power of his faith. While it is very likely that Theodosius prayed for victory, the storm that ensured the victory – often identified as the *bora*, the heavy downslope winds that blow in the region where the battle took place – is a fabrication to enhance the bogus religious element.

Following his victory, Theodosius had Arbogast and Eugenius executed. He then moved into Italy to re-establish his authority. Before leaving on campaign, Theodosius had elevated his teenaged son Arcadius to the rank of *augustus* in the east, a sign perhaps that he intended to remain in the west for some time. That was not to be. He died at Milan at age 49, in January 395 CE. Honorius, his son and successor in the west, was a mere 11 years old.

Theodosius was the last emperor who could claim to rule the territories of the eastern and western portions of the empire and their respective bureaucracies. Following his death, these lands were divided into two equal parts. The Balkan dioceses of Illyricum and Macedonia were allocated to the western empire, while Moesia and Thrace stayed with the east. With Illyricum went the land the Goths had settled after making the treaty with Theodosius. The specifics of this division would determine the future course of Roman history, for the Goths now became an exclusively western 'problem'.

POWERS BEHIND THE THRONES

Arcadius and Honorius, the sons of Theodosius, were now to reign as figureheads for the senior members of the bureaucracy. In the west this would be Flavius Stilicho, the son of a German officer and a Roman mother; he was *magister utriusque militiae* (master of both services). In the east, the leading figure at court was Rufinus, the Praetorian prefect.

The scene was not set for harmony, since Stilicho and Rufinus hated each other. It was a mutual detestation that played into the hands of Alaric, who had now emerged as leader of the Gothic army. He had learned enough about the workings of the imperial bureaucracy to realize that the only way to prevent his men from being cheated, as he felt was currently the case, would be if a Goth became *magister militum*. He volunteered himself for the position, and therefore his men could be added to the army's permanent payroll. To force the hand of the Romans, he led his army into Macedonia – a sensible move, since the bulk of the eastern army was still in the west, where it had remained after the campaign of 392 CE. Stilicho's army consisted of both regular Roman soldiers and a large number of *foederati*, who formed his personal military entourage. The compensation given to the latter group probably provided the model to which Alaric aspired when he moved into Macedonia.

Even though the provinces that Alaric was attacking were in the eastern empire, Stilicho set off in pursuit, claiming that Theodosius had intended him to act as regent for both Arcadius and Honorius. Later, he would make another claim: that Alaric's rebellious inspiration came from Rufinus. According to Stilicho's propagandists, the reason Rufinus was conspiring with Alaric to wreck portions of the empire he controlled was that Rufinus intended nothing less than the destruction of Roman civilization. Such blathering was represented by the poet Claudian. His language gives a sense of the sort of prejudice that made dealings between Rome and the peoples of Central Europe – who were pictured as eternal barbarians alienated from civilized life – so difficult:

Figure IX (opposite, left)

Arcadius was left in titular control of the eastern empire when Theodosius departed for the west in 394 CE, becoming *augustus* at the age of 17, when his father died. His advisers dominated him throughout his reign, which ended with his death in 408.

Figure X (opposite, right)

Honorius became emperor in 395 CE at the age of 11. He had his father-in-law, Stilicho – the dominant figure at court – murdered in 408. His bigotry and incompetence resulted in the break-up of the western empire.

> *The varied horde of Sarmatians and Dacians, the violent Massagetes who wound their horses that they may drink their blood, the Alans who break the ice and drink the waters of Lake Maeotis, and the Geloni who tattoo their limbs[,] marches against us: this is Rufinus's army. He does not allow for their defeat; he creates delays and postpones the appropriate season for battle. When your right hand, Stilicho, had scattered the Gothic bands and avenged the death of your brother general, when one section of Rufinus's army was thus weakened and easy prey, that foul traitor, that conspirator with the Goths, tricked the emperor and put off the imminent day of battle, so he could ally himself with the Huns, who, as he knew, would fight and rapidly join the enemy camp.*

Claudian, *Against Rufinus*, 1.310–22

The propaganda concealed Stilicho's real problem, which was that his army was dysfunctional, given that it combined forces from east and west that had recently been at war with each other. Claudian claimed that it was Arcadius's demand for the return of the eastern army that prevented Stilicho from destroying Alaric, but the likelihood is that the divisions in Stilicho's own camp forced him to break off the pursuit and send half his army to Constantinople.

Stilicho handed command of the eastern troops over to Gainas, a Goth who had risen to high command under Theodosius. When these forces reached Constantinople, Gainas promptly arranged for Rufinus to be assassinated at a military review. With a loyal supporter now in charge of the eastern army, Stilicho might well have imagined that he had succeeded, at minimal cost, in making himself effective master of the empire. This would not turn out to be the case, for Gainas formed a new alliance with the eunuch Eutropius. He was the man who dominated Arcadius's court, and who had lately been Stilicho's ally while Rufinus was still in the picture. But now Eutropius struck out on his own. In the autumn of 397 CE he convinced Arcadius to summon a meeting of the senate, at which Stilicho was declared a public enemy in the eastern empire.

That declaration did not constrain Stilicho's activities elsewhere. Between the years of 396 and 399 CE, not only was he campaigning on the Rhine, in the Balkans (against Alaric) and in Britain, but also he had to contend with a rebellion across the Mediterranean, in the Roman diocese of Africa. His propagandist, Claudian, ostensibly lauded Emperor Honorius but in the process trumpeted Stilicho as the power behind the throne, while also attacking Eutropius:

> *It happened that even as the august Honorius, assisted by his father-in-law Stilicho, answered the Germans who had come willingly to sue for peace, from his [Honorius's] lofty throne he was dictating laws to the Cauci [a northern people] and giving a constitution to the blond Sueves. He gave kings to these peoples, and, having demanded hostages, he signs a treaty with them; he adds others to the list of allies so that, with their long hair cut, the Sygambrians [another northern people] will serve beneath our banners. Joy and love so fill Roma's heart that she almost weeps, so great is her joyous pride in her illustrious foster-child. So just as when a bull fights in defence of the herd his mother lifts her own horns more proudly; and just as the African lioness gazes with admiration on her cub when he becomes the terror of the farmsteads and the future king of beasts. The goddess lays aside her veil of cloud and towers above the youthful warrior, then thus begins to speak:*

> *'I don't have to look far for examples to testify to the extent of my power now you are emperor. The Saxon is conquered and the ocean is safe; the Picts have been defeated and Britain is secure. I love to see the humbled Franks and broken Sueves at my feet, and I see the Rhine as my own, Germanicus. But what am I to do? The discordant East [Eutropius] envies our victories, and beneath that other sky, evils abound so that our realm does not breathe with a single body.'*

Claudian, *Against Eutropius*, 1.378–98

The balance of power in the east lasted just a couple of years before new tension broke it apart. In the summer of 399 CE a Gothic general named

Figure XI

Diptych representing Stilicho, his wife, Serena, and their son Eucherius. A diptych consists of two parts connected by a hinge, and this one was carved in ivory to celebrate the assumption of high office – in this case supreme command over the western armies.

Tribigild, who had been assigned to garrison duty at the head of troops in western Turkey, rebelled. While Tribigild led his men on a destructive march through the region, Gainas began negotiating with him; he even sent troops who enabled Tribigild to escape the army sent after him. Having disabled the defence of the eastern provinces, Gainas convinced Arcadius that Tribigild could not be stopped so long as Eutropius – by now a consul – remained in power. Arcadius believed him and sent Eutropius into exile. Gainas arranged for the eunuch's murder shortly thereafter.

With his ally-turned-rival eliminated, Gainas made peace with Tribigild, whose army he brought into the vicinity of Constantinople. The next year Gainas, who was now *magister utriusque militiae*, again blackmailed the imperial government, forcing the resignation of Eutropius's successor, Aurelian. Aurelian had been profoundly unhappy with the Gothic domination of the eastern army; one of his first acts had been to undo concessions made to Alaric, who had settled down in Macedonia, having reached an agreement with the eastern empire to become an imperial official.

Gainas had already moved the bulk of his troops into Constantinople's suburbs, where he remained while his relationship with the eastern imperial court deteriorated. But the people of Constantinople rose up, slaughtering thousands of his men and driving the rest from the city. When Gainas tried to lead his surviving troops back across the Hellespont, naval forces destroyed their transports, and the imperial army that he no longer controlled pursued his men into Thrace. Gainas and his surviving followers crossed the Danube looking for a new home. They did not find one. They were slaughtered by Uldin, King of the Huns, who had recently joined forces with Arcadius, and Uldin sent Gainas's head to the eastern emperor as a gift.

Alaric, meanwhile, left his Balkan lands in 401 CE and was now on the move westwards. Stilicho was in Gaul, so, with no Roman army in his way, Alaric advanced easily into northern Italy and drove Honorius from his palace at Milan to the city of Asta. There, Alaric besieged the western emperor for several months until Stilicho arrived with a portion of the field army from Gaul. At this point, Alaric withdrew into Raetia, looking to negotiate a deal that would give his people the privileges they had formerly enjoyed in the east. None was forthcoming, so he returned to the offensive in Italy the next spring.

On Easter Sunday, 402 CE, Stilicho attacked the now largely Christian Goths as they prepared for their religious observances near Pollentia on the River Tanaro. Despite being caught by surprise, Alaric managed to withdraw with the bulk of his army intact, and fought a running war with Stilicho until the following summer, when Stilicho pinned him down and defeated him near Verona. Even though Alaric had staged two uprisings within a decade, Stilicho still regarded him as being more useful alive than dead, signing a pact with him and allowing him to return to western Illyricum. Stilicho evidently retained the view that Alaric could play a useful role in furthering his own ambitions.

In 405 CE relations between the eastern and western courts broke down once again, and Stilicho decided that it was time, with Alaric's assistance, to seize the portion of Illyricum still under eastern control. The campaign was just getting under way when the northern frontier collapsed. A chieftain named Radagaisus had gathered a large army just to the north of Raetia, which was now largely devoid of defenders, and in the spring of 405 CE they advanced into Italy. According to Roman propaganda, Radagaisus was a devout pagan who routinely sacrificed to the gods – but that is as unlikely as was the account of Arbogast's pagan sympathies at the time of the Battle of the Frigidus. At a time when the leaders of Germanic states had become Christians in order to deal with the Romans, Radagaisus is likely to have been as much of a Christian as his Gothic fellows. Portraying him as a pagan, however, enhanced the idea that divine favour helped to explain the defeat of his immense horde of followers, which occurred in 406 CE. The reputed size of Radagaisus's army – put variously at 200,000 or 400,000 men in the sources – is improbable, given that the army would not survive its encounter with Stilicho's troops, which was reinforced with some Huns whom Uldin had provided, when they met outside Florence. Radagaisus was captured and killed after abandoning his army, which had been reduced to starvation in the wake of its defeat. About 10,000 of Radagaisus's men were taken into the western army; the rest were sold into slavery.

During this time, Alaric appears to have remained in the Balkans and to have been in receipt of a substantial payment from Stilicho in order to secure his loyalty. Then, on the 31st of December, 406 CE, the Rhine froze over – allowing a massive invasion wave to crash down upon Gaul. This time, the invaders were relatively new arrivals in the form of the Vandals, the Alans and the Sueves (or Suebi), all of whom came from central Europe. The bulk of Stilicho's field army was still in Italy, and there was nothing he could do to prevent the destruction of the Rhine frontier. The tribes that crossed on this occasion would never leave Roman territory, and the integrity of the frontier first established by Augustus, then stabilized by Tiberius, would never be fully restored. Around the same time, the commander of the Roman army in Britain, Constantine, declared himself emperor and moved into Gaul. Driving the recent invaders south and west, he rapidly took control of the northern regions of Gaul.

Stilicho was in a quandary. Uldin had gone home and Stilicho was unwilling to commit his own army to open battle against Constantine. Instead, he contented himself with garrisoning the passes over the Alps. Stilicho also faced several other difficulties. Honorius, now in his early twenties, had taken Stilicho's daughter as his wife but came to detest her. The emperor was also surrounded with courtiers who wanted to be rid of Stilicho, chief among them a man named Olympius, who, as *magister officiorum*, headed the civilian bureaucracy.

The events that led to Stilicho's execution and, with it, the end of effective administration in the west began when news arrived of Arcadius's death on the 1st of May, 408 CE. His successor was his seven-year-old son, Theodosius II. Stilicho proposed that Honorius would take over the eastern empire, dispatching Alaric and some Roman soldiers to do the job while the bulk of the army remained in Italy to deal with Constantine. Although Honorius approved the plan, Stilicho did nothing to put it into effect. His delay opened the door for Olympius, who told Honorius that Stilicho was planning to put his own son on the throne, and who then terrorized the

Figure XII (overleaf)

Theodosius II, a devout Christian, is seen here welcoming the remains of St John Chrysostom to be celebrated at Constantinople in 438 CE.

emperor by inspiring a mutiny of the garrison at Ticino, where Honorius was staying. In the course of the mutiny, a number of senior courtiers, some of them known to be on good terms with Stilicho, were killed. Olympius, now controlling Honorius emotionally as well as physically, convinced the emperor to order Stilicho's arrest. When Stilicho learned of this he took refuge in a church, from which imperial agents extracted him with a promise that his life would be spared. They lied. Stilicho was decapitated. In death, his reputation was at the mercy of the chroniclers and their differing agendas.

Olympius followed the assassination of Stilicho with a hunt for his surviving supporters. He also ordered the Roman troops under his command to massacre the German soldiers who had formed a major portion of Stilicho's personal army. Those who survived fled to Alaric, asking for his protection and notifying him that his arrangements with Honorius's administration had ended with the death of Stilicho.

Stilicho would remain a deeply controversial figure, as we can see from the radically different judgements offered by two historians in the aftermath of his assassination. Zosimus reflects the views of the eastern diplomat Olympiodorus, a contemporary of Stilicho, while Orosius, whose history was inspired by Alaric's sack of Rome, is speaking very much for himself:

> *He [Stilicho] was the most moderate of those in power at the time, for though he married Theodosius the elder's niece and was entrusted with the empires of both his sons, and had been magister for twenty-three years, he never sold military offices or embezzled the soldier's pay. Although he had only one son, he promoted him only so far as the rank of so-called* notarius *and tribune, and contrived no leading position for him.*
>
> Zosimus, *New History*, 5.34.6–7

> *In the meantime, Count Stilicho, born of the unwarlike, greedy, treacherous and sorrow-bringing race of the Vandals, thought it wasn't sufficient to rule under a ruler, but strove by all means possible that the throne would be passed on to his own son, Eucherius, who, as most people think, was planning to persecute the Christians, even though he was a young boy with no official position.*
>
> Orosius, *History Against the Pagans*, 7.38.12

ALARIC'S TRIUMPH AND THE SACK OF ROME

Olympius's fixation upon the removal of Stilicho meant that no effective preparations had been made to deal with Alaric. The army remaining in Italy was not strong enough to meet him in the field, and Alaric saw an opportunity to regain an arrangement through which he would obtain official status within the Roman government, and his people would receive land. Realizing that there was now no substantial Roman army between himself and Rome, Alaric bypassed the emperor and made straight for the city.

Figure XIII (overleaf)

Theodosius II, whose accession was somewhat controversial – as can be seen if we read between the lines of Themistius's speech quoted on page 264 – was the last man to rule the entire Roman Empire, albeit for only a few months.

THERE WAS SOMETHING WHICH GAVE THE BARBAROUS SAVAGERY A NEW APPEARANCE, THAT THE LARGEST BASILICAE WERE SELECTED SO THAT THEY COULD BE FILLED WITH PEOPLE WHO WERE SPARED, WHERE NO ONE WAS ABUSED, NO ONE CARRIED OFF, WHERE MANY WERE BROUGHT THERE TO BE FREED BY MERCIFUL ENEMIES, FROM WHERE NO CAPTIVES WERE TAKEN AWAY BY CRUEL ENEMIES. THIS IS TO BE ATTRIBUTED TO THE NAME OF CHRIST, THIS MUST BE ATTRIBUTED TO THE CHRISTIAN ERA.

AUGUSTINE OF HIPPO, *THE CITY OF GOD*, 1.7

IT WASN'T FAMILY CONNECTION THAT ADVANCED YOU [THEODOSIUS] TO THE PURPLE, BUT A VAST QUANTITY OF VIRTUE; NOT CLOSE KINSHIP, BUT DISPLAY OF STRENGTH AND MANHOOD. GRATIAN ACTED WISELY AND IN A WAY WORTHY OF GREY HAIRS RATHER THAN YOUTH BECAUSE HE DID NOT ASSUME ONE OF HIS NEAREST RELATIONS TO BE THE BEST MAN, BUT RATHER THE BEST MAN TO BE HIS NEAREST RELATION. NOBLY, HE HAS MADE THE VOTE HIS OWN, WHICH CIRCUMSTANCE HAD IN ANTICIPATION CARRIED.

THEMISTIUS, *ORATION*, 14, 182b

The senate voted to pay him a massive bribe and to negotiate a fresh deal with Honorius that would give Alaric new status within the Roman hierarchy. As a sign of their goodwill, the senate sent a number of upper-class hostages to the Goths. One of these was a young man, Flavius Aetius, who would become the last great general in the history of the western Roman Empire.

Even as Aetius took up residence with the Goths, the situation of the western empire was worsening. Honorius, who genuinely despised the necessity of dealing with people whom he regarded as inferiors, refused to go along with the arrangements proposed by the senate. His refusal to honour the senate's deal was a sign of the separation between the senate and the bureaucracy in Ravenna. This was despite the fact that an important member of the imperial family was living in the vicinity of Rome: Honorius' older sister, Galla Placidia.

Alaric returned to Rome with an even longer list of demands. These included a guaranteed homeland for his people in Raetia (a region they had come to know well), where they would be supported by the taxes paid by the locals, which would also mean that the Goths could guarantee the security of Italy against a repeat of Radagaisus's invasion. Alaric also wanted the rank of *magister militum* for himself. Although Honorius's officials were willing to accede to this demand – which would give them a decisive edge against Constantine in Gaul, as well as security for Italy – Honorius refused outright.

New thinking was needed to find ways of assimilating immigrants into imperial society. With many Germans serving in the army, even after the massacre of Stilicho's men in 408 CE, and many still in the officer corps, a pragmatic solution should have been possible. Indeed, after Alaric laid siege to Rome in the winter of 408/9, members of the Roman aristocracy went on an embassy to Honorius at Ravenna, looking to negotiate a settlement that Alaric could live with. Honorius seems to have recognized that Olympius was a problem and replaced him with a man named Jovius, who had served under Stilicho and had dealt with Alaric in the past. Once again, it looked as though a solution might work whereby Alaric would receive land for his people and the title of *magister utriusque militiae*. At the last minute, Honorius rejected this deal too, saying he would never confer office on Alaric.

His negotiation having failed, Alaric marched once again on Rome, where the senate proposed one of its members, Priscus Attalus, as emperor to replace Honorius. He joined Alaric on the march towards Ravenna. The senate's action underscored the tension that had developed between the central Italian aristocracy and the northern Italian court, which had taken no steps to protect its interests from Alaric. The aristocracy told the court that they wanted a solution giving Alaric a place in the administration. Bigotry and fantasy were the responses.

Alaric seems genuinely to have believed that the best interests of his people would be served by negotiating a permanent homeland and financial support within the territory of the Roman Empire. The problem was that he still lacked the wherewithal to realize these goals. Attalus had little influence with the bureaucracy, and Alaric's army had no siege equipment. These two shortcomings meant that Alaric would still have to negotiate with Honorius; however, having recently gained reinforcements from the east, Honorius refused discussions. Betrayed at every turn, Alaric deposed Attalus and appeared once more before the walls of Rome.

On the 24th of August, 410 CE, the Goths under Alaric found that a sympathizer had left the city's Salarian Gate open. For the first time in 800 years a man who was not part of the Roman hierarchy took control of the capital. His followers looted the city for three days. Being a devout Christian, Alaric allowed the basilicas of Peter and Paul to stand as refuges for Romans, while he concentrated on removing treasures left in the Capitol by previous emperors and burning some structures in the Forum. The sack of Rome was a protest against the folly of Honorius:

> *They say that a eunuch, evidently a keeper of the poultry, told the Emperor Honorius in Ravenna that Rome had perished. And he cried out and said, 'But it has just eaten from my hands!' For he had a very large rooster, 'Rome' by name; and the eunuch understanding what he was saying explained that it was the city of Rome which had perished at the hands of Alaric, and the emperor replied with a sigh of relief, 'But I thought that my bird Rome had perished.' So great, they say, was the idiocy of this emperor.*

Augustine of Hippo, *The City of God*, 1.7

The fall of Rome revealed many things. Politically, it demonstrated just how little the city now mattered. Honorius and his government were still secure in Ravenna, as was Theodosius II in Constantinople, while the field army remained encamped on the border with Gaul.

Yet, if the sack of Rome made little difference in terms of the political structure of the era, it was still an extraordinary shock. Perhaps the greatest impact of the city's fall was in its inspiration for a bishop in North Africa, once resident in Rome, to compose his greatest work. Augustine's *The City of God* would become a central exposition of Christian thought for centuries to come. He felt he had to answer the charge, levelled by pagans, that the advent of Christianity had angered the gods, who now imposed this disaster on the Roman state. Augustine's reply was that political history was of little consequence when compared with the history of God's relationship with humanity. After all, he contested, far worse things had happened in the past, before the rise of Christianity.

As for Alaric, he moved from Rome into southern Italy, where he died less than a year later at Cosentia. He was buried in the riverbed of the Busento, which had been diverted to allow his people to create a grave for him that could not be desecrated. He was interred with some of the treasures from Rome, and the river was returned to its course.

Having demonstrated that they could humiliate the Roman Empire at its historic heart, the Goths, led by Athaulf, the husband of Alaric's sister, now referred to themselves as the Visi ('strong') Goths. They remained in Italy for the rest of the year before heading to a new home in southern France.

CHRONOLOGY 364–411 CE

360 | 370

364 CE
Death of Emperor Jovian (28th of February); Valentinian I selected as *augustus*: promotes brother Valens as *augustus* of the eastern Roman Empire.

365 CE
Revolt of Procopius: defeated by Valens in 366 CE (May).

367 CE
Gratian elevated as *augustus* of the western Roman Empire.

367–69 CE
Valens' campaign north of the Danube.

372 CE
'Conspiracy' of Theodorus unmasked at Antioch.

373 CE
Confrontation between Valens and Sapor II over Armenia.

375 CE
Execution of Theodosius; death of Valentinian I; Valentinian II made *augustus* in Italy and the Balkans.

376 CE
Goths admitted to the Roman Empire by Valens; beginning of the Gothic revolt.

378 CE
Battle of Adrianople (9th of August): death of Valens.

379 CE
Theodosius I made *augustus* of the eastern Roman Empire.

```
380          390          400          410                      → CE
 |            |            |            |
```

382 CE
Theodosius I's peace treaty with the Goths: they receive lands south of the Danube.

383 CE
Gratian defeated by Magnus Maximus at Lyons and killed (25th of August).

384 CE
Maximus recognized as *augustus* of the western empire by Theodosius and Valentinian II.

387 CE
Maximus's seizure of control in Italy; Valentinian II's flight to the east.

388 CE
Defeat of Maximus (by Theodosius) at Poetovio and Aquileia; Maximus executed; Valentinian II restored as *augustus* in the west.

392 CE
Valentinian II killed; Eugenius made *augustus* in the west by Arbogast; Theodosius's ban on pagan sacrifice.

394 CE
Arbogast defeated by Theodosius at the Battle of the Frigidus (September): Eugenius executed and Arbogast commits suicide.

395 CE
Death of Theodosius in Milan (17th of January): succeeded by his sons Honorius (as *augustus* in the west) and Arcadius (*augustus* in the east); Gothic revolt in the Danubian provinces.

396 CE
Stilicho's campaign on the Rhine.

397 CE
Stilicho's defeat of Alaric in the Balkans; Gildo's revolt in Africa.

398 CE
Stilicho's campaign in Britain; Gildo defeated.

399 CE
Consulship of Eutropius in the east; revolt of Tribigild in Phrygia.

401 CE
Alaric's invasion of Italy: defeated (Easter Sunday 402 CE) by Stilicho at Pollentia.

403 CE
Alaric defeated by Stilicho again, at Verona: Alaric accepts treaty settling his Goths in Noricum and Pannonia.

405 CE
Radagaisus's invasion of Italy.

406 CE
Radagaisus's defeat; beginning of the Vandal invasion of Gaul (31st of December).

407 CE
Revolt of Constantine III in Britain.

408 CE
Death of Arcadius; accession of Theodosius II as *augustus* in the east (1st of May); execution of Stilicho (22nd of August) and massacre of Stilicho's troops; new invasion of Italy by Alaric.

409 CE
Rome besieged by Alaric, who proclaims Priscus Attalus emperor; they besiege Honorius at Ravenna.

410 CE
Rome sacked by Alaric's forces (24th of August).

411 CE
Death of Alaric.

CHAPTER 7

FINAL CONVULSIONS: VISIGOTHS, VANDALS AND HUNS

In later centuries the sack of Rome by Alaric's Visigoths in 410 CE came to be viewed as vivid and dramatic confirmation that the inevitable decline and fall of a once mighty empire was well advanced. According to the convenient periodization of history, it was when the light began to go out all over Western Europe, and when the progress of civilization that Rome represented began its retreat into the amnesia and shadows of a new Dark Age. That narrative has exerted a powerful hold on the imagination.

The truth, of course, is more nuanced and more complex; and the timescale was more drawn out, for there was another chapter to go in the story of the Roman Empire in the west. Although much territory had already fallen under the political control of the peoples who had migrated into Roman territory, there remained the possibility that they could be peacefully assimilated into Roman power structures *if* Emperor Honorius were astute, and *if* those who advised him were wise. Neither was the case. Instead, Honorius's court at Ravenna was staffed by bigoted incompetents, whose primary interest was self-advancement, which, they felt, could be best secured through the murder of colleagues and the encouragement of the emperor's pathological prejudice against 'Germans'.

A situation that might have been retrievable became unstoppable. The decades after the sack of Rome would bring an increasing divide between the eastern and western Roman regimes. The two would be, for the most part, no longer in conflict, as they had been in Stilicho's time, because the eastern regime – now the stronger of the two – sought to avoid entanglements with the west. It was telling that the eastern regime offered no relief to Honorius in the wake of Alaric's attack on Rome; neither did the east bring aid the next year, when Athaulf and the Visigoths remained in Italy until they received offer of payment to assist Honorius's regime in Gaul (precisely the deal Alaric had been refused). Officials would try, throughout the remainder of Honorius's reign, and that of his nephew Valentinian III, to restore imperial control over portions of the empire lost in the years before 410 CE. But there was to be no salvaging anything that resembled the former empire.

CONSTANTIUS AND ATHAULF: AN UNEASY ALLIANCE

The Visigoths' agreement with Honorius required them to assist the emperor's new *magister militum*, Constantius, in restoring order to Gaul. A few years previously Gaul had come under the sway of the self-declared emperor Constantine III, who had previously governed Britain. He had succeeded in driving the major groups that had crossed the Rhine at the end of 406 CE – the Vandals, the Sueves and the Alans – into northern and

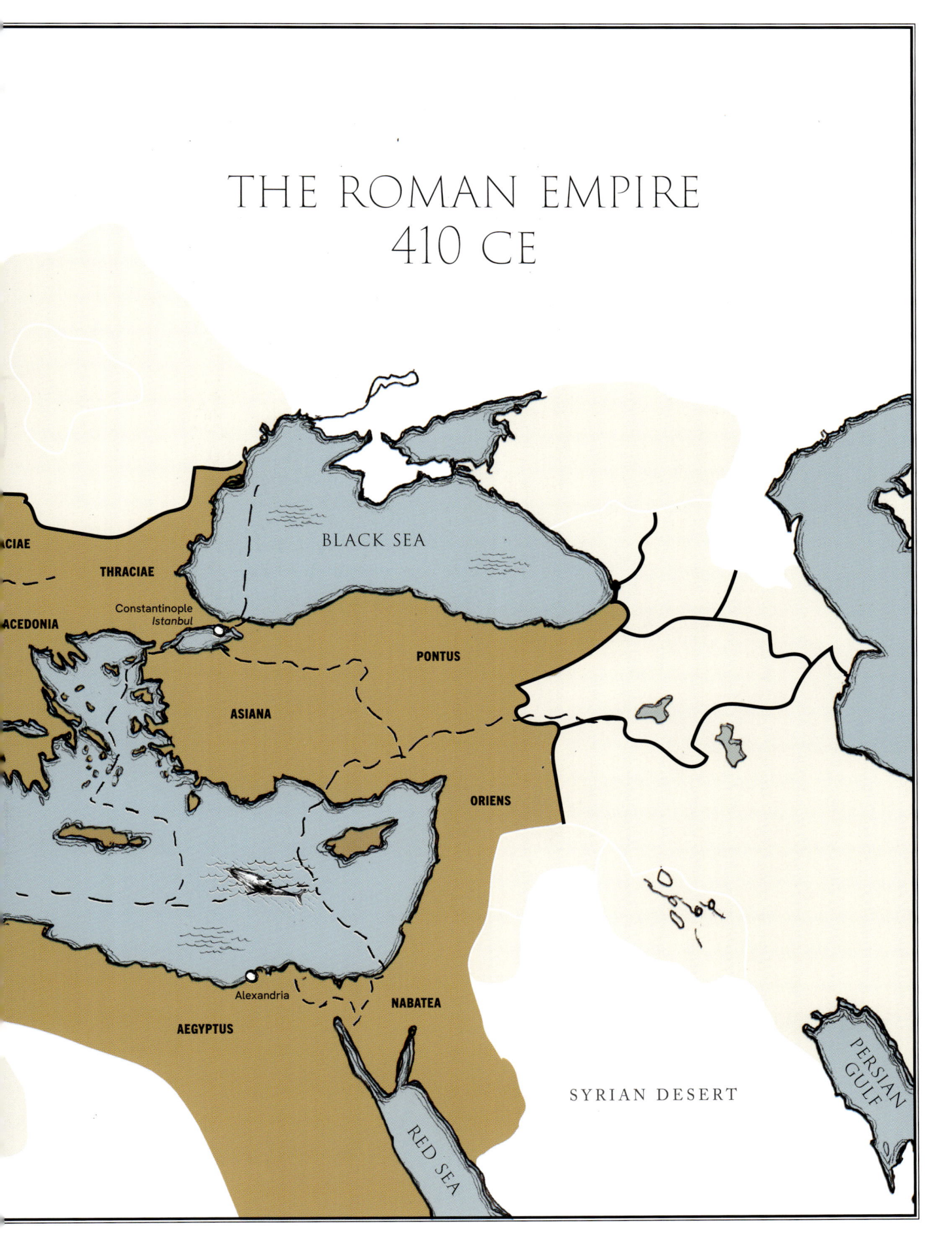

western Spain. But there was unrest within his ranks. In 409 CE Constantine had tried to replace one of his senior officials, Gerontius, who commanded his forces in Spain. The outraged Gerontius mutinied. He eschewed the option of raising himself up as an emperor, instead picking another candidate for the job – perhaps a sign that the officeholder was increasingly regarded as a figurehead.

In 411 CE Gerontius succeeded in killing Constantine's son and besieging Constantine at Arles, until the arrival of Honorius's army under Constantius forced Gerontius to withdraw. That was a mistake. Gerontius's troops took the withdrawal as a sign of weakness and mutinied against him. He committed suicide, while a weakened Constantine, in no position to resist Constantius, surrendered. Although promised his life, Constantine was murdered shortly thereafter.

Constantine's demise did not solve the crises in Gaul, for in the north a man named Jovinus took it upon himself to declare himself emperor. Athaulf, who did not get along with Constantius, initially joined forces with Jovinus, but then, in the wake of a dispute over his standing in the regime, overthrew the would-be emperor instead. Having therefore realigned the Visigoths with Honorius, they were granted land in southern Gaul as a base for their subsequent operations against the Vandals and other groups in Spain.

Athaulf's dealings with Honorius were complicated not only by his poor relations with the emperor's *magister militum*, but also by the circumstances surrounding Honorius's sister Galla Placidia, who had been a hostage of the Visigoths since her capture by Alaric. Having promised to return her to Honorius, Athaulf failed to do so when, in 413 CE, it briefly looked as though Honorius might be overthrown. The challenger was Heraclian, the governor of Africa, who invaded Italy that year. He was defeated near Rome, but the general chaos of the situation appears to have convinced Athaulf that he could do better without Honorius's patronage. Not only did he marry Galla Placidia, but also he revived the imperial claim of Priscus Attalus – the man whom Alaric had briefly installed as emperor, then deposed, in 409 CE. Priscus had remained with the Goths throughout the intervening years. Athaulf's ultimate ambition was revealed by the fact that when Galla Placidia bore him a son at the end of 414 CE, the child was named Theodosius. Since Honorius was childless, the boy would have been an obvious candidate for the imperial succession at Ravenna – had he survived infancy, which he did not.

In the wake of Theodosius's death in early 415 CE, open conflict burst out between the Visigoths and the Romans. Constantius launched a successful attack on the Visigoths, relying on similar tactics to those that Athaulf had employed against the Vandals, namely, avoiding battles in favour of raids to cut off supplies. The *magister militum* was able to drive the Visigoths into northern Spain, in a campaign that spelled the end of Athaulf's prospects; he was then murdered by his own people. His successor, Wallia, returned Galla Placidia to Constantius and the Roman orbit, while acceding to the Roman request to continue operations against the Vandals and their allies in Spain. After four years of slaughter in Spain, the Visigoths were rewarded with land of their own, around what is now Toulouse.

ROMAN HISPANIA

☆ Provincial capital
○ Capital of conventus (administrative district)
▪ Hasdingi (Vandals)
▪ Silingi (Vandals)
▪ Suevi
▪ Alans
▪ Roman Empire

FINAL CONVULSIONS

By now, the western empire was a shambles. Britain, which had expelled the representatives of Constantine III in 410 CE, was barely part of it; its tiny garrison was fully occupied defending the territory against raids by the tribes north of Hadrian's Wall (the Picts and Scots) as well as raiders from across the North Sea (Angles and Saxons). The Burgundians, a tribe that had taken advantage of the collapse of the Rhine frontier to establish themselves on Roman land, occupied a substantial portion of northeastern France. Southwestern France (the diocese of Septem Provinciae – Seven Provinces) was now the home of the Visigoths, and most of the Iberian peninsula was occupied by the Vandals and their allies.

The regime in the east, ruled by Theodosius II, was largely untroubled by these events. The western regime was in no position to intervene militarily in its affairs, and as long as Honorius was alive, the government of Theodosius II rested easy in the knowledge that there was a representative of the dynasty in place in the west. But if that dynasty were to continue, the key figure would be Galla Placidia. The thought was not lost on Constantius.

Ever since he had defeated Constantine III, the ambitious Constantius had successfully inveigled himself into ever more influential positions within the regime. He could also claim that he had rescued Galla Placidia from the hands of the barbarians, and that she should now show him due gratitude by accepting his generous offer of marriage. She, however, found him personally abhorrent and the prospect of becoming his wife deeply distasteful. But marry she must, in the view of the court. She was the key to the future of the western empire, since any son she bore would probably become emperor, thus guaranteeing that western officialdom would avoid a takeover by representatives of the dynasty from the east, or another civil war.

Galla Placidia managed to resist what was essentially a political act of rape for three years, until her brother finally forced her to take Constantius's hand, on the 1st of January, 417 CE. Their first child, a daughter named Honoria, was born within the year, followed by a son, Valentinian, in 419. In early 421 CE Constantius finally achieved his aim of being named co-*augustus* with his brother-in-law Honorius, although the eastern court refused to recognize his title. He did not have long to enjoy it, dying the same year, and leaving Galla Placidia a widow for the second time.

With Constantius's death, the tensions in government between the 'Germans' and 'Romans' resurfaced almost immediately. Honorius issued an edict forbidding anyone to wear German dress within the walls of Rome. Galla Placidia now became the focus of loyalty for the German soldiers with whom her late husband had surrounded himself, and who were now fighting regularly with Honorius's guards. It was at this point that her relationship with her brother, once allegedly too close, deteriorated to such an extent that Galla and her children were exiled to Constantinople towards the end of 422 CE.

Figure I

This consular diptych of Constantius III shows Constantius celebrating the inauguration of the games. The leaf placed on the left shows him standing with two of his officials, while that on the front displays him as the central figure with *mappa* (which he will drop to signal the beginning of a chariot race) in one hand, and sceptre in the other, flanked by two officials. Court figures sitting with Constantius are shown on the top of both parts of the diptych.

THEIR UNRESTRAINED PASSION AND CONTINUOUS KISSING ON THE MOUTH CAUSED MANY PEOPLE TO HOLD SHAMEFUL SUSPICIONS ABOUT THEM. BUT ... GREAT HATRED AGAIN AROSE BETWEEN THEM SO THAT THERE WERE OFTEN RIOTS IN RAVENNA ... AND BLOWS WERE EXCHANGED BETWEEN THE TWO SIDES.

OLYMPIODORUS, *HISTORY*, FR. 38 BLOCKLEY

CONSTANTINOPLE'S POWERFUL WOMEN

In exile, Galla Placidia found herself in a place that still had a properly functioning administration, in large part because women of the imperial family were, in the eastern empire, not dynastic puppets but actual rulers. The first woman to assert her position as *augusta* had been Eudoxia, wife of Emperor Arcadius. Although she had died in 404 CE, the precedent she set for strong female rule paved the way for her daughter Pulcheria to become, in time, effective regent for the imperial heir, her brother Theodosius (II).

Theodosius II was only eight years old when he ascended the throne in 408 CE, and his sister just a year older; but, as the years passed, Pulcheria created an aura of imperial power closely linked with the civilian institution that reached into the homes of all her subjects: the Church. Her power would come to depend not on her potential role as a spouse, but upon her relationship to God, as demonstrated by the very strongly publicized lifestyle choices she (and her younger sisters) made. Through her public proclamation of virginity, which was probably genuine, and her essentially ascetic lifestyle, Pulcheria helped to foster a growing interest in the figure of the Virgin Mary as the model for female leadership in the state. On the 4th of July, 414 CE, Theodosius II named Pulcheria *augusta*.

The alliance Pulcheria forged between the imperial office and the Church helped to reconcile different groups within the bureaucracy. German generals now stood on an equal footing with traditional aristocrats in the hierarchy of the eastern empire, while the highly Christianized version of the imperial role succeeded in bringing the concept of emperorship back into line with contemporary social values. The presentation of Theodosius II to his subjects, as an equal of the Apostles, was far more in tune with contemporary thought than the militarized imperial persona of earlier centuries, especially when it was obvious to everyone that the incumbent possessed no ability, actually, to do the job of emperor on his own.

In the west, by contrast, the presentation of the emperor to the public remained tied to tradition, no matter how obviously absurd that was. In the panegyrics written by Claudian, Honorius still embodied the traditional warlike virtues of an emperor, in place since the time of Augustus, even though everyone knew Honorius could not lead an army into battle. Another contemporary, Augustine of Hippo, wrote in his *Confessions* that when he had once given a speech in honour of Emperor Valentinian II, everything he had spoken was a lie. That was before Augustine's conversion to Christianity. But the fact that Augustine could write it so publicly suggests that the sentiment was widely held.

When Galla Placidia arrived in Constantinople, in 423 CE, she did so at a time of subtle power shifts among the court's powerful women. Two years before, Theodosius II had married. His bride was Eudocia, a talented poet and the daughter of a pagan philosopher. She was also a skilled self-publicist in her own right, and rivalled Pulcheria enthusiastically in her demonstrations of devotion. In 422 CE, after giving birth to a daughter, Eudocia was granted the title of *augusta* too. The new empress in the east seems to have seen in Galla Placidia a useful tool with which to assert her own supremacy. Eudocia's infant

Figure II (above)

Pulcheria was the daughter of Arcadius. In 414 CE, at the age of 15, she became the guardian of her younger brother Theodosius II, and was also proclaimed *augusta*. Pulcheria had significant influence during her brother's reign, especially in promoting the worship of the Virgin Mary. After Theodosius's death, she married Marcian while maintaining her vow of virginity.

Figure III (opposite)

A significant aspect of Pulcheria's religious policy was the promotion of the cult of the Virgin Mary, depicted in this sixth-century mosaic from St Apollinare Nuovo, Ravenna.

daughter was betrothed to Galla's six-year-old son, Valentinian, symbolizing the eastern court's interest in the succession to Honorius.

That question of succession arose almost immediately, for Honorius died before the end of 423 CE. Western officials tried to assert their independence by proclaiming a palace functionary named John as *augustus*, but he was a poor choice. The Visigoths declared allegiance to the cause of Galla Placidia, their former queen, and began to attack imperial territory in Gaul, while the eastern court made extensive plans to invade the west. According to the fifth-century historian Olympiodorus of Thebes, Theodosius II made Galla Placidia's son *caesar* before the expedition set out – a story that probably reflected contemporary propaganda from the eastern court.

The expedition that followed was not lacking in miraculous elements, according to official narratives. The commander of eastern forces was Flavius Ardabur, a general of Alan descent, who had made his reputation during a brief war with Persia in 422/3 CE, during which he had managed to kill several senior Persian officers. His immediate subordinates now were his own son Aspar and an officer named Candidianus. According to one version, Ardabur was captured by John's troops and brought to Ravenna, where, although a prisoner, he was able to undermine John's authority; Candidianus meanwhile captured several cities in northern Italy. John's erstwhile supporters then deserted him before murdering him, after which Valentinian III donned the imperial robes as *augustus* of the western Roman Empire. In another version – circulated to emphasize the importance of imperial piety – Ardabur was shipwrecked and captured, but Aspar, guided by an angel into Ravenna, completed John's destruction. In similar vein, the seventh-century chronicler John of Antioch (not to be confused with the fifth-century patriarch) included a version in his *Historia Chronica*, in which an angel disguised as a shepherd guides the victorious eastern general across the marshes around Ravenna:

> *Having arrived at Thessalonica, he [Ardabur] sailed for Aquileia, and suffered a reversal of fortune, which turned into good fortune as was later revealed. A contrary wind blew him into the hands of the tyrant [John], who seized him and hoped to force the emperor [Theodosius] to declare him his fellow ruler. Theodosius fell into distress as did Aspar, Ardabur's son, and the affairs of the Roman state fell into confusion. God sent an angel in the guise of a shepherd to guide the Roman army and its general and led them across the marsh surrounding Ravenna. For the tyrant resided in that city, where it is said no one had ever passed before. Thus, crossing the uncrossable swamp, and finding a passage over the dry ground, and seeing the gates were open, he took control of the city. After killing the tyrant, they reported these events to the emperor. He gave thanks to God and began to consider who he should make emperor over the western regions.*

John of Antioch, *Historia Chronica*, fragment 221 (ed. Sergei Mariev) (The translation changes the received text, in which a copyist wrongly added Ardabur's name as the general led across the swamp.)

AMBITIOUS GENERALS, BELEAGUERED EMPERORS

The armies of the east were not intended to be armies of occupation in the west. Once John was dead, it was Galla Placidia's job to govern her part of the Roman Empire in the name of her young son. But in order to do this, she had to balance the competing ambitions of three generals who had once served her late and unlamented husband, Constantius, and who had played various roles in the latest civil war: Flavius Faustus, Boniface and Aetius.

For the first five years after her restoration in the west, Galla Placidia was able to manage the three men, even as they plotted against one another. Flavius Faustus made peace with the new regime. But then, events in Africa precipitated a struggle between Boniface and Aetius. Boniface had ruled the province of Africa as a virtual principality of his own, and had sided with the eastern, pro-Galla forces against John. In 429 CE he invited the Vandal confederation, under its leader, Geiseric, to migrate to his territory from Spain. By this time, weakened by warfare, the Vandals, Alans and Sueves had been severely depleted, so much so that one of the two original Vandal tribes had virtually ceased to exist. The Alans also lost their independence as their

Figure IV

Galla Placidia, daughter of Theodosius I and his second wife, Galla, was captured by the Visigoths in 410 CE and briefly married Athaulf. Her second marriage was to Constantius III, with whom she bore the future emperor Valentinian III. She acted as regent for 12 years when he was placed on the throne of the western empire in 425, and she remained influential until her death in 450.

Geiseric was of moderate height and lame as a result of a fall from his horse. He was a person of deep thought and few words, holding luxury in contempt, given to furious anger, greedy for gain, shrewd in winning allies and skilled in sowing dissension to rouse anger.

Jordanes, *History of the Goths*, 33.168

own losses forced them to join with the Vandals to form the new confederation that crossed into Africa.

Geiseric would soon prove to be one of the dominant figures of the age. Within a year of arriving in Africa – their recent weakness notwithstanding – the Vandal confederation was besieging the city of Hippo, where its bishop, Augustine, lay dying. As for Boniface, he soon had problems other than the Vandals to deal with, when rivalry with Aetius exploded into armed conflict after Aetius accused him of treason.

Aetius had supported John in the civil war by recruiting an army of Huns, but he paid them off after John was killed, and accepted command of the army in Gaul for the new regime. Having spent much of his youth as a hostage, first with the Goths of Alaric and Athaulf, then with the Huns of Uldin, Aetius combined ambition with a genuine knowledge of the people with whom he would have to deal. But in accusing Boniface of treason, he now incurred Empress Galla Placidia's irritation and her desire to be rid of him, for which purpose she summoned Boniface – with an army – from Africa.

Galla Placidia's plan was initially successful. Boniface's forces succeeded in defeating Aetius, but Boniface himself died in the moment of victory, leaving control of Italy to his son-in-law Sebastian, while Aetius sought aid from the Huns. When Aetius arrived back in Italy with an army of Huns, Sebastian fled to Constantinople. Galla Placidia now realized that she would after all have to deal with Aetius, who, in 433 CE, took effective control of the western empire, assuming the title *magister utriusque militae*. This latest outbreak of civil war could not have come at a worse time, for it enabled the Vandals to stabilize their position in North Africa. Their advance continued until 435 CE, when Aetius made a treaty ceding them substantial territory in what is now the region of Algeria and Tunisia.

Aetius now turned his attention to the Germanic kingdoms in Gaul, where he hoped to make use of his Hunnic allies. Ever since their emergence as a major force in the 370s CE, the Huns who lived in the Balkans had more often assisted the Roman Empire than assailed it. With the exception of a brutal raid by Uldin in 407 CE, the leaders of the Huns (there were typically two) had made deals, choosing to accept large imperial payments, either to keep the peace on their side of the frontier (while controlling a coalition of other groups) or to lend significant assistance at moments of crisis. In 434 CE the brothers Bleda and Attila succeeded their uncle as leaders of the Huns, in support of Aetius's plans.

First on Aetius's list of targets were the Burgundians, whose king, Guntiarius, was duly killed in 437 CE. He had an afterlife, however, for he would join the usurper Maximus of Britain in medieval legend, being remembered twice over: first as 'Gundahar' (a victim of Attila), and second as the 'King Gunther' who married Brünhild and conspired to murder the heroic Siegfried in the German national epic, the *Nibelungenlied*. With Guntiarius dispatched, Aetius and the Huns then turned on the Visigoths, who were thoroughly defeated two years later.

Despite the loud celebration of these victories in Rome, they would be overshadowed by events in North Africa, where Geiseric had broken his treaty with the Romans, capturing Carthage even as Aetius celebrated his northern triumphs. Yet Aetius was diverted again to Gaul for a couple of

Figure V

Ruler of the Huns 434–50 CE, Attila became one of the dominant political figures of his age. He demanded respect from the Roman court and launched devastating invasions of the eastern and western empires when he did not receive what he felt was his due.

years, while Vandal fleets began raiding around the Mediterranean. Having decided action was finally needed, Aetius secured a fleet from Constantinople to tackle the Vandal threat – but the ships got no further than Sicily when news came that the Huns had launched a massive attack across the Danube.

Unable to launch his offensive, Aetius instead negotiated a fresh treaty with Geiseric in 445 CE, whereby the Roman government recognized Vandal control of the land they had seized. To ensure the peace, Geiseric continued to make nominal tax payments from the region under his control, in return for the betrothal of Valentinian III's infant daughter to his young son Huneric. Ever the astute observer, Geiseric wanted security for his people, and he had perhaps noted that Athaulf's son from his marriage to Galla Placidia would surely have been in line – had he lived – for imperial office. What was good for a Goth would be good for a Vandal, or so he might have thought.

ATTILA AND THE HUNNIC INVASIONS

The termination of Aetius's plan to invade Africa was probably connected with an emerging threat to the eastern empire from Aetius's erstwhile allies, the Huns. Under Attila and Bleda, Huns had attacked the eastern empire in 441 CE. They seemed to have benefited from seeing Roman siege techniques in Gaul, and were no longer allergic to waging 'war with walls'. Indeed, the most important source for these years, the historian Priscus, quotes no less an authority than Attila himself on the importance of his ability to capture cities in the Balkans. In 442 CE Attila conquered the city of Naissus (now Niš, Serbia) through the impressive use of complicated engineering techniques:

> *Attila threatened to go to war if the Romans did not surrender them [some fugitives] to him and they did not stop farming the land captured in the war. He claimed that this tract of land was downstream on the Danube from the land of the Pannonians as far as Novae in Thrace, a total of three hundred miles, that the breadth of the land in question was five days' march and that the market town was not to be in Illyria, on the bank of the Danube, as had previously been the case, but at Naissus, which he established as the frontier between the lands of the Huns and Romans, after it had been sacked by him.*

Priscus, *History*, fr. 7 Blockley

One casualty of Attila's depredations appears to have been Empress Eudocia. Over the previous two decades she had been able to make the emperor's sister Pulcheria share significant public space with her. It was only with the new threats on the frontiers, with their suggestion that God was unhappy, that Eudocia's position came under fire. In 443 CE her opponents at court succeeded in making a charge of adultery against her stick. She was exiled to Jerusalem, where she lived on until 460 CE. (Interestingly, Eudocia was allowed to retain her insignia as empress, an admission, perhaps, that the reason for her exile had more to do with politics than with sex.)

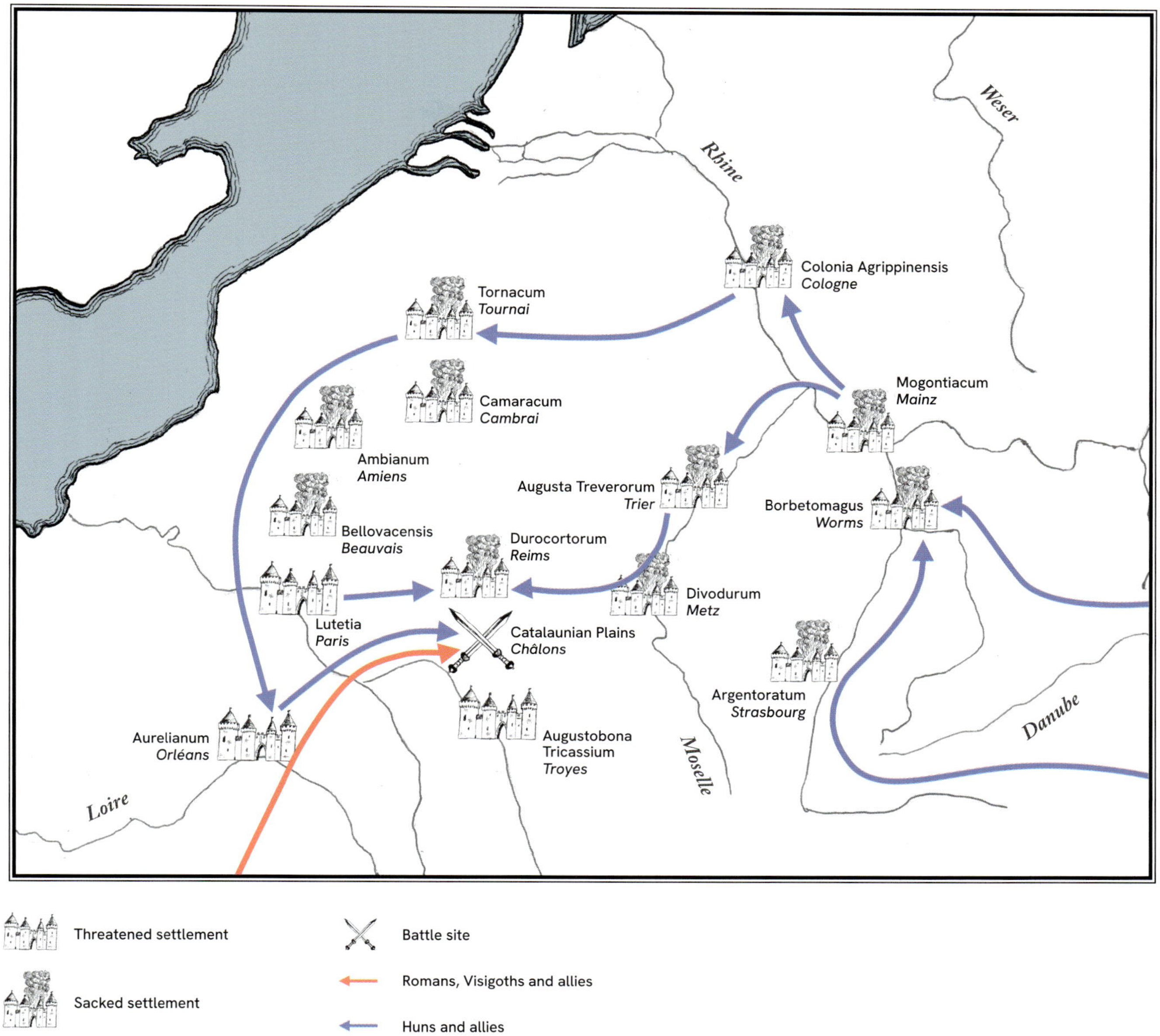

ATTILA IN GAUL

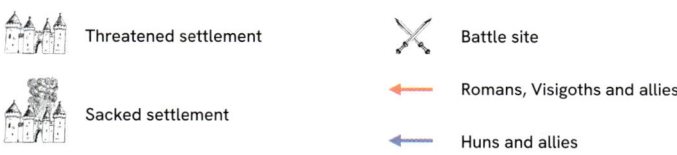

FINAL CONVULSIONS 285

The Huns and the eastern empire agreed a treaty in 443 CE, but the catalyst for renewed conflict seems to have been a change of regime among the Huns. In 445 CE Attila murdered his brother Bleda. At the same time he played up his possession of a sword that had once belonged to the god Mars, granting him supremacy in war. Two years later Attila attacked the eastern empire once more, invading Pannonia.

The result of these operations was that Attila achieved a position of clear superiority over the eastern imperial armies. Priscus, describing his embassy to Attila, reveals that an unoccupied buffer zone (requiring five days to pass through), which the Romans had insisted on in the past, had shifted in the Huns' favour and was now south of the Danube. With reason, one of Attila's ambassadors to Constantinople could boast that Theodosius II was now Attila's subject; by this time, the annual tribute paid by the eastern empire to the Huns had risen six-fold, from 350 pounds of gold to 2,100 pounds (a Roman pound equates to about 0.3 kilograms/¾ pound today). The western regime, for its part, attempted to save face by awarding Attila the title of *magister militium*, which included a payment, like the ones Alaric had been seeking, that counted as a 'salary'.

Attila was not short on ambition. Having defeated the eastern Romans, he asserted that he would invade the Persian Empire from the north – a statement indicating that he controlled territory well into Central Asia. One Roman ambassador felt that he would succeed, and furthermore would then decide to end the Roman Empire. But by the standards of a Roman aristocrat, Attila's personal style was simple. He lived in a wooden house in his chief city, as Priscus reported:

> *Crossing several rivers, we came to a large village in which Attila's dwelling was said to be more magnificent than elsewhere. It was built of timbers and smoothly planed boards and surrounded with a wooden wall built with a view for elegance rather than protection ... There are neither stones nor trees for the barbarians who live in this area, so the wood they use is imported.*

Priscus, *History*, fr. 11, lines 356ff.

Attila insisted on respect from his neighbours, however, and infringements were punished severely in his own lands. When he negotiated with the Romans in the open field, they were expected to stay mounted on their horses, as the Huns did. And while Priscus was visiting the Huns – to negotiate over some rebels that Attila thought the eastern empire was harbouring – he discovered a huge problem brewing between Attila and the western empire, because of perceived disrespect. Attila claimed that western representatives had cheated him out of a payment he was due.

That grievance might have been what motivated Attila, a year later, to intervene in a succession crisis that afflicted the Frankish kingdom in central Gaul, and to assert the authority that he felt had been challenged by the western ambassadors. But that might not have been the whole story, for he may have received from Valentinian III's sister Honoria an appeal that would have enabled him to claim a spot in the imperial family. If the chronicler

His [Attila's] stride was haughty, and he looked around him so that the power of his pride was reflected in the way he moved[;] a lover of war, he was temperate, he was a wise councillor and merciful to those who sought his forgiveness, and loyal to those whom he received as friends. He was short with broad shoulders and a big head. His eyes were small, his beard sparse and greying, his nose was flat and his colour dark, which revealed his origin.

Jordanes, *History of the Goths*, 35.182

John of Antioch is to be believed, Honoria, in disgrace after an affair with her estate manager, was stripped of her powers and married off against her will. In response, she sought Attila's paid help in rebelling against her situation, while also sending him her ring – which some have interpreted as an offer of marriage:

> *Honoria, who possessed the insignia of imperial power, was going to bed, in secret, with Eugenius, who managed her property. He was killed for his crime and she, having been deprived of her imperial insignia, was betrothed to a man named Herculanus, who was of consular rank, good character, and not suspected of having any designs on the imperial title or [being inclined] for revolution. Considering the situation a misfortune and a terrible trouble, she sent her eunuch Hyacinthus to Attila, offering him money to avenge her marriage. She also sent the barbarian a ring as a pledge.*

John of Antioch, *Historia Chronica*, fr. 223.2

Before launching an invasion of Gaul, which was a considerable distance from his usual stomping grounds in Central Europe, Attila sent embassies to Rome and Constantinople, explaining Honoria's appeal. At Constantinople, his ambassadors were met by a new eastern emperor, Marcian, who succeeded to the throne on Theodosius II's death in 450 CE. (Marcian, an experienced general, had married the late emperor's sister Pulcheria on her condition that he continue to respect her famed virginity.) Attila was received with short shrift. The new emperor told the Huns to go away. Meanwhile, in the west, the imperial court responded that Honoria had no claim to the imperial throne and that she was married to someone else, so Attila had no business dealing with her.

It is possible that a factor in Attila's decision to launch an invasion of the west was encouragement from the Vandals, specifically a message from Geiseric promising to attack the Visigoths from the south if Attila attacked them from the north. If Geiseric did send such a message, he was lying, for the Vandals would play no part in what was to come.

Aetius saw a potential advantage in the Hunnic threat to Gaul: that it would enable him to build a coalition strong enough to resist it. He created an army that united the Visigoths with the forces of one of the Frankish kingdoms and his own troops from Italy, totalling, perhaps, 50,000 men. That army may have considerably outnumbered the force Attila assembled; shortage of fodder probably limited Attila's cavalry to about 15,000 men. Attila may have had about the same number of infantrymen (although, again, food would have been a limiting factor) when the two armies met in 451 CE, at the Catalaunian Plains near Châlons, northern France (see pages 290–91). The result for Attila was his first ever serious defeat. It turned out to be the last major battle a western Roman army would fight.

In the wake of the Battle of the Catalaunian Plains, Aetius seems not to have appreciated the harm that such a setback might inflict on Attila, a ruler whose power depended solely upon others' terrified belief in his invincibility. If Attila was to maintain control of his empire, staying at home and licking his wounds would not be an option for him. And so, in 452 CE, while Aetius was still in Gaul, Attila returned but this time made straight for Italy. The

Figure VI

Hunting scene from the floor of San Giovanni Evangelista at Ravenna. Even as the empire was transformed, beast hunts remained one of the spectacles at which members of the imperial government could encounter their subjects.

city of Aquileia fell and was destroyed after a terrible siege, then Milan was taken, before Attila's attack faltered. He lacked the logistical support to advance on Rome, and disease began to take its toll on his army. After receiving an embassy that included the Bishop of Rome (now a leading figure in the Roman aristocracy), Attila agreed to withdraw.

That was Attila the Hun's last offensive. Within months, he was dead. Legend recounts that, while attending a feast to celebrate his marriage to a woman named Ilico, he overindulged in wine, burst a blood vessel and suffocated. The kingdom of the Huns – dependent as it was upon his personal authority – collapsed in civil war the next year as the many Germanic peoples who had been subject to Attila rose up and defeated their erstwhile masters in a huge battle in the central Balkans. The Huns withdrew to the north and resumed their role as occasional mercenaries in Roman service.

THE BATTLE OF THE CATALAUNIAN PLAINS

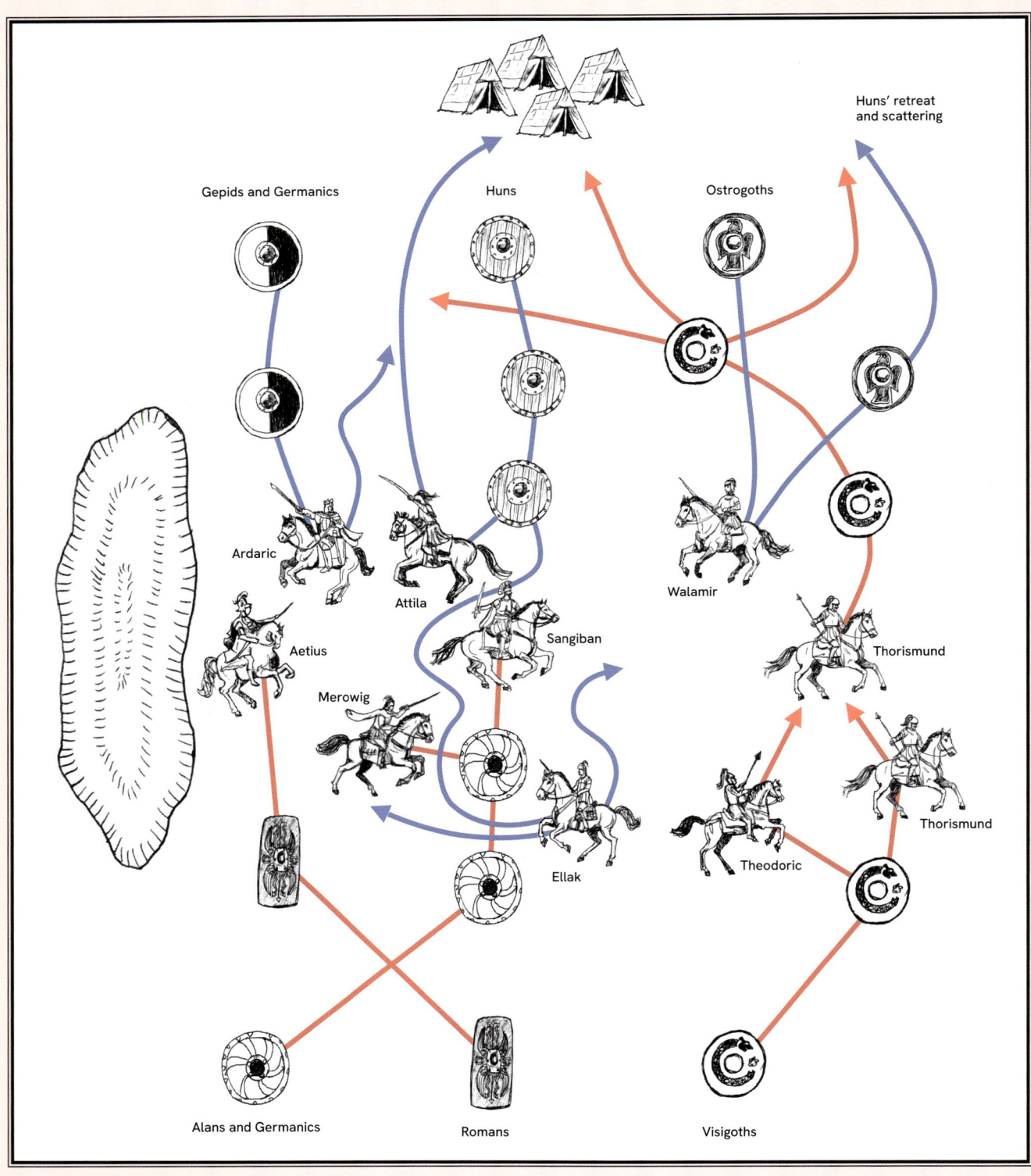

At the Battle of the Catalaunian Plains, on the 20th of June, 451 CE, Aetius's army consisted of three groups: one drawn from the smaller Germanic/Gothic communities in Gaul, along with the Franks led by Sangiban; one the Visigothic army, commanded by King Theodoric; and the third Aetius's own Roman forces from Italy.

Initially, Aetius placed Sangiban's men on his left, his own men in the centre and Theodoric's forces on the right. Facing them was the line of the Hunnic army, commanded by Attila in the centre, supported on both flanks by troops drawn from the largely Gothic communities under his control. To the left of Aetius was a steep hill, overlooking the plain, which he determined would be crucial to the outcome of the battle. Therefore, he exchanged places with Sangiban and seized the hill, driving Attila's Goths – who were also trying to occupy the place – back into the plain.

In the meantime, Attila attacked the Roman centre, which gave way, while Theodoric defeated his enemies on the right and prevented Attila from exploiting his success in the centre. With Aetius's men now joining them, the Visigoths inflicted a serious defeat on the Huns. In the course of this struggle, Attila was wounded, while Theodoric was killed. According to our main source for the course of the battle, the sixth-century Gothic historian Jordanes, Attila had been told by his prophets that he would lose the battle, but that the leader of the enemy would perish. Attila interpreted that to mean the death of Aetius, which would have made the wider loss of the battle worthwhile.

The next day opened with the Huns in their encampment, and the Romans and their allies deciding what to do. According to Jordanes again, Aetius opted to let Attila go, because, if the Huns were destroyed, the Visigoths would take over the western empire. Aetius's reasoning has not been preserved, but he did allow the Huns to withdraw, and he advised Theodoric's son and heir to return to Toulouse and stabilize his position as the Visigothic king.

VANDAL CONSOLIDATION, IMPERIAL ENDGAME

The external threat from Attila had been seen off, narrowly, but internal tension was never far from the surface. Valentinian III was evidently furious that he had not been consulted about Marcian's succession in the east. But then, it was not his empire. As Priscus makes clear in his writings, in the view of the east, the 'western' and 'eastern Romans' constituted distinct political entities, pursuing quite different policies when it suited them.

Valentinian's frustration was increasingly directed at Aetius, whose effective control of the state he resented. The most powerful senator of the time, Petronius Maximus, along with Valentinian's *cubicularius*, the eunuch Heracleius, only encouraged the emperor's antipathy. Matters came to a violent head on the 21st of September, 454 CE, when Aetius met Valentinian at Ravenna, in the presence of Heracleius, ostensibly to discuss imperial finance. Instead, Valentinian accused Aetius of treason for allowing Marcian to take over the east, and attacked him with a sword. Heracleius joined in the assault, brandishing a meat cleaver.

Having murdered Aetius, Valentinian III set about purging Aetius's senior supporters. Unfortunately for the emperor, he failed to reward Petronius Maximus in a manner the senator thought appropriate. Maximus's response was to recruit two soldiers from Aetius's bodyguard as assassins, who carried out their work on the 21st of March, 455 CE, murdering Valentinian. Maximus not only took the throne, but also forced Valentinian's widow, another Eudoxia, to marry him, and for good measure forced Eudoxia's daughter (another Eudocia) to marry his son.

This second marriage proved a terrible mistake. It was the chief reason why Maximus's reign as *augustus* lasted a mere 11 weeks. Eudocia had once been betrothed to the son of the Vandal leader, Geiseric. No sooner did Geiseric hear of the marriages in Rome than he claimed Eudocia had summoned him to her aid. The Vandal fleet sailed from Carthage and landed near Rome in May 455 CE. When Maximus tried to flee, a mob murdered him. The Vandals sacked Rome for more than two weeks, causing a level of devastation far greater than Alaric had wrought 45 years before. Among the treasures removed to Carthage now was the Ark of the Covenant, taken centuries earlier by Emperor Titus from the Temple at Jerusalem.

Geiseric also took captive Eudoxia, Eudocia and her sister Placidia, holding the three of them at Carthage and for several years refusing requests from the eastern government for their return. It was only in 462 CE that Eudoxia and Placidia were sent to Constantinople. As for Eudocia, she remained in North Africa, where she was married to Geiseric's son Huneric, thus consummating the arrangement that Valentinian III had made years earlier. She would remain there until 471 CE, when Huneric allowed her to go to Jerusalem, where she died. As in the case of Attila, Geiseric came to occupy a status that was roughly on a par with being an emperor; as is also the case with Attila, Geiseric provided a model for post-Roman rulers, joining the traditions of his own peoples with those of Rome.

The vandalizing of Rome proved to be the curtain-raiser for the final act in the drama of the western empire. In the power vacuum following the deaths of Aetius and Valentinian III, a soldier of Germanic origin named Ricimer, now *magister militum* of the west, assumed the role of kingmaker. First, he crushed the ambitions of a senator who had declared himself emperor at Arles, by defeating him in battle in 456 CE, near Placentia; then, he placed an officer named Majorian on the throne.

Majorian proved to be a success. In 457 CE he defeated a Vandal attack on Italy, and a year later he defeated Rome's old allies, the Visigoths, who were expanding their power in central France. In a series of further campaigns, Majorian reinforced Roman control of Gaul and moved into Spain, where he prepared a fleet to invade Africa. Geiseric forestalled that effort, by destroying the Roman ships at Cartagena, after which Majorian returned to Rome. Despite that rebuff, overall he had been rather too successful. Although, in the words of Procopius, the great sixth-century historian of these years, he had made himself 'an object of fear towards his enemies', he had also made himself unpopular with the senate. Ricimer turned the situation to his advantage, having Majorian executed in 461 CE and replacing him with a new *augustus*, Libius Severus (Severus III), a man who promised to be more of a nonentity.

However, the eastern emperor refused to recognize Severus, who died in suspicious circumstances in 465 CE. For the next two years the western empire had no emperor – Ricimer did not seem to feel the need of one. His success in these years seems to have derived from his ability to deal with the eastern court, which was at that time dominated by another general of Germanic descent, the Aspar whom we met when the eastern army restored Galla Placidia and Valentinian to power (now 40 years in the past). It was Aspar who had played a leading role in installing Marcian as emperor, then, after Marcian's death in 457 CE, in promoting an officer from southern Turkey named Leo to be Marcian's successor.

In office, Leo began to strike out on his own. In 467 CE he sent one of his generals, Anthemius, to fill the void as western emperor. Ricimer accepted this candidate, but in the process therefore rejected Geiseric's demand that Ricimer support his own chosen puppet. Then, Leo sent a massive naval expedition to oust the Vandals from their slice of North Africa. The result was a disaster, which ensured that the Vandals would remain the great power in the western Mediterranean.

DISASTER AT SEA

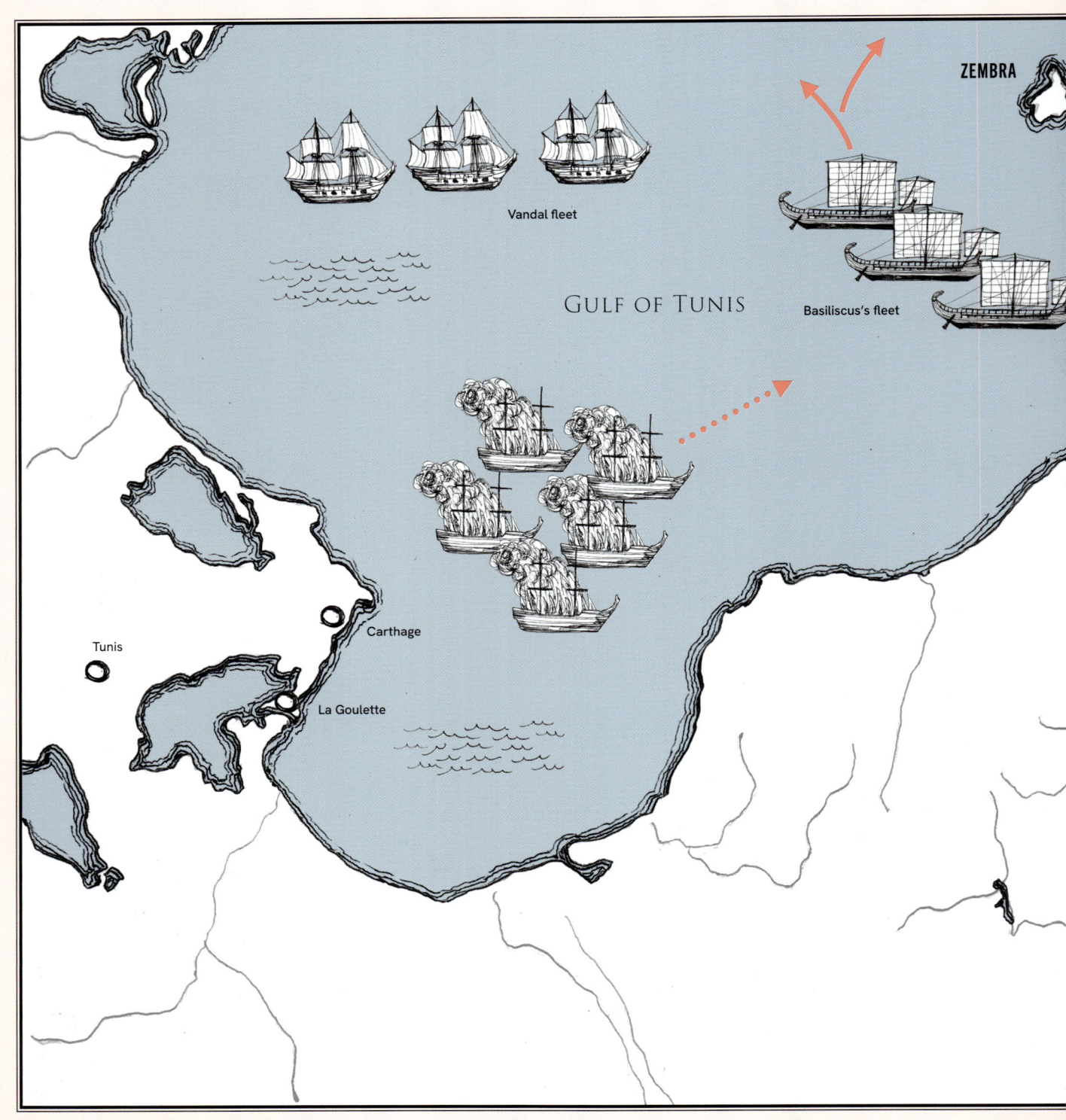

- ····◄ Vandal fireships advance
- ◄─── Roman retreat

The eastern Roman Empire's attempt to prise North Africa away from the Vandals in 468 CE would be remembered as a spectacular disaster. For generations afterwards, it dissuaded the eastern empire from venturing any further action against the Vandals. However, it started off well. The invasion was preceded by two successful operations: the capture of Sardinia and a land campaign in eastern Tunisia, which bordered the surviving Roman province in North Africa, administered from Constantinople.

The commander of the imperial fleet was Emperor Leo's brother-in-law Basiliscus. The fleet he assembled was said to have been the largest ever put together by the eastern empire, although surely not the 1,100 ships mentioned in surviving sources. However many ships there were, they arrived at the peninsula known today as Cap Bon on the eastern side of the Gulf of Tunis. Geiseric sent messengers offering a large sum of money to make peace – an offer that Basiliscus accepted, halting his operation. He played directly into Geiseric's hands. The Vandal leader was looking for an opportune moment to release fireships into the harbour, which was now crowded with imperial vessels. A millennium later, in 1588, Sir Francis Drake and his colleagues deployed very similar tactics to rout the Spanish Armada that was threatening England.

Geiseric's fireships created chaos as the imperial ships strove, without great success, to ward them off. At the same time, the Vandals had a fleet of their own warships outside the harbour, waiting to sink any Roman vessels that escaped the trap. About half of the imperial fleet was destroyed. The survivors, including Basiliscus, fled back to Constantinople.

THE END OF THE WESTERN EMPIRE

Leo remained emperor in the east until 474 CE. Over the next year, first his grandson and then his brother-in-law Basiliscus – the failed naval commander – were briefly emperor, until his son-in-law Zeno ejected Basiliscus. While the eastern empire was witnessing dynastic turmoil, the western empire faced extinction.

During the 460s Ricimer had remained a force to be reckoned with in the west. In 472 CE he revived his role as kingmaker by replacing Anthemius as emperor with the man who had been favoured by Geiseric: Anicius Olybrius. But within months both Ricimer and Olybrius were dead. A new kingmaker, the Burgundian general (and Ricimer's nephew) Gundobad, ended a five-month interregnum by persuading a man named Glycerius to become emperor in 473 CE; then, Gundobad promptly departed Rome for Gaul, where he deemed developments to be of greater importance.

The effect of Gundobad's departure was to leave the new emperor exposed. He was toppled by Julius Nepos, commander of the Balkan army. Backed by the eastern emperor, Nepos seized the throne in 474 CE, only to retreat to Illyricum within months when it became plain that he lacked the support of the commander of Italy's army, Orestes. Now, Orestes exploited the volatile situation to install his young son Romulus Augustulus as a figurehead *augustus* for his own rule. Father and son had barely a year to savor their pre-eminence, before, in 476 CE, Orestes died in a mutiny and Romulus was deposed.

The man who overthrew Orestes and Romulus was Odoacer, the son of one of Attila's generals. He now wrote to Emperor Zeno to announce that there was no longer any need for a Roman emperor in the west. Zeno was receiving entreaties of a different kind from the still-ambitious Nepos, asking the eastern emperor to recognize his continuing claim as emperor in the west. Zeno was sympathetic, being related to Nepos through marriage, but he was in no position to champion his cause. Indeed, Zeno's lack of interest in western entanglements was underscored by the 'perpetual peace' he arranged with Geiseric, which stated that the Romans and Vandals would not enter into hostile actions against each other. With his hopes of recovering the throne ended, Nepos spent the next five years claiming it, in vain, from Salona (near present-day Split, Croatia). There would be no further claimant to the Roman imperial throne in the west after Nepos was murdered in his villa on the 9th of May, 480 CE.

As for Odoacer, he continued to reign, not as emperor, but as King of Italy until his own murder in 493 CE. His personal style made a point; he would be depicted on his coins sporting a 'barbarian' moustache. It was something no Roman emperor had ever done.

Figure VII (above)

This coin shows Odoacer, bare-headed without any regalia, but with a hairstyle and moustache, an overall look that stresses his Germanic background. The legend 'FL ODOVAC', partly visible on the obverse, identifies the portrait as being of the king himself.

Figure VIII (opposite)

The scene depicted on this sarcophagus from Acilia, west of Rome, represents the honorary procession of a consul who has just taken leave of the family members represented here for his inauguration into office.

CHRONOLOGY 409–480 CE

409 CE
Entry of Vandals, Sueves and Alans into Spain; Gerontius's rebellion against Constantine III.

410 CE
End of direct imperial rule in Britain.

411 CE
Constantius's campaign in Gaul; suicide of Gerontius; surrender and execution of Constantine III.

412 CE
Revolt of Jovinus on the Rhine: Visigoths join forces with him.

413 CE
Overthrow of Jovinus by Athaulf; Visigoths granted land in southern Gaul; revolt of Heraclian in North Africa.

414 CE
Athaulf marries Galla Placidia on 1st of January; Constantius attacks Visigoths who move to Spain; birth of Theodosius, son of Athaulf and Galla Placidia; Pulcheria proclaimed *augusta* in Constantinople.

415 CE
Theodosius dies; Athaulf murdered; Wallia becomes leader of the Visigoths; Visigoths restore Galla Placidia to Rome.

417 CE
Constantius marries Galla Placidia.

418 CE
Visigoths return to Gaul; death of Wallia; Theoderic I becomes king of the Visigoths; birth of Justa Grata Honoria, daughter of Constantius and Galla Placidia.

419 CE
Birth of Valentinian III, son of Constantius and Galla Placidia.

421 CE
Vandals occupy southern Spain; Constantius declared co-*augustus* by Honorius; Constantius dies (2nd of September); marriage of Aelia Eudocia and Theodosius II.

422 CE
Galla Placidia flees east with her children; birth of Licinia Eudoxia, daughter of Theodosius II and Aelia Eudocia.

423 CE
Aelia Eudocia proclaimed *augusta* at Constantinople; Honorius dies; John becomes emperor in Italy; Boniface appointed governor of Africa.

425 CE
John overthrown by eastern imperial army; Galla Placidia and Valentinian III installed as rulers in the west; agreement of Aetius to serve the regime.

429 CE
Vandals enter North Africa.

432 CE
Civil war between Aetius and Boniface: Aetius and his Hunnic allies defeated, but Boniface dies; Bonface's successor, Sebastian, forced to flee east.

433 CE
Aetius appointed *magister utriusque militae* in the western empire.

434 CE
Attila and his brother Bleda succeed as joint leaders of the Huns: they support Aetius in campaigns against the Burgundians and Visigoths (437–39 CE).

439 CE
Vandals capture Carthage.

441 CE
Hunnic attack on the eastern empire.

442 CE
By treaty, Vandals receive most of North Africa.

443 CE
Treaty between the Huns and the eastern empire.

445 CE
Bleda murdered by Attila, who becomes sole king of the Huns; Aetius's second treaty with the Vandals, recognizing their lands.

447 CE
Attila's attack on Pannonia.

449 CE
Eastern embassy to Attila (described by Priscus); Attila made *magister militum* by Valentinian III.

450 — 460 — 470 — 480 — CE

450 CE
Honoria requests Attila's assistance; death of Theodosius II: succeeded by Marcian as emperor in the east.

451 CE
Attila's invasion of Gaul and defeat at the Battle of the Catalaunian Plains (20th of June).

452 CE
Attila's invasion of Italy.

453 CE
Death of Attila.

454 CE
Murder of Aetius by Valentinian III (21st of September).

455 CE
Assassination of Valentinian III (21st of March); his successor, Maximus, murdered within 11 weeks; sack of Rome by the Vandals under Geiseric; western throne claimed by Flavius Avitus at Arles.

456 CE
Avitus defeated by Ricimer; Ricimer promotes Majorian to emperor in the west.

457 CE
Death of Marcian; succession of Leo I as emperor in the east.

461 CE
Execution of Majorian and replacement with Libius Severus, who is not recognized by the eastern empire.

465 CE
Death of Libius Severus: the western imperial throne is vacant for two years.

467 CE
Anthemius, an eastern general, made emperor in the west.

468 CE
Battle of Cape Bon: Vandals under Geiseric destroy an eastern imperial fleet.

472 CE
Anthemius replaced as western emperor by Ricimer's candidate, Olybrius; death of Ricimer (18th of August); death of Olybrius (2nd of November).

473 CE
Glycerius appointed western emperor by Burgundian general Gundobad.

474 CE
Glycerius deposed by the eastern-backed Julius Nepos, who assumes the title *augustus*; death of Leo I; eventual succession of Zeno as eastern emperor.

475 CE
Revolt of Basiliscus in the east; Nepos ejected from the western throne by Orestes, who is proclaimed *augustus* (with his son Romulus).

476 CE
Basiliscus defeated and Zeno restored as emperor in the east; Orestes killed in a mutiny led by Odoacer, who deposes Romulus and proclaims himself King of Italy.

480 CE
Nepos murdered at Salona (9th of May).

FINAL CONVULSIONS

EPILOGUE

WHAT WENT WRONG?

Given the often lurid allegations swirling around the lives of Roman emperors, and the murderous ambition and chaos that frequently brought them to power (and ended that power), it is tempting to read the implosion of the Roman Empire as a kind of moral judgement on human venality and immorality: the rot spread from the top.

Failure there certainly was – and in plentiful supply, when it came to individual personalities, decision and actions. But accounting for the failure of the whole system, which had withstood all manner of badly behaved individuals after Augustus, requires a different judgement. Put simply, the collapse of the Roman Empire stemmed from the persistent failure of the emperors who succeeded Theodosius I, and their advisers, to understand the principles that underlay Augustus's creation of the imperial system.

According to the Augustan system, the army was to be commanded by officers who owed their positions to the emperor. That army would be a mixture of troops from different backgrounds, citizen and non-citizen. Service in the army would help to bind provincial communities and leadership groups into the government of the empire. When that relationship broke down – as it did, for example, in the rebellions by Arminius and Boudicca – the result was catastrophic. It is somewhat ironic that in the early fifth century CE the Goth Alaric, in his persistent search for legitimacy within the imperial system, showed a better understanding of the Augustan ideal than did Emperor Honorius and his courtiers.

In the Augustan system, the empire's immediate neighbours also needed to feel that they profited from their association with Rome, and thus, ideally, could act as a forward defence against external aggression. Hence the reliance on allied states that existed between the boundaries of Roman provinces and the Persians in the east, and on the economic evolution of settled peoples along the northern frontiers. When the government lost the capacity or interest to provide this support, as appears to have happened with some regularity in Britain, the result was constant instability and the solution – building a new wall – expensive.

The nature of decision-making mattered, too. Under the Augustan system, the emperor was required to take decisions based on advice he received from subordinates who had served extensively in the provinces. Provincial governors were expected to follow the policies dictated by the emperor. The grand strategy of empire that emerged from this system was based on calculations of affordability and the rational distribution of military forces to defend the frontiers. Imperial aggression was largely reactive to perceived threats from beyond the frontiers, and the peoples of the empire regarded the imperial government as providing a fortress to protect them. In the wake of Valens' mismanagement of the Thervingi and Greuthungi in the fourth century CE, the initiative passed from the imperial government to its neighbours, and Theodosius I's surrender of territory to the Goths set a precedent that undermined the ability of the imperial regime to pay for an army that would be strong enough to control the frontier.

Another major break with the Augustan system was the progressive weakening of the imperial office with respect to the imperial aristocracy. A persistent theme in the century after the death of Julian, after the mid-360s CE, was the refusal of senior officials or generals to take on the job of emperor for themselves. They appear to have felt that the real power lay elsewhere, that an emperor should be guided by the collective wisdom of senior officials, and that, if the emperor refused, those officials should be free to make significant decisions in their own interest. The result was increasing factionalization as self-interest was mistaken for the interest of the state. In the end, an Attila or a Geiseric came to occupy positions rather similar to those of powerful regional bureaucrats.

The ideology of victory that supported the Roman imperial regime had to be based, in the end, on the actuality of military success. Emperors Trajan and Marcus Aurelius won the wars that are celebrated on their columns. The crisis of the mid-third century CE stemmed from the combination of structural weaknesses arising from economic mistakes – notably, Emperor Severus's military pay rise in the late second century CE – and the losses stemming from pandemics and the military incompetence shown by a series of emperors. A critical qualification for the job of emperor was the ability to understand and direct military operations. The restoration of imperial stability by the emperors from Claudius II to Constantine underscores the point that as long as capable people filled the senior position in the state, Rome could control its relationship with its neighbours. When emperors could no longer exercise command of their armies, that relationship was again reversed after Constantine, this time permanently.

Finally, it was important that the ideology of Rome's imperial system aligned with reality. Belief that the gods – or God – secured the empire against its neighbours in the company of the emperor could be retained only when the emperor in question was actually capable of handling the job. A state cannot endure when ideology is detached from reality. The separation of ideal from real doomed the Roman Empire.

Figure I (opposite)

This mid-third-century depiction of combat stresses the violence inherent in hand-to-hand struggles as it shows a member of an auxiliary cohort victorious over a rival.

Figure II (overleaf)

A ship from the fleet of Augustus sinks a ship from the fleet of Antony and Cleopatra. This image, from the collection of the Dukes of Cardona at Córdoba, Spain, stresses the tactical superiority of Augustus's ships.

FURTHER READING

Abdy, Richard
- *Legion: Life in the Roman Army* (London, 2024)

Birley, Anthony R.
- *Marcus Aurelius: A Biography*, 2nd edn (London, 2000)

Birley, Robin
- *Vindolanda: Everyday Life on Rome's Northern Frontier* (Stroud, Gloucestershire, 2009)

Bowersock, G. W.
- *Julian the Apostate* (Cambridge, MA, 1978)
- *Roman Arabia* (Cambridge, MA, 1983)

Bowman, Alan K.
- *Life and Letters on the Roman Frontier* (London, 1994)

Brice, Lee L., and Greene, Elizabeth M., eds,
- *Women and the Army in the Roman Empire* (Cambridge, 2024)

Brown, Peter
- *The Rise of Western Christendom*, 2nd edn (London, 2003)

Brunt, P. A.
- *Roman Imperial Themes* (Oxford, 1990)

Campbell, J. B.
- *The Emperor and the Roman Army 31 BC–AD 235* (Oxford, 1984)

Corcoran, Simon
- *The Empire of the Tetrarchs: Imperial Pronouncements and Government, AD 284–324* (Oxford, 1986)

Goldsworthy, Adrian
- *The Complete Roman Army* (London, 2007)
- *How Rome Fell: Death of a Superpower* (New Haven, CT, 2010)
- *Rome and Persia: The Seven Hundred Year Rivalry* (London, 2023)

Gordon, C. D.
- *The Age of Attila: Fifth-Century Byzantium and the Barbarians*, rev. edn (Ann Arbor, MI, 2013)

Greatrex, Geoffrey, and Samuel N. C. Lieu
- *The Roman Eastern Frontier and the Persian Wars AD 363–628* (London, 2002)

Griffin, Miriam T.
- *Nero: The End of a Dynasty* (New Haven, CT, 1984)

Gurval, Robert
- *Actium and Augustus: The Politics and Emotions of Civil War* (Ann Arbor, MI, 1995)

Hart, Timothy C.
- *Beyond the River: Under the Eye of Rome* (Ann Arbor, MI, 2024)

Heather, Peter
- *The Fall of the Roman Empire: A New History of Rome and the Barbarians* (Oxford, 2005)
- *Empires and Barbarians: The Fall of Rome and the Birth of Europe* (Oxford, 2012)

Holland, Tom
- *Pax: War and Peace in Rome's Golden Age* (London, 2023)

Kelly, Christopher
- *The End of Empire: Attila the Hun and the Fall of Rome* (New York, 2009)

Lacey, James
- *Rome: Strategy of Empire* (Oxford, 2022)

Lane Fox, Robin
- *Pagans and Christians* (London, 1986)

Levick, Barbara
- *Vespasian*, 2nd edn (London and New York, 2017)
- *Julia Domna: Syrian Empress* (London, 2007)

Mattern, Susan P.
- *Rome and the Enemy: Imperial Strategy in the Principate* (Berkeley, CA, 1999)

Matthews, John
- *The Roman Empire of Ammianus*, 2nd edn (Ann Arbor, MI, 2008)
- and Cornell, Tim, *Atlas of the Roman World* (London, 1982)

Mattingly, David
- *An Imperial Possession: Britain in the Roman Empire* (London, 2007)
- *Imperialism, Power, and Identity: Experiencing the Roman Empire* (Princeton, NJ, 2011)

Maxfield, Valerie
- *The Military Decorations of the Roman Army* (London, 1981)

Millar, Fergus
- *The Roman Near East 31 BC–AD 337* (Cambridge, MA, 1993)

O'Donnell, James J.
- *The Ruin of the Roman Empire: A New History of the Emperor Who Brought It Down and the Barbarians Who Could Have Saved It* (New York, 2008)

Phang, Sara Elise
- *Roman Military Service: Ideologies of Discipline in the Late Republic and Early Principate* (Cambridge, 2008)

Pollard, Nigel, and Berry, Joanne
- *The Complete Roman Legions* (London, 2012)

Potter, David
- *Constantine the Emperor* (Oxford, 2012)
- *The Roman Empire at Bay: AD 180–395*, 2nd edn (London, 2014)
- *The Origin of Empire: Rome from the Republic to Hadrian* (London, 2019)
- *Master of Rome: A Life of Julius Caesar* (Oxford, 2025)

Syme, Ronald
- *The Roman Revolution* (Oxford, 1939)
- *Tacitus* (Oxford, 1958)

Talbert, Richard J. A.
- *Rome's World: The Peutinger Map Reconsidered* (Cambridge, 2010)
- *Ancient Perspectives: Maps and Their Place in Mesopotamia, Egypt, Greece, and Rome* (Chicago, 2012)

Tatum, W. Jeffrey
- *A Noble Ruin: Mark Antony, Civil War, and the Collapse of the Roman Republic* (Oxford, 2023)

Watts, Edward J.
- *The Final Pagan Generation: Rome's Unexpected Path to Christianity* (Berkeley, CA, and Los Angeles, 2020)

Wellesley, Kenneth
- *The Year of the Four Emperors*, 3rd edn (London, 2000)

Wells, Peter S.
- *The Battle that Stopped Rome: Emperor Augustus, Arminius, and the Slaughter of the Legions in Teutoburg Forest* (New York, 2003)

INDEX

Page numbers in *italic* refer to the captions.

A

Abgar 125
Abritus 178, 189
Acte 88
Actium 33, 38–39, 42–43, 49–51, 54, 66–67, 219
Adamclisi 116
Adiabene 125, 148, 160
Adrianople 8, 216, 218–19, *238*, 245–7, 268 *see also* Edirne
Adriatic 29, 60
Aelia Capitolina 136
Aelian Wall *see* Hadrian's Wall
Aemilianus (emperor) 179, 189
Aetius, Flavius 266, 281, 283–4, 288, 290–93, 298–9
Afghanistan 21
Africa 21, 31, 43, 174, 180, 191, 204, 211, 241, 256, 269, 274, 281, 283–4, 293, 298
· North 7, 9, *27*, 83, 121, 125, 132, 148, *154*, 160, 189, 249, 267, 283, 292–3, 295, 298
Against Eutropius 256
Age of Diocletian 18, 235
Agricola, Julius 108, 111, 126
Agrippa, Marcus Vipsanius 31–32, 39, 43, *51*, 54, *54*, *59*, 61, 63, 67, *72*
Agrippina *61*, *72*, 75, 77, 83, 88, 110
Ahura Mazda (god) *172*
Akhiva *see* bar Kokhba
Alamanni 168, 233, *238*, 248
Alans 249, 255, 259, 271, 275, 281, 290, 298
Alaric 251, 255–6, 258–9, 262, 266–7, 269, 271, 274, 283, 286, 292, 301
Albinus, Clodius 160, 163, 188
Alemanni 227
Alexander, Marcus Aurelius Severus (emperor) 170, *170*, 172–3, 188–9
Alexander the Great 9, 160, 165, 169, 176
Alexandria 32, 33, 42, 66, 97, 169

Alexianus *see* Alexander, Marcus Aurelius Severus
Algeria 133, 170, 283
Allectus 197
Alps 22, 51, 67, 96, 205, 211, 249, 259
al-Tabari: *History* 224
Altar of Peace 43, 54
Altar of Victory 251
Amandus 194
Ambrose 250–51
Amida 227–8, 233
Anagnina 154
Anastasia 216
Anatolia 148, 160, 174, 222, 235
Anatolian plateau 216
Angivarii 74
Angles 276
Anglesey 83, 87, 111
Annals 75–76, 89, 126
Anthemius (emperor) 293, 296, 299
Antinous 137, 148
Antioch 125, 141, 148, 163, 170, 178, 189, 198, 226, 235, 243–4, 268
Antonine dynasty 215
Antonine Wall 140, 149
Antoninus, Marcus Aurelius *see* Caracalla
Antoninus, Marcus Aurelius (grandson of Julia Maesa) 170
Antoninus, Titus Aurelius *see* Antoninus Pius
Antoninus, Uranius 178
Antoninus Pius (emperor) 7, *137*, 137–8, 140, 148, 149
Antonius, Lucius 31
Antony, Mark 22, 24–27, 29, 31–33, 37, 39, *42*, 42–43, 50, 66–67, *302*
Aosta Valley 51
Apollo 215
Apostles 200, 278
Appian (historian) 29
Appian Way 204
Aquileia 174, 218, 250, 269, 280, 289
Aquitania 51
Arabia 49, 122, 132, 140, 148, 180
Arbogast 250–54, 259, 269
Arcadius (emperor) 254–6, *255*, 258–9, 269, 278, *278*

Arch of Constantine 211, *211*, 214, 214–15
Arch of Galerius *198*, 198–9
Arch of Septimius Severus 215
Arch of Titus 100
archers 76, 92, 121–2
Ardabur, Flavius 280
Ardashir (king) *172*, 172–3, 176, 188–9
Argentoratum *see* Strasbourg
Ariobarzanes (king) 59
Arius 221, 251
Ark of the Covenant 292
Arles 204, 274, 293, 299
· Council of 211
Armenia 32, 50, 59–60, 67, 76, 88–89, 110–11, 122, 124, 126, 140–41, 148–9, 172–3, 176, 198, 222–3, 232–3, 244, 268
Arminius, Flavius 63
Arminius, Julius 59, 61, 63, 67, 72, 74–76, 301
Arsacid 141, 170, 172, 176, 198
Artabanus 172, *172*
Artashat 89
Artavasdes (king) 32
Artavasdes II (king) 32
Artaxas (king) 50
Asia 29, 88, 180, 286
Aspar 280, 293
Asta 258
Athaulf 267, 271, 274, 281, 283–4, 298
Athens 29, 50, 182, 189
Atia 66
Atrebates 79, 80
Attalus, Priscus (emperor) 266–7, 269, 274
Attianus, Publius Acilius 125
Attila (king) *283*, 283–92, 296, 298–9, 302
augusta 113, 278, 298
Augustan (system) 7, 43, 64, 77, 93, 301, 302
Augustine of Hippo 267, 278, 283
· *City of God, The* 263, 267
· *Confessions* 278
Augustulus, Romulus 296
augustus 197, 202–5, 216, 222, 228, 232–3, 235, 238, 241, 243, 248–50, 254, *255*, 268–9, 276, 280, 292–3, 296, 298–9

308 ATLAS OF THE ROMAN EMPIRE

Augustus (emperor) 7, *22*, 27, *27*, *33*, 42–43, *43*, 47, 49–51, 53–54, 59–60, 63–64, 67, 69, 72, *72*, 77, 79, 110, 126, 132, 155, 173, 259, 278, 301, *302*
· *The Deeds of the Divine Augustus* 42, *49*, 49–50
Augustus of Prima Porta 50
Aurelian (emperor) 165, 178, 182, 185, 187, 189, 191, 194, 202, 211, 219, 258
Aurelius, Marcus (emperor) 7, *122*, 138, 141–2, *142*, 145–7, *146*, 149, 151, 159, 163, 197, 215, *302*
· *Meditations* 138, *142*, 147, 151
Aurelius Victor, Sextus 197
Austria 51, 133
Autun 16–18
Axidares (king) 122

B
Baden-Württemberg 51
Baghdad 32, 125
Balbinus (emperor) 174, 189
Balearic Islands 121
Balkans 43, 51, 54, 61, 132, 141, 160, 176, 178, 182, *182*, 185, 189, 198, 204, *216*, 222–3, 232, 241, 243–4, 248, 250, 256, 259, 268–9, 283–4, 289
Ballista 181
bar Kokhba 136–7, *137*, 148
Basiliscus 295–6, 299
Basingstoke 79
Bassiana, Julia Soaemias *170*
Bassianus 216
Batavians 98, 104, 134
Baths of Diocletian (Rome) *191*
Battle of Abritus 189
Battle of Actium 33, 38–9, 42, *42*, 50–51, 66, 219
Battle of Adrianople 246, 268
Battle of Calvatone 111
Battle of Cape Bon 299
Battle of Carrhae 49
Battle of the Catalaunian Plains 288, 290–91, 299
Battle of Colchester 80, 83
Battle of the Frigidus 251–2, 259, 269
Battle of Harzhorn 175

Battle of the Milvian Bridge 205–6, *206*, 215, 232
Battle of Philippi 28–29, 66
Battle of Singara 233
Battle of Tapae 111
Battle of Teutoburg Forest 61–2, 72
Bavaria 51
Bay of Naples 31, 88
Bede 100
Belgium 21, 134
Beroia 218
Bishop of Rome 210, 251, 289
Bithynia 115, 180
Black Sea 21, 142, 219
Bleda 283–4, 286, 298
Bologna 22, 25
Boniface 281, 283, 298
Bonosus 194
Bosnia 51, 54
Bosporus 219
Boudicca (queen) 83, *85*, 85–88, 95, 104, 111, 176, 301
Brigantes 80, 83
Brindisi (Brundisium) 31
Britain (Britannia) 7, 18, *27*, 79, 80, 83, 87–88, 95, 104, *104*, 108, 110–11, 126, 132–3, 140–41, 148–9, 154, 160, 168, 176, 182, 188, 197, 203, 241, 249, *249*, 256, 259, 269, 271, 276, 283, 298, 301
Brundisium *see* Brindisi
Brutus 22, 25, 27, 29, 66
Brutus, Decimus *see* Decimus
Brutus, Marcus Junius *see* Brutus
Bulgaria 51, 178, 216, 244
Burgundians 276, 283, 298
Busento 267
Byzantium (Constantinople; Istanbul) 219, 221, 233

C
Caecina, Aulus 74–75, 97–98
Caenis, Antonia 92, 154
caesar 7, 16, 160, 163, 167, 174, 194, 197, 200, 202–4, 216, 218, 222, 226–8, 232–3, 280
Caesar, Gaius 59, *59*, 60, 67

Caesar, Gaius Julius *see* Octavian
Caesar, Germanicus 61, *61*, 63, *64*, 67, 72, 74–77, 79, 110, 256
Caesar, Julius 7, 9–10, *10*, 21–22, 25–26, 29, *31*, 31–32, 42, 50–51, *51*, 66, 79, 96, 104, 122, 165, 205
Caesar, Lucius 59, *59*, 67
Caesarea 95
Caesarion 32
Caesars, The (Sextus Aurelius Victor) 197
Calabria 32
Calgacus 109
Caligula (emperor) 7, 77, 79, *79*, 83, 110, 197
Calpurnii Pisones 107
Calvatone 97–98, 111
Campania 180
Campus Martius 145
Camulodunum *see* Colchester
Candidianus 280
Cap Bon 295
Capitoline Hill 98, 165, *165*, 170
Cappadocia 88–89, 110, 140, 149, 180
Capri 76–77, 79, 110, 151
Caracalla (emperor) 163, 167, *168*, 168–70, *169*, 188
Caratacus 80, 83
Carausius 197, 219, 232
Carinus (emperor) 187, 191, 194, 232
Carnuntum 133, 142, 149, 188
Carrhae 32, 49, 169–70, 180–81, 198, 232
Cartagena 293
Carthage 8, 43, 174, 283, 292, 298
Cartimandua (queen) 80, 83
Carus (emperor) 187, 189, 191, 235
Cassius 22, 25, 27, 29, 66
Cassius, Avidius 141, 146, 149
Castelfranco Emilia *see* Forum Gallorum
Catacombs of Domatilla *200*
Catalaunian Plains 288, 290–91, 299
Catus, Decianus 87
Catuvellauni 79, 83
cavalry 32, 62–63, 76, 104, 116, 121–2, 124, 130, 133, 135, 182, 200, 206, 238, 242, 247, 249, 288
Ceionius 137

Cerialis, Flavius 134–5
Cerialis, Petilius 104, 108
Châlons 185, 288
Characene 125
Charax 140
Chatti 54, 74
Cherusci 59–60, 63, 74, 76
Chester 131
Chichester 80, 83
Chosroes (king) 172
Christians 8, 179, 189, 200, *200*, 202–3, 210–11, 214–16, *216*, 221, 223, 228, 232, *235*, *241*, 251, 253, *259*, 262, 267, 278
· Church 8, 179, 228
· God 206, 211, 253
· Goths 258
Cibalae 216, 223
Cicero, Marcus Tullius 27
Cilicia 125, 180, 216
Cilician plain 216
Circus Maximus 92, 113, 116, 154
Cisalpine Gaul 21–22
City of God, The (Augustine of Hippo) 263, 267
Civilis, Julius 104
Classicianus 87
Classicus, Julius 104
Claudian 255–6, 278
Claudius, Marcus Aurelius 182
Claudius (emperor) 13, 79, 80, 83, 88, 110, 126
Claudius II (emperor) 182, 185, 189, 191, 205, 232
Cleander 154, 188
Clemens, Flavius 108
Cleopatra (queen) 29, 31–33, *33*, 39, 42, 66, *302*
cohorts 24, 62, *69*, 76–77, 115, 122, 134, *302*
Colchester 80, 83, 87, 104, 111
Cologne (Colonia Agrippinensis) 51, 113, 133
Colonia Commodiana 154, 188
Colosseum *98*, 100, *100*, 111, 113, 151, 154, 215
Column of Marcus Aurelius 145
comitatenses 200, 202, 222, 228

Commagene 141
Commodus, Lucius Ceionius *see* Ceionius *and* Commodus
Commodus (emperor) 7, 146–7, 149, 151, *154*, 154–5, 159–60, 188
Confessions (Augustine of Hippo) 278
Conquest of Britain 79, 80, 83
Conspiracy of Murena 67
Conspiracy of Sejanus 110
Conspiracy of Silvanus 233
Conspiracy of Theodorus 268
Constans (emperor) 222–3, 226, 233
Constantia 216, 219
Constantine I (emperor) 8, 13, 16, *197*, 200, 202–6, *203*, *206*, 210, 210–11, *211*, *214*, 214–16, *216*, 218–19, *221*, 221–2, 230, 232–3, 251, 302
Constantine II (emperor) 218, 222–3, 232–3
Constantine III (emperor) 259, 266, 269, 271, 274, 276, 298
Constantinople (Byzantium; Istanbul) *13*, 18, 27, *221*, 222, 233, 238, 245, 247–8, 250, 256, 258, *259*, 267, 276, 278, 283–4, 286, 288, 292, 295, 298 *see also* Byzantium
Constantius, Flavius *see* Constantius I
Constantius I (emperor) 16, 19, 191, 197, *197*, *198*, 200, 202–4, 215, 218, 232
Constantius II (emperor) 222–3, 226–8, *228*, 233, 235, 238, 296
Constantius III (emperor) 271, 274, 276, *276*, *281*, 298
Constitutio Antoniniana 167
Corbulo, Domitius 88–89, 92, 110–11
Cornelianus, Atidius 141
Corsica 31
Cosentia 267
Council of Nicaea 8, 221, 233
Crassus 26, 67, 96
Cremona 98
Crispus 203, *203*, 218–19, 221–2, 232–3
Croatia 51, 191, 221, 296
Ctesiphon 32, 125, 141, 148–9, 165, 187, 228
cubicularius 151, 154, 188, 292
Cunobelin 79, 80, 83
Czech Republic 60

D
Dacia 116, *120*, 120–21, 132, 148, 180
Dacian wars 122
· First 116, 148
· Second 121, 148
Dacians 108, 111, 116, 120–21, 145, 255
Dadastana 235
Daia, Maximinus *202*, 203, 205, 211, 216, *216*, 232
Dalmatia 50, 54, 79, 191
Dalmatius 222
Danube (river) 51, 54, 64, 67, 108, 113, 116, 122, 126, 132, 141–2, 145–7, 149, 151, 160, 168, 178–9, 222, 227–8, 241, 243, 244, 248, 258, 268–9, 284, 286
Darius III (king) 160, 169
Dark Age 271
Decebelus (king) 108, 116, 121, 132
Decimus 22, 24–25
Decius (emperor) 176, 178–9, 189
Deeds of the Divine Augustus, The (Augustus) 42, 49–50
Devnya (Marcianopolis) 244
Dexippus, Publius 178, 181–2
Diana 215
Dio, Cassius 37, 115, 147, 163, 170
· *Roman History* 87, 156, 163
Diocles, Gaius Aurelius Valerius *see* Diocletian
Diocletian 8, 18, 134, 187, 189, 191, *191*, 194, *194*, 197–8, *198*, 200–4, *202*, 215–16, 221, 222, 222, 230, 232, 235, 238, 248
Dionysius, Papirius 154
Divine Mind 211
Domitian (emperor) 71, 98, 100, 108, 111, 113, 116, 197
Domna, Julia 160, *169*, 170, *170*
Domus Aurea 100
Draco 16
Drake, Sir Francis 295
Drusilla, Livia 22
Drusus 49, 51, 54, *54*, 59, *64*, 67, 72, 76–77, 110
Drynovets 178
Dura-Europos 176, *179*

E

Eclectus 154, 159–60
Edessa (Urfa) 165, 169, 180
Edict of Milan 216
Edirne 8, 247 *see also* Adrianople
Egypt 29, 31, *33*, 42–3, 49, 67, 95, 125, 132, 137, 146, 148, 165, 169, 185, 188, 198, 219, 232
Elagabalus 170, *178*, 179, 185, 188
Elbe 51, 54, 63
Elegeia 141
Emesa (Homs) 160, 170, 179, 185
Ems 74, 76
England 79, 130, 133, 295
English Channel 197
Epaphroditus 108
Ephesus 122
Ephrem Syrus (Ephrem the Syrian) 226
 · *Hymn Against Julian III* 229
Eucherius *256*, 262
Eudocia, Aelia 298
Eudocia (Empress) 278, 284, 292
Eudoxia 278, 292
Eudoxia, Licinia 298
Eugenius (emperor) 269, 288, 250–51, 253–4
eunuchs 256, 258, 267, 288, 292
Euphrates (river) 50, 60, 125, 140–41, 149, 173, 176, 178, 230
Europe 8, 164, 197, 206, 218
 · Central 7, 43, 51, 67, 108, 255, 288
 · Western 51, 271
Eusebius (Bishop) 211, 219, 221
 · *Life of Constantine* 211, 219
Eutropius 256, 258, 269

F

Fars 172
Fausta 204, 216, 221–2, 232–3
Faustina 146
Faustus, Flavius 281
Fectio *see* Vechten
Field of Mars *see* Campus Martius
Fifth Legion 51
First Cohort of Tungrians 134
Firth of Clyde 140
Firth of Forth 108, 140
Flaccus, Hordeonius 96, 104
Flavian dynasty 98, 100, 108, 160
Flavus 63
Florence 259
Florus, Gessius 95, 111
Forma Urbis Romae 16–17, 19
Forum (Rome) 50, 163, *165*, 215, 267
Forum Boarium 13
Forum Gallorum 24
Forum of Trajan 120, *120*
France 7, 10, 21, 51, 203, 267, 276, 288, 293 *see also* Gaul
Franks 168, 194, 204, 219, 222, 232, 238, 256, 291
Frigidus 253 *see also* Battle of the Frigidus
Fritigern 244, 247
Frontinus 108
Fuscus, Cornelius 97

G

Gainas 256, 258
Gaius Vibius Pansa Caetronianus *see* Pansa
Galatia 110, 180
Galba, Sulpicius (emperor) 93, 96, 104, 111, 113
Galen 155
Galerius (emperor) 197–200, *198*, *202*, 202–6, *216*, 230, 232–3
Galilee 95, 111
Galla *see* Placidia, Galla
Gallienus (emperor) 179, 181–2, *182*, 189, 191, 200, 202, 219, 248
Gallus 222, 226, 233
Gallus, Cestius 95, 111
Gallus, Trebonianus (emperor) 178–9, 189
Gaul 10, 21–22, 24–25, 31–32, 50–51, 67, 79, 80, 87, 93, 95, 104, 111, 179, 189, 194, 204, 216, 223, 227–8, 232–3, 241, 248–50, 258–9, 266–7, 269, 271, 274, 280, 283–4, 286, 288, 291, 293, 296, 298–9
Geiseric 281–4, 288, 292–3, 295–6, 299, 302
Gemellus 77
Geoffrey of Monmouth 249
Georgia 88
Germania
 · Inferior 96, 104, 182
 · Superior 79, 93, 96, 104
Germanic states *see* Germany
Germany 8, 18, 43, 51, 54, 59–64, 67, 72, 74–77, 79, 88, 95–97, 110–11, 113, 126, 132–3, 149, 160, 168, 174, 180, 182, 188, 203, 227, 256, 259, 266, 271, 276, 278, 283, 289, 291, 293, *296*
Gerontius 274, 298
Geta (emperor) 168, *169*, 188
Gibbon, Edward 7, 53
Gladiator (film) 151
gladiators 7, 92, 100, 113, 147, *154*, 154–6
Glycerius (emperor) 296, 299
Gordian (emperor) 174, 189
Gordian III (emperor) 174, 176, 189
Gospel of Matthew 72
Goths 178, 182, 189, 219, 241, *242*, 244–8, 250–51, 253–6, 258–9, 266–7, 268–9, 274, 283–4, 291, 301, 302
Grammaticus 83
Gratian (emperor) 238, 241, *241*, 243–5, 247, 248–9, *249*, 268–9
Greece 21, 29, 39, 51, 90, 92, 95, 111, 148, 199
Greuthungi 241, 244, 248
Gulf of Tunis 295
Gundobad 296, 299
Guntiarius 283

H

Hadrian (emperor) 18, 13, 48, 113, 120, 122, 125–6, *126*, 130, 132–4, 136–7, 140, 215
Hadrian's Wall 16, *18*, 130–31, 133–4, 140, *164*, 276
Hampshire 79
Hannibal (the Carthaginian) 104, 176
Hannibalianus (king) 222
Hanover 74
Harran 32, 168
Harzhorn 174 *see also* Battle of Harzhorn

Hatra 125, 165, 172
Helena *197*, 221, *221*
Hellespont 216, 218, 258
Heracleius 292
Heraclian 274, 298
Herculaneum *33*, 42, *106*, *107*
Herculanus 288
Hercules 42, 151, 154, 194, 197, 202, 215
Herculius *see* Maximian
Herod (of Judaea) 67, 95, *137*
Herodian: *History* 173
Herodion *137*
Hesse 54, 74, 168
Hippo 283 *see also* Augustine of Hippo
Hirtius, Aulus 22, 24
Hispania *see* Spain
Historia Chronica (John of Antioch) 280, 288
Historiae Adversus Paganos see History Against the Pagans
Histories (Tacitus) 98
History (al-Tabari) 224
History (Ammianus Marcellinus) 243, 247
History (Herodian) 173
History (Olympiodorus) 277
History (Priscus) 284, 286
History Against the Pagans (Orosius) 250, 262
History of the Goths (Jordanes) 282, 287
Homs 160 *see also* Emesa
Honoria 276, 286, 288, 298–9
Honorius (emperor) 254–6, *255*, 258–9, 262, 266–7, 269, 271, 274, 276, 278, 280, 298, 301
Hormisdas (Hormizd) 228
House of the Faun (Pompeii) 107
House of the Papyri (Herculaneum) *106*, *107*
House of the Vettii (Pompeii) *74*, *106*, *107*
Housesteads 131, 134
Huneric 284, 292
Hungary 51, 116
Huns 8, 244, 255, 258–9, *283*, 283–4, 286, 288–9, 291, 298
Hyacinthus 288

I
Iberia (Iberian peninsula) 88–9, 276
Iceni 80, 83, 87
Idistaviso 76, 110
Ilico 289
Illyricum 51, 54, 205, 248, 254, 258, 296
Imperator Caesar Augustus *see* Augustus; *see also* Octavian
imperium maius 49, 67
Inchtuthil 108
India 18, 49, 140
infantry 24, 62–63, 76, 122, 200, 238, 242, *245*, 288
Invincible Sun *see* Sol Invictus
Ionian Sea 39
Iran 8, 172, 180
Iraq 32, 124–5, 169, 173, 223, 227, 230, 232
Iron Gates gorge 116
Isauria 180
Isle of Wight 83
Israel 21, 136, *179*
Issus 160
Istria 180
Italy 9–10, 13, 21–22, 25, 27, 31, 39, 42, 51, 61, 77, 97, 104, 107, 125, 142, 149, 174, 176, 179, 182, 187, 191, 194, 204–5, 211, 216, 218, 222, 232, 241, 243, 248–50, 254, 258–9, 262, 266–9, 271, 274, 280, 283, 288, 291, 293, 296, 298–9
İzmit *see* Nicomedia

J
Jaghjagh 223
Jerusalem 92, 95, 98, 100, 111, 136–7, 284, 292
Jesus 54, 67, 72, 200, 221, *221*, 251
Jewish Revolt 111, 140, 148
Jewish Temple 95, 136
Jews 125
John (emperor) 280–81, 283, 298
John of Antioch 280, 288
 · *Historia Chronica* 280, 288
Jordan 122
Jordanes 291
 · *History of the Goths* 282, 287

Jovian (emperor) 230, 233, 235, *235*, *238*, 268
Jovinus (emperor) 274, 298
Jovius 197, 266 *see also* Diocletian
Judaea 54, 67, 79, 92, 95, 97–8, 100, 111, 133, 136, 148, 180
Julia (daughter of Augustus) 51, 54, *59*, 60, 67, 72
Julian (emperor) 222, 226–8, *228*, 230, 233, *235*, 235–8, 302
Julianus, Didius (emperor) 159–60, 188
Julio-Claudian era 215
Julius Caesar (Shakespeare) 29
Jupiter 98, 136, 170, *194*, 197, 203, 215
Justina 250
Justus-Liebig University of Giessen 168

K
Kalkriese 63
Kartir 185
Kent 80
kings 8, 42, 49–50, 59, 76, 79, 87–89, 95, 110, 116, 122, 125–6, 132, 141, 160, 165, 169, 172, 188, 198, 204, 215, 221–2, 226–8, 230, 232, 246, 291, 296
 · of Armenia 141 *see also* Ariobartzanes, Artavasdes, Artavasdes II, Artaxas, Axidares, Chosroes, Hannibalianus, Tigranes *and* Tiridates
 · Arthur 249
 · of Dacia *see* Decebelus
 · Gunther 283
 · of the Huns 258, 298 *see also* Attila *and* Uldin
 · of the Iceni *see* Prasutagus
 · of Italy *see* Odoacer
 · of Media 32
 · of Noricum 54
 · of Parthia *see* Vologaeses, Osroes *and* Phraates IV
 · of Persia *see* Ardashir, Sapor *and* Sapor II
 · of the Visigoths 298 *see also* Theodoric
Kosib, Simeon Ben 136

L

Lactantius 200, 211, 221
- *On the Deaths of the Persecutors* 203

Laetus, Quintus Aemilius 159–60
Lambaesis 133
Langres 51
Last Days of Pompeii (Edward Bulwer-Lytton) 107
Latin 7, 26, 120, 134, 160, 182
Leo I (emperor) 293, 295, 296, 299
Lepidina, Cornelia 164
Lepidina, Sulpicia 135
Lepidus, Aemilius 25–27, 31, 66
Leptis Magna 160, *160*
Libya 21, *160*
Licinianus, Piso 96, 111
Licinius (emperor) 204–5, 211, 215–16, *216*, 218–19, 221, 223, 232–3
Lieu, Samuel N. C. 235
Life of Constantine (Eusebius) 219
Life of Nero (*Lives of the Caesars*) (Suetonius) 90
limitanei 222
Lippe 54
Livia 49, 51, *54*, *61*
Livy 79
Lollius, Marcus 51, 67
London (Londinium) 80, 83, *85*, 87, 104, 111
Longinus, Gaius Cassius *see* Cassius
Lucilla 146, 151
Lugdunum *see* Lyons
Lupicinus 244
Lusitania *see* Portugal
Lycaonia 180
Lycia 180
Lydia 180
Lyons 67, 163, 188, 249, 269

M

Macedonia 21–22, 29, 51, 54, 169, 254–5, 258
Macer, Aemilius 133
Macrianus 181
Macrinus (emperor) 169–70, 173, 188
Macro, Sutorius 77
Macsen Wledig *see* Maximus, Magnus
Maesa, Julia 170, *170*
magister equitum 238
magister militum 238, 241, 250, 255, 266, 271, 274, 286, 293, 298
magister officiorum 259
magister peditum 238, 243, 244
magister utriusque militiae 255, 258, 266, 283, 298
Magnentius (emperor) 223, 228, 233
Main (river) 54
Mainz (Mogontiacum) 54, 126
Majorian (emperor) 293, 299
Mamaea, Julia 170, *170*
Manichaeism 8, 202
Marcellinus, Ammianus 223, 226, 241–3
- *History* 243, 247

Marcellus, Marcus Claudius 49
Marcellus, Neratius 134
Marcia 154, 159
Marcian (emperor) *278*, 288, 292–3, 299
Marciana, Ulpia 113, 120
Marcianopolis *see* Devnya
Marcomanni 60, 132, 145–7, 149
Margus 194
Mariades 178
Maroboduus 60–61
Mars 50, 286
Marseilles 204
Masada 95
Mauritania 180
Maxentius (emperor) 204–6, *206*, 211, *211*, 215–16, 232
Maximian (emperor) 189, 194, *194*, 197, *197*, *198*, 202–6, 219, 232
Maximinus, Gaius Julius (emperor) 173–4, 176, 189
Maximus (general) 244
Maximus, Magnus (emperor) *241*, *249*, 249–50, 269, 283
Maximus, Petronius (emperor) 292, 299
Maximus, Tiberius Claudius 116
Meditations (Marcus Aurelius) 138, 142, 147, 151
Mediterranean 10, 21–22, 74, 77, 219, 256, 284, 293
Megiddo *179*
Menorah 100
Meredetes 140
Merobaudes 241, 244
Mesene 125, 140, 148–9
Mesopotamia 124–5, 141, 165, 172–3, 176, 180–81, 188–9, 198, 228
Milan 182, 194, 197, 205–6, 215–16, 227, 232, 250, 254, 258, 269, 289
Minden 61, 63, 76
Minervina *203*, 203–4
Miseno 31
Mithras (god) *191*
Mithridates *see* Meredetes
Modena *see* Mutina
Modestus 107
Moesia 51, 97, 116, 178, 180, 194, 199, 254
Mogontiacum *see* Mainz
Mona *see* Anglesey
Mopsuestia 228
Morocco 21
Mosul 169
Mount Cenis 205
Mons Graupius 108
Mucianus 97–98, 104, 111
Mursa 223, 233
Musa, Thea 60
Mutina 22, 24
Mygdonius *see* Jaghjagh

N

Nabataean kingdom 122, 132, 148
Naissus (Niš) 182, 189, 284
Naples 92 *see also* Bay of Naples
Naqsh-e Rostam 180
Narcissus 80
Narses (king) 198–9, 230, 232
Near East 7, 9, 89
Neoplatonism 8
Nepos, Julius (emperor) 296, 299
Nero (emperor) 7, 83, 87–89, *89*, 92–93, 95–96, 98, 100, 104, 108, 110–11, 113, 115, 140, 215
Nerva, Cocceius (emperor) 108, 111, 113, 148
Neuss (Novaesium) 54
New History (Zosimus) 249, 262

Nibelungenlied 283
Nicaea 8, 221, 233
Nicene Creed 221, 233, 241, 251
Nicomedia (İzmit) 187, 191, 194, *194*, 197, 200, 203, 216, 219, 221, 232
Nicopolis 39
Niger, Pescennius 160, 188
Nile Delta 146
Ninth Cohort of Batavians 134
Niš *see* Naissus
Nisibis (Nusaybin) 160, 165, 170, 223, 226, 230, 232–3, 235
Noricum 51, 54, 180, 269
North Sea 76, 197, 276
Northumberland 134
Novaesium *see* Neuss
Noviomagus Reginorum *see* Chichester
Numerian (emperor) 187
Nusaybin *see* Nisibis

O
Octavia 32
Octavian 21–22, 24–27, 29, 31–33, 39, 42, 66–67 *see also* Augustus (emperor)
Octavius, Gaius *see* Octavian
Odaenathus, Septimius 181–2, 189
Odoacer (king) 296, *296*, 299
Olybrius, Anicius (emperor) 296, 299
Olympia 93
Olympic Games 92
Olympiodorus 262, 280
· *History* 277
Olympius 259, 262, 266
On the Deaths of the Persecutors (Lactantius) 203
Oration (Themistius) 262, 264
Orcistus 221
Orestes 296, 299
Orosius 250, 262
· *History Against the Pagans* 250, 262
Osrhoene 124–5, 141, 148–9, 160, 180
Osroes (king) 122, 125–6, 132
Otho, Salvius (emperor) 96–97, 111

P
Pacorus 141
Paetus, Caesennius 89
Palatine Hill 206
Palestine 97, 125, 136, 140
Palma, Cornelius 122
Palmyra 140, 181, 185, 189, 121
Palmyrene (regime) 136, 185, 187, 194, 248
Pandateria 60
panegyrics 16, 204–5, 211, 226, 278
Pannonia 51, 54, 59–61, 64, 69, 72, 97, 110, 149, 160, 174, 178, 180, 269, 284, 286, 298 *see also* Slovenia
Pansa 22, 24
Paris 194, 228, 249
Parthamasiris 122, 124
Parthamaspates 125–6, 132
Parthia (Parthian Empire) 21–22, *22*, 29, 31–32, 39, 49–50, 59–60, 64, 66–67, 76–77, *88*, 88–89, 110, 122, *122*, 124–6, 132, 140–41, 146, 148–9, 165, 169–70, *172*, 188–9
Passover 95
Paterculus, Velleius 59–60
Paulinus, Suetonius 83, 87–8, 97, 111
Pedius, Quintus 25
Peloponnese 31
Perennis 151, 154, 188
Pergamon 155
Persia (Persian Empire) 8, 33, 160, 170, 172–3, 176, 181, 185, 187–9, 191, 198, *198*, 202, 206, 221–3, *222*, 226–8, 230, 232–3, 235, 244, 280, 286, 301
Pertinax, Helvius (emperor) 146, 159–60, 188
Perugia 31
Peutinger, Konrad 18
Peutinger Table see Tabula Peutingeriana
Philip (emperor) 176, 178, *180*, 189
Philippopolis (Plovdiv) 178
Phoenicia 180
Phoenix, Joaquin 151
Phraates IV (king) 32, 49–50, 59–60
Phraates V (king) 60
Phrygia 180

Piazza Colonna (Rome) 145
Picts 256, 276
Placentia 293
Placidia, Galla 250, 266, 274, 276, 278, 280–81, *281*, 283–4, 293, 298
Placidus, Vetutius 107
plague 7, 141–2, 147, 149
Plautianus 165, 168, 170, 188
Plautius, Aulus 79, 80, 83
Pliny the Elder 107
Pliny the Younger 107, 115
Plotina, Pompeia 113, 120, 125
Plotinus 176
Plovdiv *see* Philippopolis
Po Valley 22, 97, 206
Poetovio *see* Ptuj
Pola 221, 226
Pollentia 258, 269
Pompeianus, Claudius 146
Pompeii 27, *74*, *106*, 106–7
Pompey, Gnaeus (Pompey the Great) 9, 10, 13, 21, 26, 29, 32, 50, 96, 165
Pompey, Sextus 29, 31–32, *51*, 66
Portico of Agrippa *see* Porticus Vipsania
Porticus Vipsania 13
Portugal 21, 96
Pozzuoli 92
Praetorian Guard 77, 79, 93, 96–98, 113, *159*, 159–60, 174, 238
Praetorian prefect 77, 92, 96, 108, 110, 113, 125, 135, 151, 154, 159, 165, 169–70, 174, 180, 187–8, 197, *197*, 238, 250, 255
Prasutagus (king) 83, 87
Primus, Antonius 97–98, 104
Priscinus 134
Priscus (historian) 284, 286, 292, 298
· *History* 284, 286
Priscus, Statius 141, 176
Probus, Marcus Aurelius (emperor) 187, *187*, 189, 191, 194, 219
Procopius 235–8, 268, 293
Proculus 194
Ptuj 97
Pulcheria 278, *278*, 284, 288, 298
Pupienus (emperor) 174, 189

Q

Quadi 132, 145–7, 149, 241
queens 33, 60 280
· Cleopatra of Egypt *see* Cleopatra
· of the Brigantes *see* Cartimandua
· of the Iceni *see* Boudicca
Quietus, Lusius 125

R

Radagaisus 259, 266, 269
Radamistus 110
Raetia 51, 126, 180, 258–9, 266
Ravenna 98, 266–7, 269, 271, 274, *278*, 280, *289*, 292
Remi 51
Republic *see* Roman Republic
Rhine (river) 21, 43, 51, 54, 59, 63–64, 69, 72, 75–76, 79, 96, 98, 104, 108, 110, 126, 133, 140, 148, 173, 194, 204, 228, 245, 249, 256, 259, 269, 271, 276, 298
Rhineland 132
Rhodes 59, 67
Rhone (river) 27
Richborough 80
Richomer 244
Ricimer 293, 296, 299
riparenses 200, 222
Roma (goddess) 215
Roman History (Cassius Dio) 87, 156, 163
Roman Inscriptions of Britain (online project) 134
Roman Republic 8, 21, 42–43, 64, 169
Romania 108, 116
Romulus (emperor) 296, 299
Rubicon (river) 21
Rufinus 255–6
Rufus, Egnatius 67
Rufus, Verginius 93, 96–97, 111

S

Sabina 113, 126, 136
Sabinus, Flavius 98
Sabinus, Julius 104
Sabinus, Nymphidius 92–93, 96

Sacred Way *see* Via Sacra
St Albans 87, 111
St Bernard Pass 51
St John Chrysostom 259
Saints Cosmas and Damian *see* Santi Cosimo e Damiano
Salarian Gate 267
Salona 296, 299
Samos 50
San Giovanni Evangelista, church (Ravenna) *289*
Sangiban 291
Santi Cosimo e Damiano 13
Saoterus 151, 154
Sapor I (king) 172, 176, 178–81, *180*, 185, 189, 198, 221
Sapor II (king) 221, *222*, 223, 227–8, 230, 233, 243, 268
Sardinia 13, 31, 295
Sarmatians 132, 145–6, 149, 248, 255
Sarmizegetusa 108, 116
Sasanian dynasty 172, 176, 185, 199
Saturnalia 135
Sava 54
Saxons 256, 276
Saxony 54
· Lower 74, 174
Scordisci 54
Scotland 108, 241
Scots 276
Scythica 178
Sebastian 283, 298
Second Legion 83
Segestes 63, 74
Segusio 205–6
Segusium *see* Segusio
Sejanus, Aelius 77, 110
Seleucia 165
Selinus 125
senate 9–10, 21–22, 24–25, 33, 42, 49–50, 67, 69, 77, 79, 83, 93, 96, 111, 125, 137, 140, 151, 159–60, 173–4, 211, 243, 251, 256, 262, 266, 293
Seneca 87
Septem Provinciae 276
Serbia 51, 54, 116, 182, 194, 284
Serdica *see* Sofia
Serena (wife of Stilicho) 256

Sermon on the Mount 72
Seven Provinces *see* Septem Provinciae
Severa, Claudia 135
Severianus 141
Severina, Ulpia 185
Severus 203–4, 232
Severus, Alexander *see* Alexander, Marcus Aurelius Severus
Severus, Avidius 149
Severus, Cassius 141
Severus, Libius 293, 299
Severus, Septimius (emperor) 13, *16*, 134–5, 160, *160*, 163–5, *165*, 168, *168*, *169*, 170, 173–4, 179, 215, 302
Severus III *see* Severus, Libius
Shakespeare, William 21, 29
· *Julius Caesar* 29
Short History of Rome (Velleius Paterculus) 59–60
Sibylline Oracles 206, *206*
Sicily 29, 31, 284
Sigimir 63
Silchester 79
Silius, Publius 54
Silures 83
Silvanus 215, 226, 233
Silvester (pope) 210
Singara (Sinjar) 223, 227 *see also* Battle of Singara
Sirmium 216
Slovenia 51, 97, 251, 253 *see also* Pannonia
Sofia 216
Sohaemus (king) 141
Sol Invictus 211
Solway Firth 126, 130
Spain 7, 10, 21, 43, 49–51, 59, 67, 93, 104, 111, 113, 132, 180, 274, 281, 293, 298
Spanish Armada 295
Split 191, 296
Sri Lanka 18
Staffordshire Trulla (Staffordshire Moorlands Pan) 16, *18*
Stephanus 107
Stilicho, Flavius 255, 255–6, *256*, 258–9, 262, 266, 269, 271

Strasbourg (Argentoratum) 227, 233
Sudan 49
Suetonius (biographer) 126
· *Life of Nero* (*Lives of the Caesars*) 90
Sueves (Suebi) 256, 259, 271, 281, 298
suicide 29, 42, 60, 66, 92, 93, 96, 111, 121, 160, 204, 216, 223, 232, 233, 250, 269, 274, 298
Sulla, Lucius Cornelius 9, *9*, 31
Sun God 100, 170, 215
Switzerland 51, 227
Syria 7, 21–22, 29, 32, 43, 49–50, 63–64, 67, 88–89, 95, 97, 111, 122, 125, 136, 140–41, 148–9, 160, 163, 170, 176, 178–81, *179*, 185, 187, 198, 221, 223, 232, 245

T
Tabula Peutingeriana 13, 18, 27
Tacitus, Cornelius 7, 69, 72, 75, 76, 83, 87, 89, 107–9, 126, 133
· *Histories* 98
Tacitus, Marcus Aurelius (emperor) 185, 187, 189
Tanaro 258
Tapae 108, 111, 116 *see also* Battle of Tapae
Tarsus 216, 235
Taurus mountains 160
Tazoult 133
Temple of Capitoline Jupiter 98
Temple of the Divine Trajan *120*
Temple of Hadrian 13
Temple of Mars the Avenger 50
Temple of Mater Matuta 13
Temple of Peace 100
Temple of Tellus 13
Termini station (Rome) 77
Tetrarchy 18, 197, 199
Tetricus 185, 194
Thames (river) *27*
Themistius: *Oration* 262, 264
Theodora 197, 200, 203, 222, 232
Theodoric (king) 291
Theodorus 243–4, 268
Theodosius I (emperor) 241, *241*, 248–51, 253–4, *255*, 256, 268–9, 281, *281*, 298, 301–2

Theodosius II (emperor) 259, *259*, *262*, 269, 274, 276, 278, *278*, 280, 286, 288, 298–9
Thervingi 238, 243–4, 248, 301
Thessalonica 198–9, 219, 248, 250, 280
Third Legion 170
Thirteenth Sibylline Oracle 181
Thornycroft, Thomas *85*
Thrace 51, 178, 180, 218, 245, 249, 254, 258, 284
Thusnelda 74
Tiber (river) *13*, 54, *206*
Tiberius (emperor) 43, 49–51, 54, *54*, 59–61, *61*, *64*, 67, 69, 72, *72*, 76–77, 79, *79*, 110, 116, 173, 259
Ticino 262
Tigellinus, Ofonius 92, 96
Tigranes III (king) 50, 59
Tigranes IV (king) 59
Tigranes VI (king) 89, 110
Tigranocerta 89, 110
Tigris (river) 32, 124–5, 163, 223, 226, 228
Timesitheus 174, 176
Tiridates (king) 49, 88–89, 92, 110–11, 198, 232
Titius, Lucius 26
Titus (emperor) 95, 97–8, *98*, 100, *100*, 108, 111, 136–7, 292
Tivoli 136
Togidumnus 80, 83
Torah 95
Toulouse 274, 291
Trajan, Ulpius (emperor) 7, 113, *113*, 115–16, *116*, 120–22, 124–6, 132, 136, 140–41, 148, 173, 197, 215, 228, 302
Trajan's Column *113*, *120*, 121, 145
Tribigild 258, 269
Trier 133, 204, 211, 216, 221–2, 248
Trieste 54
Trinovantes 79, 83, 87
Triumvirate 31–32
· First 26, 96
· Second 26, 66
Tunisia 21, 283, 295
Turin 205–6
Turkey 7–8, 21, 29, 32, 49, 115, 160, 163, 168, 187, 191, *194*, 221, 228, 238, 258, 293
Tyne (river) 126

U
Uldin (king) 258–9, 283
Ulpian (jurist) 168, 170, 188
Ursicinus 226

V
Vaballathus 182
Valens, Fabius 97–98
Valens (emperor) 8, 218, 235–8, *238*, 241, 243–5, 247–8, 268, 301
Valentinian I (emperor) 235, 238, *238*, 241, *241*, 243, 268
Valentinian II (emperor) *249*, 249–50, 268, 278
Valentinian III (emperor) 271, 276, 280, *281*, 284, 286, 292–3, 298–9
Valeria 197, 232
Valerian (emperor) *179*, 179–82, *180*, 185, 187, 189, 219, 221
Vandals 8, 259, 262, 271, 274, 276, 281, 283, 288, 292–3, 295–6, 298–9
Varronian 235
Varus, Quinctilius 63–64, 67, 72, 74–75, 110, 178
Vechten 54, 74, 76
Veleda 104
Verecundus, Julius 134
Verica (king) 79
Verona 178, 206, 215, 258, 269
Verulamium *see* St. Albans
Verus, Lucius (emperor) 140–42, 146, 149, 151
Verus, Marcus Annius 137
Verus, Martius 141
Vespasian (emperor) 80, 83, *83*, 92, 95, 97–98, *98*, 100, *100*, 104, 108, 111, 113, 115, 122, 154
Vespasianus, Flavius *see* Vespasian
Vesuvius 107, 111
Vetera *see* Xanten
Vetranio (emperor) 223
Via dei Fori Imperiali (Rome) 13
Via Sacra (Rome) *98*, 100, 215
Victor, Aurelius 197
Victoria (goddess) 145
Vienne 250
Vindex, Julius 93, 95, 111

Vindolanda 133–5, 164, *164*
- Writing Tablets 133–4

Vipsania 67
Virgil 34, 67
Virgin Mary 278, *278*
Visigoths 271, 274, 276, 280, *281*, 283, 288, 291, 293, 298
Vitellius, Aulus (emperor) 96–98, 104, 111
Vologaeses (king) 88–89, 110–11
Vologaeses III (king) 132
Vologaeses IV (king) 140–41
Vologaeses V (king) 165

W
Waldgirmes 54
Wales 80, 83, 87, 108, 116, 249
Wallia 274, 298
Wallsend 130
Weser (river) 76
Westminster Bridge *85*

X
Xanten (Vetera) 54, 61, 72, 75, 104

Y
Yemen 49
York 126, 131, 133, 168, 204, 232
Yorkshire 83, 108

Z
Zagros mountains 125
Zaitha 176, 189
Zeno 296, 299
Zenobia 185
Zeus 136
Zliten mosaic *154*, 154–5
Zosimus 249, 253, 262
- *New History* 249, 262

ACKNOWLEDGEMENTS

I am very grateful to Daniel Mills for the invitation to write this book with UniPress. Mark Hawkins-Dady did a wonderful job in the copy-editing phase, while Rosanna Fairhead has been a splendid colleague throughout the production process, which she has overseen with gracious skill. I thank Sandra Zellmer for the design of the book, Alexandre Coco for art direction, Anna Walsh for her marvellous illustrations, Julia Ruxton for her conscientious picture research, and Agatha Tweedie for her help with gathering the images. As always I owe a great debt to my family: my wife, Ellen, our daughters Claire and Natalie, our son-in-law Michael and now Bennett Potter-Schneider, who joined the family in the summer of 2025 and brings joy to us all.

PICTURE CREDITS

The publisher thanks the following for permission to reproduce copyright material and for the use of reference material for illustrations. All reasonable efforts have been made to contact copyright holders and to obtain their permission for the use of copyright material. The publisher apologizes for any errors or omissions and will, if notified, gratefully incorporate any corrections in future reprints.
l = left; r = right; t = top

akg-images/Andrea Jemolo 146; /André Held 200; /Erich Lessing 113, 303
Alamy Stock Photo /Adam Eastland 78, 121, 139, 220; /Album 279, 281; /Danita Delimont 105; /Floriano Rescigno 74-75; /Hanan Isachar 137; /Heritage Image Partnership Ltd 249 i & ii; /Paul Broadbent 164; /Peter Horree 239; /Prisma Archivo 58l, 265; /RealyEasyStar/Claudio Pagliaran 289; /Richard Slater 172; /Rik Hamilton 84-85; /Sonia Halliday Photo Library 180; /The Print Collector 240; /Tuul and Bruno Morandi 218; /Vito Arcomano 23; /YAY Media 48; /Zev Radovan 179
Araldo de Luca, Rome 99, 102-3, 107tl, 144, 165, 208-9, 214; (Ara Pacis Museum, Rome) 44-45; (Archaeological Museum, Cyrene, Libya) 196, 54r; (Capitoline Museums, Rome) 30, 65, 73, 82, 91, 117, 127, 143, 157, 161, 166, 183, 186, 213; (Dar Buk Amméra, Sliten, Tripoli, Libya) 155; (Egyptian Museum, Cairo) 171; (Museum of Roman Civilization, Rome) 69; (National Museum of Rome) 297; (Vatican Museums, Rome) 35
The Art Institute of Chicago /Gift of Martin A. Ryerson 1922.4889 170iii; /Purchased with funds provided by the Classical Art Society, John T. Vaughan and Jeffrey R. Darna (2016.189) 202i, ii;
Bridgeman Images 16, 52; /© Erich Lessing 254l; /© Iberfoto 241; /© Photo Josse 283; /Granger 238; /Luisa Ricciarini 11, 257; /Pictures from History 260-61; /Tarker 210; /Vincenzo Pirozzi 216; /© NPL - DeA Picture Library 18
© The Trustees of the British Museum 17, 55l, 55r, 58r, 134, 296i, ii
Classical Numismatic Group https://cngcoins.com 9tl, 203i, ii, 228, 278
Flickr/Carole Raddata CC-BY-SA 9tr, 33, 40-41, 61, 88, 107tr, 123, 191, 195, 198, 304-5
Getty Images/traveler1116 199
© Kulturstiftung Sachsen-Anhalt & Falk Wenzel, Halle 277
Metropolitan Museum of Art, New York Bequest of Joseph H. Durkee, 1898 (99.35.218) 170l; /Fletcher Fund, 1965, (65.126) 225; / Rogers Fund, 1923, (23.160.52) 114
© Nicomedia-Çukurbağ Archaeological Project (TÜBİTAK 115K242)/Kocaeli 194
Österreichische Nationalbibliothek, Vienna (Cod. 324 HAN MAG) 13, 14-15, 26-27
Wikimedia Commons Anagoria 169;/Ángel M. Felicísimo 36;/Christophe Jacquand 158; /Coin Archives 235i, ii; /Münzkabinett, Staatliche Museen zu Berlin/Reinhard Saczewski 178i, ii
Yale University Art Gallery Ruth White Fund, (2021.84.151) 170iv; /The Ernest Collection in memory of Israel Myers (2007.182.424) 170ii

ABOUT THE AUTHOR

David Potter is Francis W. Kelsey Collegiate Professor of Greek and Roman History and Arthur F. Thurnau Professor in the Department of Classical Studies at the University of Michigan. His research has focused on the interaction between people and institutions in the ancient world, and the presentation of that research in a form that is accessible to all readers.

His early work on oracles was designed to illuminate the dialogue between the imperial government and its subjects, and that the commonplace process of reasoning about the possibility of divine action depended upon the view that oracles represented authentic divine revelation. His *The Victor's Crown: A History of Ancient Sport from Homer to Byzantium* (2011) looks at the history of sport in the Greco-Roman world from a comparative perspective, while in *Literary Texts and the Roman Historian* (1998), he shows how the work of historians of the early modern period, especially those espousing the 'vulgar Marxist' approaches of E. P. Thompson and Eric Hobsbawm, is especially useful in reading ancient texts as the product of a very limited class of authors – that class bias rather than rhetorical interest tends to shape the narratives that have survived from the Roman Empire. In *The Roman Empire at Bay: AD 180–395* (2004), he shows how modern management theory can be deployed to analyse the way in which the Roman Empire worked over the course of more than two hundred years, from the late second century to the late fourth century CE. The comparative perspective also informs his *The Origin of Empire: Rome from the Republic to Hadrian* (2019), tracing the rise of Rome from the mid-third century BCE to the early second century CE, looking at how the government of the Republic was transformed into a contractor state in the middle of the second century and then into a bureaucratic monarchy, making use for this analysis of work by Charles Tilly. In *Disruption: Why Things Change* (2021), he explores the way radical change results from the collapse of the political centre. This is explored through a series of case studies, including the conversion of the Roman Empire to Christianity, the rise of Islam, the Protestant Reformation, the French and American Revolutions, and, finally, the rise of Bolshevism and Nazism. Each case study begins with an exploration of the ideals that will be adapted in a period of disruption – such as the constitutional theories of John Locke and Jean-Jacques Rousseau, Marxist thought or Social Darwinism – followed by a discussion of what happened in each case.

Potter's three biographies offer fresh perspective on well-known characters. In *Constantine the Emperor* (2012), he argues that the impact of Constantine's conversion was shaped by the way in which he worked Christianity into the traditional system of government, rather than using his new faith to reshape the empire's government. In *Theodora: Actress, Empress, Saint* (2015), he shows how Theodora (despite what was suggested by her vitriolic critics) played a positive role within the administration of the empire. His most recent book, *Master of Rome: A Life of Julius Caesar* (2025), presents the career of Caesar, based on Caesar's writings, as a product of a failing democratic system.

First published in 2026
by Riverside Press, an imprint of
UniPress Books Ltd
World's End Studios
London SW10 0RJ
United Kingdom

Copyright in the Work © 2026
UniPress Books Ltd
Text copyright © 2026 David Potter

The moral rights of the author and artist
have been asserted.

ISBN: 978-1-917226-19-6
ISBN e-book: 978-1-917226-20-2

All rights reserved. No part of this book
may be reproduced, stored in an retrieval
system or transmitted in any form
or by any means, without prior written
permission from the publisher.

This book is distributed throughout
the UK and Europe by
Abrams & Chronicle Books,
1 West Smithfield, London, EC1A 9JU and
57 rue Gaston Tessier, 75166 Paris, France.
www.abramsandchronicle.co.uk
info@abramsandchronicle.co.uk

Artwork: Anna Walsh
Designer: Sandra Zellmer
Cover Design: Sandra Zellmer
Project Manager: Rosanna Fairhead

Printed in Malaysia
riversidepress.co.uk

10 9 8 7 6 5 4 3 2 1